THE WORST OF FRIENDS

Colin Shindler is the author of the bestselling autobiography *Manchester United Ruined My Life*, which was shortlisted for the William Hill Sports Book of the Year prize. He has enjoyed a long and distinguished career as a film screenwriter and television producer, and teaches film history at Cambridge University. He lives in London.

THE WORST
OF FRIENDS
THE BETRAYAL OF JOE MERCER

A NOVEL BY
COLIN SHINDLER

MAINSTREAM
PUBLISHING

EDINBURGH AND LONDON

This edition, 2010

Copyright © Colin Shindler, 2009
All rights reserved
The moral right of the author has been asserted

First published in Great Britain in 2009 by
MAINSTREAM PUBLISHING COMPANY
(EDINBURGH) LTD
7 Albany Street
Edinburgh EH1 3UG

ISBN 9781845965693

This book is a fictional account based on true events.
In some limited cases names of people have been
changed to protect the privacy of others

A catalogue record for this book is available
from the British Library

Typeset in Big Noodle and Palatino

Printed in Great Britain by
CPI Cox and Wyman, Reading RG1 8EX

1 3 5 7 9 10 8 6 4 2

This book is for my grandson, Oliver Shindler. For the sins of the fathers are visited on the children even unto the third and fourth generation and even with all those petrodollars.

ACKNOWLEDGEMENTS

Although this is a work of fiction, it is clearly based on real events in the lives of Joe Mercer and Malcolm Allison, both of whom I got to know briefly in the summer of 1971. They offered me a memorable glimpse into a world I have never forgotten.

I am grateful to Eric Alexander, Sidney Rose, Bernard Halford, Ian Niven, Peter Gardner and Tommy Docherty, all of whom generously gave of their time and shared their memories of the events of 1965–73. Manchester City has always been liked as a family club, and my treatment by the staff there over ten years and four books has at all times been highly valued.

I am particularly indebted to Geoff Watts and Howard Davies, whose knowledge of those times is as vivid as my own, and who read the book in manuscript form and offered greatly appreciated critical comments. John Dolan in the computer office of the History Faculty at Cambridge University saved this technophobe from utter despair with his impressive mastery of the technology needed to reproduce the results and attendant detail of the eight seasons, and Ruth Blair provided vital suggestions in the field of 1970s fashion that had passed me by completely. The Mike Summerbee stories were provided by my good friend Mike Summerbee, who ought to know. In addition, the writing of this book has brought home to me how much was added to my experience of those days in the sun and rain by the much valued friendship of fellow-travellers David Green, Michael Chadwick and Jeffrey Cohen.

At Mainstream, I have received exemplary support from Bill Campbell, Karyn Millar and Fiona Atherton. For imposing on Amy and David and now Oliver my love of Manchester City, I have always felt a little guilty. My love for them, however, exceeds the guilt.

THE WORST OF FRIENDS

Finally, I wish to acknowledge my thanks to Joe and Malcolm. Without their partnership, my life would have been greatly impoverished. What they achieved together remains an imperishable memory for me and for the 30,000 others who remember those days.

PROLOGUE

10 MARCH 1973

'**D**id you want it that badly, Mal?' they asked him. 'Did you have to destroy Joe to get it? Now you've got it, was it worth it? All the heartache and the misery you caused?'

They crowded round the new yellow E-Type Jag, pressing their faces, their notebooks, their cheap biros against the window, jostling him so he could barely get out of the car. He thought he knew every football reporter in the country, but there were some here he'd never seen before. Not football reporters at all. Not journalists, not proper journalists. Scandal seekers, sensationalists, looking for headlines, looking for bad news. They could start with the dent in the passenger door where some bastard had side-swiped him when he was harmlessly parked on a Manchester street. This fucking car was jinxed – like he felt he was these days.

'Don't you think it's funny? You want somebody else's job for five years, you want it so badly that you can barely sleep or eat, and when you get it you find out you're a gigantic fucking disaster?'

They pursued him like a pack of animals, jostling, pushing, crushing up against his new cashmere overcoat. This was what Bestie had to put up with all the time. Paul Newman, Robert Redford, Steve McQueen: this is what big stars had to deal with. Ali and Sinatra were never free of the press – and they hadn't been knocked out of the Cup by Second-Division Sunderland or beaten 5–1 by Wolves last week.

On second thoughts, no, it wasn't like that. McQueen and the others were the adored ones. This was more like the pack that surrounded Christine Keeler in her glory days. The memory of his brief liaison with the woman who had allegedly caused the collapse of Harold Macmillan's

9

government brought a brief smile and a glow of satisfaction to his face. That infamous night of passion was nearly three years old, but the memory warmed him still. She had wanted him because he was on the telly and in the papers. She understood the demands of that kind of notoriety and found it arousing. Would she find it a turn-on reading about him in today's press? Somehow he doubted it.

He had been expecting it. Some version of it. The press had been all over the story for days. Joe was coming back. Back to the ground he had graced for seven years. Joe, who had hired Malcolm in the first place, was coming back to Manchester with his bright new shiny Coventry City team to see what a pig's ear Malcolm had made of Joe's old job. There was no point answering even one of their shouted questions. He would just be opening the floodgates.

'Do you still hate Joe?'

'What's your relationship with Joe like now, Malcolm?'

'Have you started talking to each other again?'

'Is it true your bank manager's taken your cheque book away from you again?'

Christ, how did they know about that? No football reporter would ask a bloody question like that. He was being set up. He'd used the press for years. Now they were using him.

Malcolm was no longer surprised by his bad press. It hadn't been like that at all for the first five years, the good years when he and Joe had won everything except the Grand National, but things had been going wrong for a while now, and, quite frankly, he was increasingly tempted to tell that lot in the boardroom that they could stick the job up their arses. Those bastards up there had buggered him about something rotten as soon as they'd got their feet under the table. All those dreams he'd told them about, all the plans for the future, for the club, for the supporters, for himself and for them, what were they worth now? About as much as his much-vaunted 20-year contract. In other words, fuck all.

'Do you think the board will sack you if you lose to Coventry today?'

'Have you lost the players' respect since Sunderland knocked you out of the Cup?'

'Do you regret signing Rodney Marsh now?'

That question, that one question above all others, drove him crazy. He fled up the steps and through the main entrance. He slipped out of the cashmere overcoat and shook it as if he were trying to rid it not just of the crushing by the journalists but also the insistent questions that clung to the fabric as surely as they stayed in his mind, revolving, demanding, judging. Always judging. He was free of the pack for now – until after the game, the one game he dared not lose. Now all he had to worry about was 30,000 angry, bitter, disappointed, frustrated, hostile supporters.

The fact was, there was some truth in those shouted, harassing questions. The players *had* let him down, though neither the supporters nor the press would see it like that. It was hard for him to put his finger on why it had happened. They'd had a slow start in the League, but they'd shown their usual appetite for the FA Cup. Stoke had been dispatched in the third round and, to his great satisfaction, Liverpool in the fourth, but Sunderland had been their undoing in the fifth round, when it was just starting to feel like this was their year for the FA Cup again. Joe must have loved that, *loved* it!

Well, Joe was hardly a miracle worker, so he didn't have much to chortle about. His Coventry team were battling the prospect of relegation, and at least City didn't have that nightmare to worry about. Still, they were trapped in one of the worst runs Malcolm had known since he'd arrived at the club with Joe nearly eight years before. The team was losing games, and he was losing . . . losing his fucking mind, he thought as he darted into an empty office to avoid the Chairman and the Secretary, whom he could see at the end of the corridor, huddled together, conspiring, whispering about him, about how they wished they'd never sided with him and forced Joe out.

Why was he even doing this job? This job, which he had coveted for five long years. It wasn't for the money. He spent more than he earned without trying too hard. Mind you, he always had. He was invariably broke, but he was never poor. He never stinted on clothes or cigars or booze, and his taste in women was expensive, too. Not like Joe: middle-aged, semi-detached Joe with his sports coats with the leather elbow patches and his beige-coloured Rover 2000 with the towbar on the back, which he would drive sedately home to Norah every night of his life. He'd show Joe what a great manager he was. He had Bell, Lee and Summerbee at his disposal – to say nothing of Corrigan, Doyle, Booth and his big signing, the superstar Rodney Marsh, as well as the highly promising youngsters Towers, Jeffries and Donachie. He had a great side with great players. It was an unfathomable mystery why they kept turning in bad performances.

THE WORST OF FRIENDS

He sat in the empty office and looked again at the team sheet, shaking his head in disbelief. It had been nearly three years since they had won anything, but these were mostly the same players who had won those five trophies in five years. How could they play like they were strangers who had just been introduced to each other? If they played like they did last Saturday, he was finished. 'Not today, lads, not today,' he muttered to himself as he opened the office door and clattered down the narrow stairs that led from the main corridor to the dressing-rooms. Not with Joe sitting smiling in the directors' box behind him. That fucking smile of his . . .

This was the game that really mattered. Going out of the FA Cup at Roker Park the previous week had killed the season stone dead. At least with the points they'd gathered before Christmas they were safe, but there was nothing left to play for – just this game. A mid-table finish to a season of mind-numbing mediocrity was virtually certain. It was so disappointing compared with the excitement he and the players had served up for the previous seven seasons. A victory in today's game would get him through the last ten matches. If he beat Joe's Coventry, he would re-establish his credibility. If they drew, if, unbelievably, they lost at home to this bunch of deadbeats from the West Midlands, then it would all get so much worse – the chanting on the terraces, the protests of Mal's Malcontents outside the ground after the game, the letters in the *Manchester Evening News*. 'How can I lose?' he asked himself. 'I've got Lee, Bell, Summerbee and Marsh; who's Joe got? Willie Carr? Dennis Mortimer? Do me a favour!'

He opened the door to the dressing-room. The familiar comforting smell of liniment and nervous tension hit him as soon as he walked in. He looked at himself in the mirror. The cameras would be here today for certain. He wanted to be sure he looked like Big Mal: the flash Cockney geezer with the big cigar and the grandiloquent style, the big, charismatic, handsome man who had been compared to George Lazenby – the bloke who did the 'Big Fry' adverts and *On Her Majesty's Secret Service*. The players understood his need to look sharp. None of the other managers had his innate sense of style – Joe, Cloughie, the Doc, Shanks, Revie with his stupid car-coat and his lucky blue suit: fashion disasters the lot of them. He looked in the mirror and approved of the wide Italian-silk tie and the smart cut of his check sports jacket. It would draw admiring looks from the likes of Marsh and Summerbee. They'd listen to him even more because he impressed with his lifestyle as well as his football knowledge.

'I'm going to the library,' remarked Mike Doyle as he picked up a programme from the stack that lay on the treatment table and disappeared into the toilet. Malcolm looked at his dressing-room full of internationals, men who had won dozens of caps and played in World Cups, and young lads of immense promise who would no doubt follow in their footsteps. It was, as the press always liked to write, the perfect mixture of youth and experience. How, then, could they have played so badly for most of this season, when last season they had been six points clear at the top of the table before Easter and missed the Championship by a single point? Even more worryingly, what did he have left to say to them that they hadn't heard a hundred times before? Maybe the fault didn't lie with the players. Maybe the fault was his. He shuddered. If they knew that was what he was thinking, they were finished before they even went out there. What if it was true that Joe was the reason . . . It couldn't be. It just couldn't.

'This lot are a piece of shit!' he thundered as the chatter of the dressing-room fell silent. 'I've just talked to Joe,' he lied, 'and even he says they're a piece of shit.' It wasn't exactly psychoanalysis, but he knew players and he knew that this sort of stuff generally worked, because it was what they wanted to hear.

In the away dressing-room, Gordon Milne gave the speech that was designed to send Coventry City out onto the pitch ready to take on the world. Joe always felt uncomfortable with that Churchillian rhetoric. He used to do it, of course. He'd had to when he'd been in sole charge of Sheffield United and then Aston Villa. He'd been much more intense then, ten, fifteen years ago. Malcolm's arrival had allowed him to take a step back, so Joe was doing what he now did best: geeing up the players individually, checking that each player was aware of his specific task on the day. He believed that he got the best out of players by taking the crippling nervous tension away. He'd been thinking about this moment ever since the fixture list had been published a few days after his arrival at Coventry.

It wasn't as if Manchester City was the only club in his long life in the game. He'd played for Everton and the Arsenal, and managed Sheffield United and Aston Villa, but Manchester City had given him the best, most satisfying years of his career. To leave in the way he had, diminished and humiliated, his car parking space taken away, his office handed over to someone else even when he thought it still belonged to him, cut him to the quick. Ever since the fixture list had been published last summer, he had focused on this day. It was the chance to go back and receive what was rightfully his – the respect of the club and the supporters for what he had achieved there.

'Is it good to be back in Manchester, Joe?'

'Do you regret walking out on the club last summer?'

'What are you going to say to Malcolm when you see him, Joe?'

Departing almost unnoticed the previous June, leaving Malcolm in sole charge after the disappointment of losing the Championship to Derby County by a point, his own presence an embarrassing encumbrance to the people who had previously lionised him, was no way to say goodbye. He was a man who revelled in making people smile, who delighted in the warmth of the embrace that a club, that special football family, could provide.

He and Norah had returned to Manchester in the autumn for the Supporters' Club's annual dinner, at which he was the guest of honour, the grateful recipient of a silver tea service. But that didn't count. The very fact that he had been specially invited had made him feel confident that his reception would be a warm one. Two hundred fans in best bib and tucker gathering to honour a past manager was no test of general popularity. Today he was going to Maine Road, to the stadium, as the manager of the visiting side whose job it was to deprive these fans of two points and inflict upon them yet another home defeat in a season that had been scarred by such outrages – rare in his time, except for that difficult 1966–67 season, when they had had to consolidate the promotion so thrillingly won in his first year, but becoming increasingly familiar to a set of fans who had been understandably lulled into expecting better over the seven years of his time there. Today's performance would tell him how his own team would bear up under the pressure, and his reception by his former staff as well as the home fans would tell him what people really thought of him.

'Do you think the fans will boo you, Joe?'

'Do you think the fans hate you for walking out on them, Joe?'

'Did you always think Malcolm would be as bad a manager as he's turned out?'

Ironically, Malcolm knew better than Joe that it was pointless for him to worry. Even if City won 6–0, Joe would be hailed as a hero. Especially if they won 6–0, thought Malcolm grimly, knowing that after such a victory even the most churlish supporter would discover new reserves of magnanimity inside himself. Joe was a man apart, not so much the manager of the visiting side as the hero returning to the battlefield where he had won so many famous victories. What could there be but a guard of honour, a procession of applause into the hearts of the faithful who remembered the great times and conveniently forgot the mistakes? It was Malcolm who was going to be lumbered with those.

He had been given a foretaste of what might lie ahead back in October, when City had gone to Highfield Road and lost 3–2. Both sides had started the season poorly, but ten months ago Coventry had only just avoided relegation while City had finished only a single point behind the fortunate champions, Derby County. Expectations in Manchester and Coventry were very different. Coventry had failed to win any of their first six games, but their supporters seemed quite unfazed by the results; City had won one and lost the other five, and the crowd was immediately on Malcolm's back. Christ! The fans could make your life a fucking misery. Even after all the success he had brought them, he felt that he had built up no credit with them. A bad run at the start of the season and he knew they were thinking that it was all his fault, though he could hardly claim to be surprised after a humiliating 2–0 defeat by lowly neighbours Bury had knocked them out of the League Cup in the early stages.

The game at Coventry had been more open than either manager had really wanted. Coventry had scored through Carr early in the first half, and after an hour Colin Stein had brought Highfield Road a rare moment of ecstasy with a magnificent goal that doubled their lead, but Marsh and Summerbee had scored two scrappy goals to equalise for City, and the home crowd, familiar with the acrid taste of disappointment, sensed that the day might yet yield only further frustration. Fortunately, a goal from Brian Alderson 12 minutes from time had brought them a deserved victory, and at the end of the game both sets of supporters had applauded Coventry off the field.

Malcolm knew well enough what they were thinking. Joe's team had played exciting football and won the game scoring three goals. This was how City fans wanted their side to play. It was how City sides had used to play. His City sides. Coventry looked like a young team just starting to gel, as City had done in the first two years that Joe and he had worked together, before the incredible, thrilling Championship year that set them all off on their road to glory. Now City looked like a tired, cynical team, unwilling to chase and harry, to do the hard but vital work necessary to win the ball and retain possession. The inescapable conclusion in the minds of these idiots was that Joe had been the brains behind the great City side and he, Malcolm Allison, was just the understudy. Faced with promotion to the top job, he'd blown it. He'd show the twats!

'Allison, fuck off back to Cockneytown!'

'You stabbed Joe in the back, Allison, you cunt!'

'You're fucking useless, Allison!'

He didn't have the energy now to wave and smile at the crowd, put two fingers up at them and blow them a kiss. They depressed him, they drained him of his good humour, messed with his head, confused him, clouded his thinking. If they hated him, he hated them back with interest. 'Stabbed Joe in the back'? What a load of bollocks. If they'd known what Joe had done to him . . . for years he'd kept his mouth shut . . . You couldn't tell anyone Joe wasn't a man of his word . . . Joe had broken a promise faithfully made . . . Joe was a shit who couldn't be trusted. The world loved Joe. Who would believe him? Results. His only response, his only safety, lay in results.

Unlikely though it seemed, that defeat back in October had been the springboard for City's best run of the season so far. They won five of the next nine fixtures, losing only to Leeds United, and one of those victories was a convincing 3–0 win over Manchester United, who were thrashing about wildly in the lower reaches of the division. Unfortunately, being knocked out of the Cup at Sunderland and the embarrassing 5–1 hammering at Wolverhampton that had followed four days later had given undue importance to this return match against Joe's Coventry.

He looked at the faces in front of him. How many of them still rated him, he wondered. They knew what he'd done for them in the past, but what did that count for now? Football wasn't a game played in the past except by middle-aged supporters nostalgic for faded glories. It was about the next match, the next half-hour, the next goal. You were never done. Even at the top, there was always another season ahead of you – a season where you were more likely to be let down by the players and be sacked than be rewarded with the garlands of victory.

For the managers who had won nothing for a while (or ever), next season was a time to be eagerly anticipated, a fresh start, a new page. But Malcolm had won it all: championships, cups, a European trophy. He had nothing to prove, but still he had to do it. Juventus had been desperate to sign him as their manager – Juventus! Outside of Real

Madrid, and begging Manchester United's pardon, Juve were the biggest team in Europe. If Agnelli wanted him in Turin, how bad could he be? 'United aren't the biggest team in Europe,' he was fond of saying to the fans in the days when they adored him. 'They're not even the biggest team in Manchester.'

Every week, every Saturday, he sent out his lads to play as well prepared as any in the land. The failures were theirs, not his. It wasn't Malcolm who missed a sitter, misplaced a header, sent the ball into the crowd behind the goal instead of the back of the net. Judging by their harsh, unforgiving reactions, those bastards on the terraces obviously thought it was. They had no fucking idea. They saw the pictures in the paper of the cigars and the clothes and the birds, and they thought that was all he was: Big Mal, a bigmouth, a big-time Charlie. They'd be amazed to learn that he spent as many nights in the living room of his flat in Sale reading books as he did drinking champagne in the Cabaret Club. They might be flattered that he spent the time he did thinking about them, perhaps even by how much he resented the power they held over him.

He tried to focus his antagonism on Joe, the man who had taken him from obscurity and given him the chance to make his name. It was easy to do. This match had been preying on his mind since the fixtures had been announced, and he was certain that the same applied to Joe. He'd always been grateful for the opportunity Joe had given him nearly eight years ago, but his critics made the false assumption that somehow Joe was the genius behind City's remarkable run of trophies, and he had been some kind of cheerleader – the man who bellowed from the touchline and antagonised the referee and the opposing supporters.

Joe might have kept his trilby on and smiled at the world, but he had only been able to play that game because Malcolm had done all the hard work behind the scenes, the work the papers never wrote about. They made the perfect 'good cop/bad cop' team only because he was prepared to risk the loss of popularity that came from constantly playing the bad-cop role. Without Malcolm, Joe would have been back in hospital. Malcolm had saved Joe's career and his health. Look how that ungrateful bastard had repaid him! Why was it that the rest of the world couldn't see it like that?

The referee knocked on the dressing-room door and talked briefly to the team while the linesmen checked the studs on the players' boots. He was as aware as the crowd of the provocative nature of the game, and he was concerned lest each of the managers had wound up their teams to win at all costs, but looking at the faces of the players he could detect nothing special about this occasion. It was Malcolm's face that was lined with anxiety. The referee walked across to the away dressing-room and made almost the same speech, but it was Gordon Milne who appeared to be in charge. Joe Mercer wasn't even there.

In fact, Joe Mercer was upstairs talking to the City directors, the men who had sided with Malcolm and pushed him out of the club he had built. He smiled at them; he always smiled. He knew what a disarming smile he had and what a powerful weapon it could prove to be, but this was the smile he reserved especially for the directors of football clubs – the vain, invariably pompous, self-important men who had made a few bob and thought it might be fun to run their local football club. They had been the bane of his life. They knew nothing about the game but thought they did, and the money they put into the club gave them the power to make decisions that invariably proved disastrous because they didn't have the sense to listen to the people who knew what was really important in football. People like him.

He knew them all: Joe Smith, Mr Weatherseal Windows, the man whose money had unseated the old Albert Alexander regime that had backed him; Ian Niven, the publican who thought the sun shone out of Malcolm's rear end; Chris Muir, the belligerent Scotsman who ran a stationery business; and Peter Swales, the smarmy chap who sold television sets. Smiling bloody assassins. He wouldn't tell that twerp Swales how to sell a television set. How was it possible that these twerps had presumed to tell him how to run a football club?

These were the men who had ended the most successful managerial regime in the history of Manchester City Football Club. These were the men who had thought they could feather their own nest by kicking him out and installing Malcolm as sole boss. Well, when he was there they'd won five trophies in as many years. Now where were they? He wanted to ask them, but he restrained himself, as he always did.

'Do you think City will ever be as successful under Malcolm?'

'What are you going to say to the directors who sacked you, Joe?'

'Will you shake hands with Swales, Joe?'

He didn't like directors because he didn't like the politics that they revelled in. What he liked was football and players and people who knew about players, really knew about them: some journalists – the older ones, obviously – the managers, the coaches, the trainers, the scouts and the old players. That's why he'd liked Malcolm. It was clear from everything that people had told him about Malcolm, long before he hired him as his assistant, that Malcolm was as besotted with the game as he was. If football was composed entirely of such people, he would never have had to go into hospital for the hypertension he still suffered from. If Malcolm hadn't listened to the blandishments of men like the new directors, Joe would never have been forced to leave the best job he'd ever had. But Malcolm had done more than listen, and, much as Norah had feared it might, Joe's sickness came back with a vengeance. And, whenever he'd felt stress at Maine Road on a match day, he would go down into the bowels of the stadium and have a cup of tea with Rose. The sight of the directors he still held responsible for the deterioration of his health and the loss of his job was enough to hasten his passage down the stairs to Rose's kitchen.

Rose was the tea lady, and for years she had been Joe's first port of call on match days. He felt safe in the little room under the main stand just off the tunnel, next door to the small gym the players used to warm up before the match. Rose was the sort of woman he had met on every Football League ground: down to earth, a good listener and, above all, a good tea-maker. Rose also made the best scones he'd ever eaten, and now, 15 minutes before kick-off, he was rediscovering the taste of her home baking.

'I don't know what you're worrying about, love,' she said, refilling his mug from the large teapot. 'Everyone loves you round here.'

'But you know the way things were last summer. The directors . . .'

'Oh them!' interrupted Rose immediately. 'You don't want to listen to them. When did a director ever say anything worth listening to?'

'They've been the bane of my life. They've been the bane of every football man in the country. You should listen to what Matt says about his lot at United.'

'It's gone quarter to, Joe. Shouldn't you be talking to the players?'

'Nah, Gordon Milne does that. Like Malcolm used to.'

'There's something queer about Malcolm . . .'

Joe raised an eyebrow. 'Malcolm? He's the last person I thought you'd ever say that about.' He smiled mischievously. Rose looked blank for a moment, then blushed, her face covered in confusion.

'Oh, Joe, you know, I never . . .'

'I'm just teasing.' He smiled, getting to his feet and draining his mug. 'You still make the best tea in the Football League, Rose, love.'

THE WORST OF FRIENDS

As he came out into the tunnel, he turned and looked across the pitch to the far side where the hardcore City supporters were already gathering in their numbers in the Kippax Stand. Who would they go for today, he wondered. Him or Malcolm? He thought about popping into the home dressing-room to have a word with the boys he still thought of as his. He knew he'd get a warmer welcome there than perhaps anywhere else. Summerbee, Bell, Oakes, Pardoe: these were players he knew so well, would trust with his life, or at least his career.

Joe had been born in 1914, the same year as George Summerbee, Mike's father. They'd played wartime football together when Joe was stationed at Aldershot and George was working in a factory in Portsmouth. He'd wondered what would happen to George's two sons when he had died of Addison's disease at the age of forty. He was delighted to find that the younger one, Mike, had become a player, and a good one at that: a fast, hard, skilful winger, as brave as a lion. Mike had rung him up that first summer Joe had taken over at Maine Road and had become his second signing, repaying the £35,000 transfer fee many times over.

He'd known and liked a great many players over his long career in the game, but none inspired more affection in him than Mike Summerbee. When Summerbee had done something wrong either on or off the field, Joe found it almost painful to tell him off. It was like disciplining David, his own son. Once, returning home from a match in Europe, Summerbee and his best friend Francis Lee had persuaded a stewardess to deliver a note warning Joe that the man in the seat next to him was a hijacker and he must keep him talking till the plane landed.

Joe felt fear course through his veins, but he never flinched from the task in hand. It never occurred to him that perhaps a committed hijacker wouldn't be deflected from his mission by Joe telling him endless tales about Cliff Britton and Tommy Lawton and the Championship-winning Everton side of 1939. On landing, the hijacker shook his hand and introduced himself as part of the relief crew. Joe stood up to see Lee and Summerbee doubled over in mirth.

He'd been angry with them for about 30 seconds, then he had joined in the laughter. He could never be angry with this bunch of lads. They were talented players and decent young men – all of them. Everyone was decent at this club. In the aftermath of the unpleasant events that had driven him out of Maine Road the previous year, he had forgotten how many people around the place he genuinely liked. He was about to go back upstairs to find Norah, who had been sitting with the other wives in the players' lounge, when he heard someone calling to him.

'Boss!' He turned abruptly to see Harry Godwin and Johnny Hart walking up the tunnel towards him. Harry had been the chief scout who had signed so many talented youngsters: Stan Bowles, Tommy Booth, Tony Towers, Derek Jeffries and, further back, Glyn Pardoe, David Connor and Mike Doyle, stalwarts of the teams who had won all the trophies. Johnny had been at City since before the end of the war, first as a player, then as a coach for the youth teams and reserves, and finally as the first-team trainer. It would be impossible to find two more honest or loyal men in any club in the land, but after a brief conversation and many expressions of mutual regard he wandered along the main corridor more anxious than at any point in this fraught day. Harry, Johnny and Malcolm . . . What a team he'd had at his command. Even now, he didn't know why they weren't still all together.

'Hello, Mr Mercer. Welcome home. Mrs Mercer's looking for you.'

Home? Well, yes. Admittedly he was an itinerant football man who went where the jobs were, but since he'd given up playing nearly 20 years ago this place was as near to home as he'd ever found. He smiled at the familiar face of the steward who stood guard over the entrance to the lounge. What was his name? Steve? Norman? He was hopeless with names, always had been, but there was no mistaking the warmth of his reception. People seemed genuinely pleased to see him back. Would the crowd feel similarly? He'd know in a few minutes.

He passed a familiar-looking door, but the name painted on it was entirely unfamiliar. This had been his office, from where he'd presided over the resurrection of a club whose descent had been regarded as irreversible. This was the office from which he'd been evicted nine months ago, his files piled up in the corridor as if waiting for the dustbinmen. How could those bastards have kicked him out after what he'd done for this club? The more he thought about it, the more bitter became his resentment.

'Joe, where have you been? I've been looking all over for you!' It was the familiar, soothing tones of Norah, who had put up with him for over 30 years, quietly enjoying his triumphs and consoling him in his defeats. She knew how anxious he had been about this day, but she had been treated with such warmth and generosity herself that her own anxieties had soon evaporated.

'Everyone's been so kind to me here. It's like coming home again, isn't it?'

'I should never have let them kick me out.'

'Now, Joe, don't start all that again. Enough's been said. It's nearly five to. We'd best get ourselves seated.'

As they turned to walk through the little door that led into the directors' box, a familiar figure mounted the stairs from the dressing-room. It was like a scene from a film where the good guy and the bad guy square off against each other while everyone else falls back and goes silent. Malcolm Allison and Joe Mercer looked at each other for the first time since October and the Coventry City victory at Highfield Road. Malcolm had been curt and uncommunicative then. Joe looked warily at his face for clues to see if his old colleague had thawed a little in the intervening five months, but he saw only a steely hatred. How could Malcolm hate him? After all they'd been through together? Joe thrust out his hand.

'Hello, Mal, nice to see you. Good luck out there.'

Allison let the hand stay unshaken for a pointed second or two before he grasped and shook it perfunctorily.

'Thanks. Same to you. Hello, Norah,' he muttered, and then disappeared into the stand to take his seat in the front row, directly over the tunnel. He had applied to the FA to have his lifetime ban from the touchline overturned as soon as he had been confirmed as manager in his own right, but the FA were implacable. On match days, he was still stuck in the main stand.

Joe turned to Norah with a half-smile on his face. He wasn't entirely sure what had just happened, but his question was stilled as he heard his name called again.

'Joe!'

He turned to see Eric Alexander, the young chairman of Manchester City, the son of Albert, the chairman who had hired him, coming towards him wearing a large grin.

'We want you to go onto the pitch so the crowd can applaud you.'

'Well now, Chairman, I'm not sure that's such a good idea.'

'It's a wonderful idea, Joe,' said Norah, her eyes sparkling with happiness for her husband. Joe might be worried about his reception, but she wasn't. She knew exactly what would happen out there.

'What about the board?'

'Never mind about them. You were here seven years. You deserve it.'

'You don't think they'll throw things at me?'

'Joe, there has never been a manager so loved by the crowd as you in the history of this football club.'

Joe was still undecided. He had planned to sneak into his seat in the directors' box when the crowd's attention was focused on the players. If people recognised him and shouted a cheery greeting so much the better, but he had left Maine Road under such unhappy circumstances that he didn't see how it would ever be possible to return to that earlier state of grace. His last two seasons as manager at City had been fraught with tension and fighting. It had been horrible, and he didn't want to reawaken any of those memories.

His wife and his former chairman stood there waiting for him.

'Come on, Joe,' said Norah quietly. 'Just go onto the pitch for a few seconds, wave at the crowd and then come off.' He nodded. He trusted Norah's judgement in nearly all things, even in football. They walked back down the stairs and into the tunnel. Passing the dressing-rooms, he could hear the sound of someone, probably Joe Corrigan, throwing a ball against the wall. He saw the referee and linesmen in earnest conference, and down at the far end of the tunnel he could see the crowd in the Kippax, excited, always anticipating victory, desperate for a first sight of the boys in blue. Well, they were getting a 58-year-old man in a coat and a trilby hat.

Eric and Norah stopped as they approached the end of the tunnel. They knew whose day it was. Joe continued steadily but nervously. It was like being a player again, the nerves of the match to come causing all his muscles to tense even though he had spent the last half an hour trying to loosen them. The crowd was an amorphous blur in front of him, though from all sides he heard the sound of his name.

'Joe!'

'It's Joe!'

'Here's Joe!'

'Good old Joe!'

'Thanks for everything, Joe!'

He felt the first prickle of tears in his rheumy old eyes. There was no room for sentiment in football. Hadn't his chequered career been testament to that old saying? Hadn't he left here nine months ago knowing in the pit of his stomach the truth of it? But it wasn't true. Not today. It wasn't only Joe Mercer who was feeling it. He could sense it all around the ground.

He emerged from the tunnel alone and walked over to the white touchline. 'Once you cross that white line you're on your own,' he would always tell the players, encouraging them to make their own decisions, to think out the game for themselves. Well, he was on his own now, but it was going to be all right. He walked a couple of yards in from the touchline, where Summerbee would pick up the ball and begin his run down the right wing towards the Platt Lane end. Tentatively, he raised his trilby hat in the direction of the Kippax. It was the gesture of a modest man – not the arms-aloft triumphalism of Malcolm Allison.

The terraces exploded with applause. All the spectators in the other stands who had been sitting down rose to their feet and clapped and shouted. Everywhere he looked there were smiles. He could hear his name again. They chanted it in chorus like a litany. Well, why not? This was their church, their cathedral. They came here to worship, to be absolved, to find comfort and eternal truths, to discover a purpose to their straitened, frequently mean lives in the glory that was football.

'Joe! Joe!!'

He was home. He lifted his trilby to the Platt Lane Stand and then to the new North Stand. He would never be forgotten. The last few months were history. They would remember the good times, the great times.

He turned and walked back towards the touchline, where Norah was waiting for him, Eric Alexander having already returned to the directors' box. Glancing upwards, he saw the glowering face of Malcolm Allison, who had clearly suffered as his own crowd lavished their affection on the manager of today's opposition. He knew what Malcolm was thinking: if 30,000 fans had all that love for Joe, how much could possibly be left for him? The next 90 minutes would tell him. Joe smiled. Joe always smiled. He wished Malcolm would try smiling a little more often. Even if he was hurting inside, as he knew he must be now. Joe still felt compassion for his old colleague, even after all the misery of their last two years together. They had travelled so far together, they had brought so much pleasure to so many people, it was a tragedy that their relationship, for so long the envy of the rest of the football world, should lie in dust at their feet. It was nearly eight years since the two of them had started out on the journey of a lifetime. The memory of those early days of uncertainty, that intoxicating mixture of irrepressible hope and paralysing fear, was as vivid now as it had ever been. Before his eyes the crowd in the main stand seemed to dissolve and all he could see was the rotting iron and steel hulk of a ground that was falling rapidly into a state of disrepair, a deeply depressing mausoleum, just as it had been that day in July 1965 when he had walked into it for the first time.

ONE

Sidney Rose stood by his seat in the directors' box and looked across the deserted Maine Road ground. It was a cold, damp July morning, yet another cold, damp morning in the miserable summer of 1965. Looking at the ground without the presence of the goalposts and the white lines marked out in their familiar geometrical shapes, and at the unkempt grass waiting for the order that would be imposed by the motor-mower still locked up in the groundsman's hut, Sidney wondered if he had ever seen a sadder sight. He wondered if he was witnessing not the beginning of a new season, with all the optimism that invariably accompanies it, but the last mournful rituals of a club whose day was done.

The previous season, the worst in his memory – which went back to the opening of the Maine Road stadium in 1923 – had concluded with a match against Charlton Athletic in front of an embarrassingly small crowd of 8,409. City had finished 11th in the Second Division. Across town, Manchester United were winning the First-Division Championship in front of full houses and with their new triumphant triumvirate of Best, Law and Charlton in the apogee of their glory. Calls for City to merge with, or rather into, United had been heard on the terraces, in the press and, to Sidney's discomfort, in the City boardroom.

The one man on the board that he knew from endless board meetings would never countenance such a spineless submission was the Chairman, Albert Alexander, a small, loquacious man in his 70s, who was currently recovering in hospital from an operation. His health was fragile but not his dedication to the cause, and when Sidney Rose saw him later that morning on his rounds as consultant surgeon, Albert was sitting up in bed and full of plans for the future.

'Do you think we could get Don Revie back to Maine Road, Sidney?'

Sidney had no wish to inhibit his patient's post-operative recovery, but the prospect of persuading City's star player of ten years ago to abandon his current post as the manager of the increasingly successful Leeds United, last season's FA Cup finalists and First-Division runners-up, seemed highly unlikely.

'Well . . .' he began slowly, but Albert's mind was racing. The appointment of a new manager to fill the vacancy caused by the sacking of George Poyser in April was of paramount urgency.

'If you don't think he'll come, what about Joe Mercer?'

'Albert, he's ill. He has hypertension. I doubt he'll ever be well enough to manage again.'

'I've been ill, but I'll be there for the first match of the season.'

'He's, well, older than 50 . . .'

'For heaven's sake, Sidney, look at me. I'm much older than Joe Mercer. Do you see any reason why I shouldn't be the manager of a football club – if I wanted to?'

Sidney smiled. Albert's enthusiasm was infectious, even if his judgement needed serious questioning.

'I think Joe Mercer was a wonderful player and a decent manager, but above all he's a gentleman. I think if his health is up to it, we could do much worse. But is his health up to it?'

It was a conversation that would be repeated at higher volume in a semi-detached house just outside Birmingham later that week.

'Why, Mum? He's been desperate to get back into football.'

'Because I think it'll kill him!'

'You think he's happy now?'

'No, but he's alive, isn't he?'

Norah was rarely roused to extreme emotion. It was the way she had learned over the years to live with Joe, but David was taking his father's side, ostensibly oblivious to the death sentence a return to football management could mean.

David raised his hand in partial apology. 'Mum, he's been so miserable this year. Even if . . . something happened, he'd die happy.'

'Was he so happy at Villa? Or Sheffield United?'

'He can't live without the game!'

'And he won't live with it. Dr Brown said the stroke's left him with a scar.'

'He's got a scar the length of his shin from when Billy Milne broke his leg. He's got a scar on his soul from the relegation seasons. What's one more scar?'

'It's on his brain, and I don't want to be a widow.'

'Mum, please.'

'He's put you up to this, hasn't he?'

David didn't answer. There was no point really. He'd overheard his father's end of the first phone call with Walter Griffiths, the Secretary of Manchester City.

'For God's sake don't say anything to my wife. She'll bloody kill me when she finds out.'

The ignorance lasted five minutes. As soon as Joe had suggested she run him into Manchester, Norah knew perfectly well the only reason was that there was a job on offer somewhere. She had pleaded with him not to take it. 'Manchester City?' she queried with a note of astonishment in her voice. 'Are you crazy?' Joe couldn't help admitting that she might be right, but he wasn't up to driving from Birmingham to Manchester, and he needed Norah to take him there.

'Let's just see what they have to say,' he said cautiously.

'You know what they'll have to say. If they're serious about offering you the job they'll expect you to work miracles with no money – just like at Villa, just like at Sheffield.' Joe knew in his heart that Norah was right, and the irritation this provoked nearly caused him to lose his temper even with this woman whom he loved so much.

'Norah, I need football!'

'More than me?'

'Yes! . . . No, of course not. It's different. You know that. Please.'

'Six months, Joe. Give it six months more.'

'There are no jobs in the middle of the season. Or if there are, it's some club in deep trouble.'

'And this lot aren't? Matt's not playing for them these days. Neither is Peter Doherty. They're a load of rubbish, and the very fact that they've come to you shows they're scraping the bottom of the barrel.'

'Oh, thanks very much.'

'I don't mean it like that, Joe. But you're still sick. Everyone in football knows that, and that's why no First-Division club's been asking about you and why this lot'll take the chance.'

'Norah,' said Joe quietly and with surprising calmness, 'if I don't get back into football now, I'll be dead in six months.'

Norah looked at him and smiled. She loved him so much, and she knew what he said was true – maybe not literally, he was only 51 after all, but he was dying inside, shrivelling up in his heart and mind and soul where the football used to be.

'Go and put a different tie on,' she said with resignation. 'Go on. Smarten yourself up a bit. You can't be the manager of a big football club in a torn cardigan and with an egg stain on your tie.'

He kissed her. He felt alive again. It wasn't a job or even the offer of a job. It was just a chance to talk about returning to football again as a manager. It was enough.

Norah was waiting for him in the car on the Maine Road forecourt when he came tripping down the steps from the front entrance, his face almost cracked in two with that broad grin she loved so much. She knew he'd got the job even before he raised his trilby with a mock ceremonial bow.

'Get in. We've got rush-hour traffic to drive through.' Joe did as he was told. Norah had to admit that he looked entirely different from the ashen figure who had been stumbling around the house, getting under her feet for the past 12 months.

'I suppose you're going to tell me you've got the job.'

'Two years I told them. That's all I want. And they're going to hire me an assistant to do a lot of the hard work with the players.' Norah was pleased. At last Joe seemed to be learning a bit of sense.

'What's the money like?'

'A bit less than the Villa job.'

'Less!'

'Well, be fair, love, City are in the Second Division and Villa were in the First.'

'How much less?'

Joe told her. Norah sighed. He was hopeless with money.

'Is that OK?' he asked anxiously.

'I'm glad they didn't ask you to pay them. You'd probably have agreed, wouldn't you?'

Joe smiled and didn't answer. He looked out of the side window at the streets of Moss Side – the endless rows of back-to-back terraced houses built in Victorian times, the little cobbled alleyways running between them, the occasional small parade of shops with their unappealing goods in the window. The television commentators and the newspaper columnists told the country that Britain was living in the so-called Swinging '60s, a decade of unparalleled prosperity, but he could see no sign of it in this part of

Manchester. It might be different a few miles away in the leafy suburbs of Cheadle and Gatley, but this stretch of the inner city seemed as depressed and as deprived as it had ever been. The Maine Road stadium rose out of these mean narrow streets like a cathedral, towering over the tiny dwellings of the impoverished people who formed its congregation.

Joe knew what football meant to the working people of the country because he was one of them and he knew what it meant to him. City was a great club fallen on hard times, and to his way of thinking there was only one way it could go from its current position: and that was up. And he was the man to take them there. He'd been a great player, captain of his club, captain of his country, but he hadn't been a great manager. In the nine seasons he'd been in charge of two different clubs, he'd known his moments of relative success, but he knew in his heart he hadn't fulfilled expectations in the manager's role – not like his friend Matt Busby, now his rival across the city.

He knew from the start that United were going to be one of his biggest problems. The directors had told him as much during his interview. They had also told him that Derek Kevan, who had been City's top goalscorer for the past two seasons, wanted a transfer – and Matt Gray, Jimmy Murray, David Connor, Alan Ogley and Neil Young had expressed concerns about their futures, which they thought would be better served away from Maine Road.

'How many professionals have we got on the playing staff?' Joe had asked.

'Twenty-two,' answered Walter Griffiths, the Secretary.

'Well, if we transfer them all it's going to leave us a bit short of putting out a first team and a reserve team on Saturdays.'

'How were they?' asked Norah as she guided the car onto the A6 to Stockport. Joe didn't need to be told who 'they' were.

'I liked the Chairman,' said Joe, attempting to put a positive spin on things for Norah, who knew how he despised and feared football club directors as a breed. 'He's tiny, not much more than five foot, but very . . . warm and kind, I think.'

'What about the others?'

'Oh well, you know . . .' Norah knew well enough. They needed Joe right now, but as soon as results started to disappoint and the crowd turned sullen and then resentful, all the fine words and backslapping that accompanied the signing of the contract would be replaced by cold shoulders and avoidance of eye contact as they searched the contract for the clause that would enable them to get out of it at minimum cost. Joe would lose his cheerfulness, start to worry, become ill again . . .

'Chairman said they'd turned down Shankly and Revie to get me.' Joe laughed. Even Norah couldn't help smiling at the absurdity. What a ridiculous game football was, and how crazy it was that 22 men in shorts behaving like overgrown schoolboys could so affect both their lives.

'Isn't Bill Shankly happy at Liverpool?'

'You would have thought winning the League last year and the Cup this year might have kept him there for a while longer. According to Mr Alexander, him and Revie would have given their right arms to manage this team.'

'Eh?'

'Directors!' And he smiled again at the absurd idea that the two managers who had walked out at Wembley at the head of their teams in the Cup final played a few weeks previously would gladly throw up two of the best jobs in the country to come and manage a team of little talent floundering in the middle of the Second Division, playing out their home games in front of fewer than ten thousand supporters in a stadium designed to hold over sixty thousand.

'You know you had Ray Shaw and Dick Taylor and Jimmy Easson to help you out at Villa, and the work still nearly killed you. If you're going to be out every night of the year again, driving thousands of miles all over the country, you'll have a stroke. And this time you won't recover.'

'I won't be out that often. I'm going to delegate.'

'Joe! Delegate? You? Don't make me laugh.'

'I mean it, Norah. The board agreed. They even offered me Johnny Hart, but I told them the chap I'm thinking about is more than a trainer or a scout, and he's young and hungry.'

'What's his name?'

'Allison.'

'That's a girl's name.'

'Malcolm Allison.'

'And who's he when he's at home?'

'He's the manager of Plymouth Argyle.'

'Well, if he's already a manager why would he want to come and be your dogsbody?'

'Because he's just been sacked and he's as mad as hell. He wants to prove the whole world wrong.'

Norah gave Joe a sideways look. She wondered if he was aware of how closely that description fitted him, as well as his new coach. She'd never heard the name Malcolm Allison before, but from what Joe had told her about him her first instinct was that her husband had made a very grown-up decision. She drove back to Birmingham along the A34 in a slightly more optimistic frame of mind. If this chap Allison could take some of the worries off Joe and let him stand back and do the PR he was so good at, maybe this partnership would work out after all.

TWO

'Fuck them! Who gives a shit about Plymouth Argyle anyway?'
Malcolm Allison faced the prospect of unemployment with the
insouciance of a man who knew that his horizons stretched further
than Home Park and the south-west corner of England. As he drove
away he smiled, recalling the first time he had driven into the car park
to find two detectives waiting in his office to arrest him over a small
matter of £94 in unpaid parking fines. He wrote out a cheque for the
full amount despite knowing perfectly well that his bank account did
not have sufficient funds to cover it. Something would turn up. It
always did.

Plymouth had never seen anyone quite like Malcolm Allison, and the
board of directors were quite sure they never wanted to do so again. His
flamboyant behaviour had split the board down the middle, and despite
a season in which they had reached the semi-final of the League Cup and
challenged strongly for promotion to the First Division until the New
Year, Plymouth decided they could dispense with the services of their
ebullient young manager before the end of the campaign.

Allison was hardly devastated. On Easter Monday, the directors had
told him to select John Leiper in goal instead of his preferred choice,
Noel Dwyer. That was enough. They could bugger about all they wanted
in the boardroom, but the moment they started to think they could pick
his teams for him he knew the time had arrived to move on.

'Who's picking this fucking team?' he demanded of one of the
directors.

'Not you, sunshine!' came the instant reply.

A few days later, and well before the final whistle blew at the end of
the last match of the season, he was on his way out of Home Park. As
soon as he had extracted his pay-off of £1,650, his contracted salary for

what would have been his second season in charge, he was as keen to be off as the Plymouth directors were to see the back of him.

He was quite sure it wasn't the football he'd coaxed out of the players that was the reason for his dismissal. He almost hugged himself when he recalled that magical moment in the 3–2 home win over Manchester City in November. Exactly as he had taught them on the training pitch, the captain and centre-half, John Newman, stepped up to take the penalty that had just been awarded. But instead of shooting at goal, he simply rolled the ball a few inches forward for Mike Trebilcock to storm into the box and hammer it past the startled Alan Ogley, who had sprinted from the City goal fractionally too late to block the shot. For a moment, a stunned silence reigned in Home Park, broken only by the sound of a roar from Malcolm Allison climbing out of the dugout and bellowing his triumph into the afternoon sky. The Manchester City players were shortly to get a closer look at the large figure in an overcoat with both arms raised above his head as he saluted his own bold cunning, removing his Russian 'Cossack' hat and bowing low in the direction of the Plymouth directors' box, whose inhabitants, after their initial exultation, remained unimpressed by the crowd-pleasing antics of their manager. The referee realised that no infringement of the rules had taken place and pointed to the centre spot as the crowd applauded one of the most original goals ever scored in the south-west of England.

In the opposition dugout, Jimmy Meadows, the Manchester City trainer, seethed. He didn't like Malcolm Allison at all. The previous night, Meadows had been drinking quietly in a Plymouth bar when Peter Gardner, the *Manchester Evening News* reporter on the City beat, drew his attention to the large, grinning figure at a corner table. He had each of his arms around an attractive blonde woman, occasionally, and with some reluctance, removing one of them from a bare shoulder to flick the ash from his Montecristo cigar. On the table in front of them stood one empty and one recently opened bottle of champagne.

'Isn't that their manager, Allison?' asked Gardner innocently. Meadows turned to stare. This was no way for the manager of a Football League club to behave.

'What a fucking twat he is.'

'We'll see how big a twat he is at twenty to five tomorrow,' observed Gardner sagely.

At twenty to five the following afternoon, as the referee was about to blow for full-time, Jimmy Meadows picked up the bucket of cold water he kept by his side, extracted the 'magic' sponge and walked across to stand in front of the Plymouth Argyle dugout, where the cigar-smoking ponce from the previous night was wearing the broadest of grins. He was about to engage in chortling banter with the opposition when the referee's whistle sounded. As he opened his mouth to impart his humorous commentary on Plymouth's 3–2 victory, Meadows emptied the entire bucket of cold water over him and ran off down the players' tunnel. Behind him he heard a bellow of anger that sounded as though it had emanated from an enraged beast.

Meadows ran into the dressing-room with his players, who were shuffling in slowly, heads bowed in the time-honoured show of disappointment displayed by any losing side. They were astonished to see their trainer slam the door shut and then hurl his body against it.

'What the fuck's going on, Jimmy?' asked Dave Bacuzzi, the blond-haired right-back.

'C'mere, Kev!' exhorted the trainer. Derek Kevan was a big lad and the obvious bloke to put his shoulder against the door. 'I think . . .' Meadows's speculation was ended by the sound of an animal roar and fists pounding on the door of the dressing-room. 'Kevan, all of you, get over here and keep this fucking maniac out. Come on!'

The urgency of his tone prompted an instant response from the nearest three players, who were glad enough that the prospect of the traditional post-mortem of defeat had been indefinitely postponed.

'Which fucking maniac, Jim?' asked Alan Oakes reasonably.

'Is it Albert Alexander?' The players laughed at Bobby Kennedy's humorous suggestion that City's elderly 5 ft 2 in. Chairman, with his obsession with tea in china cups and smoked-salmon sandwiches, was pounding the dressing-room door with both fists and now boots.

'It's their fucking twat of a manager. He wants to kill me.'

'Why? Have you been making him do laps of the pitch?' It was Meadows's favourite way of torturing the players, and now that their trainer was in trouble they were gleefully taking advantage of a rare opportunity to watch him squirm.

'I threw a bucket of water over him. I don't think he liked it.'

'I'll fucking slaughter you, you cunt,' came the shouted promise from the other side of the barricaded door as the kicks increased in intensity. They stopped only when the muffled voice of someone in authority, possibly the Plymouth chairman or the referee, spoke sharply to Allison. The players thought the whole escapade was a tremendous joke, but

THE WORST OF FRIENDS

Meadows stayed nervously by the door, opening it only once to let in a bemused George Poyser, City's nonentity of a manager.

Once he had dried off in the home dressing-room, Malcolm Allison recovered his former good spirits quite quickly. The fact that the opposition could only respond to the cleverness of his football brain by throwing a bucket of cold water over him seemed to him, on reflection, the final proof that the world of football was there to be taken by a man with the courage to think laterally about the game. Jimmy Meadows had been reduced to the actions of a frustrated kid because he had been out-thought by a clever tactician and had no reply.

Malcolm's players, of course, increased their respect for their innovative manager. But the water incident didn't endear him any more to his own directors, who spoke to him sharply about his reaction to it. That just confirmed Malcolm in his belief that directors were to be ignored with the contempt they deserved. He would continue to demonstrate to the Plymouth supporters that he had the most original football brain in the game. No, he knew perfectly well that it certainly wasn't the quality of the football on display that caused Malcolm Allison to be relieved of his position as the manager of Plymouth Argyle.

The affair with the wife of one of the directors probably didn't advance his cause much in the boardroom. He had, he could have truthfully protested had he been minded to do so, made none of the running. That was all her. In fact, she had made such a direct play for him that even he, not the most subtle of men, had been put off. His dismissal of her simply increased her determination to have him, and finally he had submitted. The fact that she was attractive made the decision easier, but even he, with his experience of the duplicity of humanity, was unprepared for what she did next. They had spent the afternoon in bed together at the cottage of one of her girl friends. He had barely dressed and let himself out of the house before the woman had rung her husband to proclaim triumphantly what she had done and with whom.

He was shocked by his own behaviour, knowing instinctively that it had been a mistake to have become involved even briefly with a woman like that. Though apologetic to the directors, it took some effort on his part to calm the hostility in the boardroom. It was as if the new sexual morality that had excited even the readers of the *Daily Telegraph* had come to a sudden halt on the Exeter bypass.

He was prepared to concede that the enjoyably athletic afternoon in bed with the director's wife had been a mistake, but these same moralistic prudes also seemed to take it amiss that he had formed a relationship with the 16-year-old Serena Williams, just because she was a little over 20 years younger than he was. It had been one of his more memorable first encounters. He had just taken the manager's job and was staying in a Plymouth hotel when he noticed a very striking young woman in an orange dress who was accompanying a bookmaker to his annual dinner dance. As she passed him on her way to the cloakroom, he took hold of her arm and said in the domineering tone of voice that had invariably proved successful in the past, 'I'd like to take you to dinner, young lady.' She stopped and looked at him. In the two seconds it took her to appraise him, he had clearly passed the test. It was only the directors of Plymouth Argyle who thought he'd failed.

But despite his initial indifference at his termination, as May turned into June and the phone didn't ring, the old doubts began to flood back. Malcolm had always felt driven by football, always knew he was meant to achieve great things. He'd not done so as a player, but that wasn't just about the football; it was also about the illness, the TB, having a lung removed. It had started during a night match against Sheffield United, one of the first he had played under floodlights – a magical, thrilling atmosphere. Just before half-time, a Sheffield forward had shown him the ball and taken it past him. He turned to chase, but though he pumped his arms he couldn't run. It was as if his legs were wading through treacle. It was terrifying, but he quickly attributed it to playing too soon after being out for some matches with a nasty bout of Asian flu. He managed to get through the rest of the game, but he was struggling for breath after every run. All night he lay awake in the Sheffield hotel room coughing – coughing his career away, for he knew it was serious and that his room-mate and closest friend in the game, Noel Cantwell, was right when he advised him to go to a hospital as soon as they got back to London.

He could never find the words to convey to anyone the utter devastation he felt at having his career, his principal reason for living, taken away from him in the time it took a harassed consultant at the London Hospital to look at an X-ray and say, 'Mr Allison, you have a severe case of TB. I'm going to need to remove a lung, so you'll have to forget about playing football again.' All that time in the sanatorium in Sussex, he felt that he didn't belong there, especially when he saw other patients who were in a worse condition than he was, but this was the start of the depression that periodically afflicted him for years afterwards. When he later read a biography of Churchill and learned about the wartime leader's 'black dogs', Malcolm felt a shiver of recognition. So terrifying were these moods of utter despair that once he went of his own volition to a small church near the sanatorium seeking an explanation for why this terrible catastrophe had befallen him, but no answer was provided – not one he immediately appreciated, at any rate. He never confessed this unique if short journey into the world of spirituality to his teammates, and he couldn't help observing how uncomfortable were those West Ham players who had bothered to make the trip to see him in the heart of the Sussex countryside. He might have felt as though he didn't belong in the sanatorium in Midhurst, but he knew well enough that West Ham United felt strongly he didn't belong at Upton Park any longer, either.

He went to the banquet at the Café Royal to celebrate the winning of the Second-Division Championship and the club's promotion to the First Division only to be told that he hadn't played sufficient matches to justify the award of a Championship medal. He was being challenged for the number 6 shirt by the 17-year-old Bobby Moore, an intelligent kid who listened when Malcolm talked to him about the game. The kid was certainly talented, arguably more talented than he was, but Malcolm was 29 and at the peak of his career when the illness struck. Undaunted, he started training again; nothing was going to stop him getting back into the first team, but when injuries eventually caused a vacancy in the West Ham defence, the first team's number 6 shirt went to Bobby Moore. That was the end of Malcolm Allison the footballer, but it was the making of Malcolm Allison the coach.

Nobody could 'see' football like he could. He knew plenty of other players who lived and breathed the game as he did, but none who had his vision. The men who ran football in England never understood the significance of the defeat in the 1950 World Cup or the 6–3 hammering by Hungary at Wembley in November 1953. Malcolm had been at Wembley that day and knew he was seeing the start of a revolution in how football was played, not just a poor performance by an ageing England team. Throughout the decade in which he earned his living as a professional footballer, he was conscious that things were done so much better abroad. The lightweight boots, the streamlined kit, the realisation that football was about tactics and what happened in the players' minds as much as strength and what happened on the pitch: these developments were taking shape in South America and all over Europe, but there was no reflection of this in the English game. When Chelsea, the 1955 English champions, were invited to take part in the first European Cup competition, the English Football Association declined on their behalf.

For two or three years Malcolm Allison deserted the game that had meant so much to him. He became by turns an unsuccessful car salesman and then a professional gambler. On good days, he had his fill of champagne and cigars and the sort of women who were attracted to that kind of lifestyle. On bad days, he tried to do the same with fewer funds at his disposal. Then there was the Artists and Repertoire nightclub off Charing Cross Road, which he opened with a loan of £2,000 from the Queens Park Rangers chairman, Jim Gregory. The A&R soon attracted Malcolm's favourite clientele, a mix of showbiz personalities such as Harry Secombe and Dorothy Squires, as well as various members of London's criminal underworld and footballers. The measly earnings of the underpaid footballers didn't contribute much to A&R's income, which rarely exceeded its expenses. It pained him to see how easily football seemed to manage without him. Tottenham Hotspur did the double, playing a brand of attacking football of a quality he could not help but admire, but he doubted that the English game in its ossified state was ready for his own innovative ideas.

He had not abandoned football altogether during those days at Kempton Park and Ascot and behind the bar in Tin Pan Alley. There were games in non-League football for Romford and a spell of coaching with Cambridge University. It was a most unlikely combination – the son of an electrician from Bexleyheath and a bunch of young gentlemen, mostly from the great public schools of the country – yet it worked. He observed their rituals with silent astonishment, comparing their relative sophistication with the behaviour of football professionals of a similar age. More to the point, the boys were intelligent. He liked that. He liked the way they listened to him, the way they respected his ideas and their willingness to put his ideas into practice. He knew how sceptical professional players could be, and he was glad of the opportunity to try out his ideas on players who were happy to cooperate.

And he won the big one. At Wembley, he took his team of Light Blues to play their traditional opponents, the Dark Blues of Oxford, and he sat on that bench below the Royal Box where he had seen the underestimated and unfairly maligned England manager Walter Winterbottom sit so many times during the 1950s. At least he had the satisfaction of picking his own team, which was more than had been granted to Winterbottom, who had been forced to watch impassively as a team that had been handed to him by the blazered fools of the Football Association struggled to come to terms with opponents who did not play in the classic 'WM' formation that had stereotyped British teams since the time of Herbert Chapman.

The other benefit was that the young men under his control had a self-discipline that came hard to young professionals. Although he only travelled up to Cambridge for training sessions and matches, he understood well enough that for an undergraduate to be awarded a Blue was as great a mark of estimation as an international cap was for a professional player. When he left players out, he told them why he had done it. That must have diluted the bitterness of their disappointment, and Malcolm was rewarded with a nod of understanding for his trouble. It probably came from being beaten at public school, he thought, before he realised how little the corporal punishment inflicted upon him had affected his own behaviour. If you didn't have self-discipline, you needed a coach or a manager who would keep you in line. But then Ted Fenton had tried that at West Ham, and Malcolm had resented it. In the end, the best coaches were those who could strike a balance between teaching players to be self-disciplined professionals while allowing them to express themselves freely on the pitch.

Winning the Varsity match at Wembley twice caused no headlines anywhere other than in the Cambridge student newspaper, but for Malcolm it relit the flames of ambition to coach at the highest level. Soon there came the chance to display his talents first with Bath City, then in Toronto during the Canadian summer, and finally at Plymouth Argyle he seized the opportunity to show the world what he could do with a Football League club. At a time when managers sat and fumed quietly in the stand rather than the dugout and understood the importance of the bland diplomatic comment when in conversation with the local press, what Malcolm Allison could do with consummate ease was to outrage his board of directors, get involved in disputes with linesmen and referees over their decisions, tell a BBC interviewer that 80 per cent of all referees were biased towards the home side and run his eye over every attractive woman within a 50-mile radius of Home Park.

Well, there were plenty more beautiful women in the country, plenty of as yet unopened bottles of champagne, more exciting nightclubs and, more importantly, better players than those he had worked with so far. Above all, he knew that he was destined for the top, and the fact that the small businessmen who ran a Second-Division club in the south-west corner of England – where football was less highly regarded than rugby union – had sacked him only served to reinforce his conviction about his ultimate destiny.

In the weeks after his dismissal from Plymouth, however, the foundations of that confidence were shaken. Even after he put the feelers out, the phone remained obstinately quiet. He ran out of money, of course, but that had never bothered him before, though it did tend to strain relations with his long-suffering wife, Beth, whose tolerance for the big gesture and the empty wallet was starting to wear out. There was an odd call from a club in Amsterdam called Blue-White, who wanted to talk about the prospect of coaching in Holland, but a firm offer never materialised. Raich Carter rang to see if he fancied coming up to Middlesbrough as coach, but again he was unsure. He'd been a manager; did he want to be someone else's number two?

Then Joe Lowery called and invited him to spend the day at Doncaster Racecourse. It was a welcome return to old times and familiar faces. He had first met Joe at Hackney Dog Track, where he was happy to act as his runner, putting his money on dogs and collecting the winnings in return for a small percentage, which in most cases was greater than his weekly wage from West Ham United. Malcolm had an idea that Joe might have been involved in a doping ring – such talk was common on the training ground and in the press – but he never asked Joe, and Joe never volunteered the information. There was one infamous night when Joe won a lot of cash and was approached by two men in the car park who made it clear to him that he would not be welcome in the future at any dog track in the country. Thereafter Joe and Malcolm turned their attention to horses.

Malcolm had grown up in a part of the world in which some form of criminal activity was unremarkable, and he had always been grateful that his talent for football had kept him from being sucked into the vortex of crime. As far as he was concerned, Joe Lowery was a friend who had never got him into trouble, and he was determined to behave equally well when, as he returned to his car after the last race at Doncaster, he found two policemen waiting for him.

'Mr Allison?'

'Yes.'

'I'm Detective Inspector Hargreaves and this is Detective Sergeant Chalmers. We'd like you to answer a few questions.'

'What sort of questions?'

'Questions relating to your association with Joe Lowery.'

'He's just a friend. We were talking about old times.'

Malcolm continued to answer in the same vein for the next four hours, which he spent at a Doncaster police station. The inexplicable failure of the favourite in the last St Leger Stakes had aroused suspicion, and Joe had been under observation for many weeks. It was clear that the police were determined to nail Joe Lowery and equally clear that Malcolm Allison had no intention of helping them to do so. Eventually a young woman constable came into the room to say that a very insistent man was on the phone and had to speak to Malcolm Allison urgently. The interrogating officer thought it might be helpful to his line of inquiry to allow the witness a brief moment to relax and think about something else. He allowed Malcolm to leave the room.

Malcolm walked to the station desk and picked up the telephone receiver that was lying on its side.

'Hello?'

'Malcolm?' came a vaguely familiar, warm but distant voice.

'Yes.'

'It's Joe Mercer here. What the bloody hell are you doing in a police cell?'

THREE

I made my First-Division debut here, you know.'

'I didn't know. Did you win?'

'Christmas Eve 1949. We got stuffed 2–0. Andy Black and Roy Clarke.'

'Good players.'

'Yeah, but the problem was at the other end. We couldn't have got anything past their keeper that day if we'd played till midnight.'

'Big Frank wasn't still playing, was he?'

'Nah. It was some Kraut they'd just signed called Trautmann.'

Joe laughed, Malcolm smiled. It was so good to talk football again and with someone who, he felt, instinctively understood the way he talked and thought. Joe was thinking similarly warm thoughts.

'So what do you think? You owe me for bailing you out.'

However timely the phone call, Malcolm had not been entirely surprised to get it. He knew exactly why Joe had wanted him to stop off in Manchester on his way up to Middlesbrough to discuss Raich Carter's job offer and not on his way back down again, and he was already attracted by the prospect of working at Manchester City even before he drove onto the Maine Road forecourt. Everyone in football knew that Joe Mercer had been seriously ill, and the chances were he'd be able to offer Malcolm more responsibility than Raich Carter. Even though coaching and working with the players would be his main duty, he was certain he could persuade Joe Mercer to make him assistant manager. Besides, Manchester City meant something to him as a club. When he was a young lad, they'd reached the Cup final twice in successive years in the 1930s, and he'd heard on the wireless their 3–0 defeat to Everton and their 2–1 victory over Portsmouth. He knew they had a bit of history about them in the way that Middlesbrough didn't, and, a significant consideration this, the nightlife was bound to be better in Manchester.

THE WORST OF FRIENDS

'Let's have a look at the place,' said Malcolm and walked down the tunnel towards the echoing vastness of the covered terrace known as the Kippax. No matter how many times he walked down a tunnel and onto a football pitch, the pleasure rarely diminished. Of course, he would have preferred to have been holding a ball and running out with ten teammates behind him, but at his age his career would have been finished even if the tuberculosis hadn't got him first. He stared at the scoreboard on top of the open terrace behind the goal to his left. There were no goalposts and no net, just empty rows of concrete steps broken by the occasional crush barrier, but in his head he heard the roar of 60,000 voices as they saluted the great team he had built showing off the trophy they had just won to their adoring fans. Was it the FA Cup? The European Cup? That wasn't the point. The point was winning – winning with style, winning with a team that had begun in his mind, a team of kids and has-beens, wannabes and never-beens, brought together, brought to glory by his imagination. That was what he wanted, and the more he thought about it the more he believed that Manchester City could offer him that.

'There's not much money in it.' Joe's warning demolished the fantasy instantly. They started to walk round the empty stadium together. Football grounds are meant to be full of supporters, and when they are nobody notices much whether the place is in good decorative order. All that matters is the green grass and the actions of the 22 players on it. Outside of 21 days or so a year, the grounds are mostly empty, and that is when their flaws are dramatically visible. The grass growing out of the cracks in the car park, the peeling paint, the crumbling terraces: here was incontrovertible evidence of a club in steep decline. Malcolm liked a challenge, but for a moment he saw just how far they would have to go merely to get the club back on its feet again. The more money they spent on doing the ground up, of course, meant less money for him and Joe to spend on players. Still, paying two managers a decent wage was going to be cheaper than buying new players.

'When you say "not much" . . .' began Malcolm slowly.

'Maybe 50 grand.' Malcolm stopped, amazed. For a moment, his mind saw images of nightclubs awash with champagne, blonde bunny girls leaning over his shoulder as he pushed a wad of notes over the green baize in front of a spinning roulette wheel. If it was good enough for James Bond, it was good enough for him.

Joe's face broke into a broad grin. He knew exactly what Malcolm was thinking.

'For players,' he laughed. 'That's two decent ones or three or four crap ones, and they've got enough of them at this club already.'

'What do you think they'll offer me?' asked Malcolm, reluctant to let go of the image of Sean Connery and his bevy of blonde beauties.

'Thirty quid a week I think they said.'

'Any players getting that?'

'I think Crossan's on forty or forty-five, and he's the top earner.'

'Crossan's a really good player. What the fuck is he doing here?'

'I think we should make him captain. I've always rated him. I wanted him when I was at Sheffield United and then again at Villa.'

Malcolm nodded and looked around sadly at the crumbling mausoleum.

'You know, this place once held over eighty thousand for a cup tie.'

'They were getting less than ten thousand last season. D'you think they'll ever come back?'

'Joe, I guarantee, within two months we'll be getting over thirty thousand here.'

'Does that mean you'll take the job?'

Malcolm held out his hand. Joe clasped it. He liked the younger man's gesture.

'Me and you, Joe. We could take on the world.'

'Maybe. But you'll have to take on the board of directors first.'

Malcolm dressed carefully. A fawn suit with an open-necked blue shirt. Respectful, but still his own man. There was no reason to suppose that the directors of Manchester City would, in essence, be any different from the directors of Plymouth Argyle, so the fawn suit would show them he could behave responsibly. The lack of a tie proclaimed that he belonged to nobody but himself.

The five directors seemed old. They wore old suits; they sat in old chairs in an old boardroom. Most of them were in their 70s, and they all behaved as though they had been in charge for the 32 years since the Maine Road stadium had been built. They belonged to the 1930s, when he was in primary school, when the world had been a drab black-and-white affair. Maybe that was why they felt so comfortable with Joe Mercer. They had seen him play before the war, and they had seen him continue his career into his 40th year, a veteran in the early 1950s.

Malcolm belonged to now – to a world of pop music and champagne and nightclubs, to a world of flowered ties and mini-skirted girls with long straight hair, to a world of television and advertising, to a world suffused in bold primary colours. The pale blue of Manchester City bothered him a little as he contrasted it with the dynamic blood-red of the shirts worn by Manchester United.

'. . . assurance that no such repetition will take place in Manchester?'

He was mystified as to what they had been talking about. Some escapade involving him in Plymouth that had made its way to Moss Side by bush telegraph, presumably. He decided that the best response was one of dignified silence. For ten seconds, nobody in the room spoke, then the silence was broken by a funereal voice.

'Would you care to hear about our profit and loss accounts for the past two seasons?' asked one of the elderly directors.

Malcolm said nothing, knowing perfectly well that he was going to get the figures whether he wanted them or not, and, judging from the tone of the director's voice, they were not going to be very good.

'In the season 1963–64 we lost £18,796. Last year we lost a further £10,229.'

'So you're going in the right direction,' said Malcolm jovially. He could tell that the directors were not impressed with the levity. Fuck them, the miserable gits!

'In 1963–64 we made over £2,000 from our run to the semi-finals of the Youth Cup. Last year we were knocked out in the first round, so revenue was scarcely more than £100.'

'You should be thrilled with those kids. If they're good, they'll save you money in the long run.'

'Do you and Mr Mercer plan to sell them all for peanuts and replace them with expensive transfers?'

'I think we should give them a chance to show what they'll do in the first team if we think they're good enough.'

'George Poyser played nine of that 1964 youth team last year, and you saw where we ended up.'

Malcolm was becoming irritated by the gloom and despondency. It was past the middle of July. The new season was less than a month away. They could win the Second-Division Championship and be promoted with big crowds and silverware to show. Why did these morons concentrate on the negatives of life? He forced his teeth into a grin.

'I can see you gentlemen know how to negotiate.' He thought he ought to start by buttering them up. Besides, in a perverse manner, it suited his plan. 'Gentlemen, I'll do you a deal . . .' he began and looked up to find all five elderly faces showing cautious interest. A deal was good for them by definition, they must be thinking. 'How much were you going to pay me?'

The directors looked at each other. They didn't like the direction this conversation was taking. What they paid their employees was their business. He would be told his wages in due course.

'Well . . .' The Chairman, Albert Alexander, cleared his throat. 'We haven't as yet decided . . .'

Malcolm had calculated that if they'd told Joe they'd pay him £30 a week that meant they'd be prepared to go up to 40. Maybe he could push them a little higher. 'I was on 45 quid a week at Plymouth.' It was an outrageous lie, but he waited for the challenge. It never came; instead, they argued a technicality.

'Ah, but you were the manager there. Here we are talking about a relatively minor position, and as such you must . . .'

'I'll take 40. If we're in the top two at Christmas, you pay me fifty quid a week.'

'That seems a little . . .'

'You've got nothing to lose. If we're in the top two at Christmas that means we're winning, and if we're winning that means the crowds are coming back.'

'My dear Allison,' began one of the suits, 'are you acquainted with the attendance figures at this ground last season? At one point we barely managed eight thousand, and for the last match of the season . . .'

'It was 8,409. I know. If Joe and I get this right we'll be getting thirty thousand through the turnstiles for every League match, and I'm asking for a pay rise of ten quid.'

There was a brief pause as the directors digested the offer and examined it for potential flaws.

'Well, that certainly seems in line with the government's prices and incomes policy,' observed the Secretary, Walter Griffiths, eventually. Malcolm was astonished by the response but felt he was winning the argument, so he kept quiet. There was a general air of agreement in the room, and if it needed Harold Wilson to approve his salary he wasn't going to argue.

The directors looked at each other with some satisfaction. Forty was indeed what they were prepared to pay him, and if he thought he was giving his services away on the cheap – which he obviously did – that was another point in their favour. They didn't much care for the manner in which he came to the boardroom, a professional man's place of work, without the courtesy of wearing a tie, but he was young and he wasn't their manager; he was only the coach or whatever it was Joe wanted to call his new dogsbody. He wouldn't be representing the club; Joe would. This chap's job was strictly to work with the players and nothing else. He'd be like Johnny Hart, a figure on match days they would nod to. He wouldn't be coming to board meetings to report on team affairs. That would be Joe Mercer's job. This Malcolm Allison chap would just be another employee.

And they rather liked the fact that he knew the crowd figures. Admittedly, he was using them as a lever to press his own case, but it showed an attention to detail, an awareness of the importance of the attendance figures and the role that money had to play in the club's future. With a bit of luck he wouldn't turn out to be one of those radicals who would encourage Joe to come to the board with ever more outrageous demands for money to fund player transfers when the board was using all its ingenuity in working out ways to pay the electricity bill. The directors looked at each other and nodded.

'Mr Allison,' began Albert Alexander and stood up. At 5 ft 2 in. the gesture was barely perceptible, but Malcolm was glad of the chance to get to his feet and tower over the Chairman. To him it was symbolic of how he wished the future to be, but he took the proffered hand and shook it gladly.

'Welcome to Manchester City. I hope we shall achieve great things together.'

'I know we shall,' smiled Malcolm. 'Now, how much is in the kitty for transfers? The sort of player we need is someone like Dave Mackay of Spurs. He's had two broken legs, and I think we could get him for fifty or sixty grand . . .'

Joe was not thrilled to hear that Malcolm had tried to sell the board on the idea of buying Dave Mackay. He tried to explain as much over a particularly unpleasant cup of tea at the greasy-spoon café across Claremont Road. Malcolm justified himself passionately.

'He's a great player.'

'Malcolm, one step at a time. Do you remember what I told you the very first time we met, at Lilleshall?'

'No.'

'I was down there with Matthews, Morty and Jimmy Hagan on one of those courses Walter Winterbottom organised. We were all getting our coaching qualifications, and I saw you practising a banana kick from a dead ball. Only we didn't call them banana kicks back then.'

'Yes, I do remember. You weren't too impressed, were you?'

'I told you to try seeing if you could kick it straight first.'

'I was right though, wasn't I? Soon as Garrincha did it against England in the World Cup everyone thought it was great.'

'I still think you need to kick the bloody thing straight first. Same applies to buying players. We're in the middle of the Second Division. If we win the First Division and we're in the European Cup, then we go out and buy Dave Mackay.'

'You said we had 50 grand. Why not spend it on one great player?'

'Because Dave Mackay plays for Tottenham Hotspur, who also have Greavsie, Gilly and Mullers, and they'll probably get Mike England because Matt won't pay what Spurs'll offer Blackburn. Why on earth would Mackay come to a club in the middle of the Second Division when he can play with men like that?'

'Because you're here, and you were a great wing-half. You could make him a better player. I know I can.'

Joe raised an eyebrow. He had always liked Malcolm's brash self-confidence, but telling one of the best wing-halves in the world that this relative nonentity could make him a better player he knew would invite a fairly dismissive response.

'Bill Nick was a wing-half too you know, Mal, and he's not done a bad job with him.'

'Give it a try! What have you got to lose?'

Joe smiled and picked up his tea cup, cradling it in his hands. 'I did. I rang Bill Nick the day I got the job. Before I got hold of you in the cop shop.'

'And?'

'I asked. He's not coming.'

'So who is coming?'

'I fancy Ralph Brand.'

'Too slow.'

'Scores goals. Lots of them.'

'In Scotland. He'll lose a yard of pace down here.'

'Not in the Second Division. Maybe in the First, but we'll deal with that when we get up. In any case, if he scores enough goals to get us up this year, we'll sell him for more than we paid for him.'

'The deal's done?'

'Not yet. Scott Symon's not returning my phone calls, and Brand says Villa have approached him. He's not decided which, but he's definitely not re-signing with Rangers, and he's definitely coming south.'

'How much?'

'I've offered 20, but they won't take it, so it'll be nearer £25,000.' Joe could see the pain on Malcolm's face. He was affronted that the younger man was already questioning his judgement.

'Who would you have wanted?'

'Lad at Bury.'

'Colin Bell?'

'Came to Home Park and ran rings round us on the heaviest pitch of the year, and he's still only 18. He's going to be a great player. Trust me.'

'They want 40 grand for an 18 year old. They won't get it from me.'

'Somebody'll pay it, and they'll have a bargain.'

'He's only had one full season. Go and watch him this year. If he improves, tell me and I'll go, only we can't go together. Soon as we do that, Bury'll know we're serious, and the price'll go up.'

'How's it going to work then?'

'How's what going to work?'

'The way we work together. You buy the players and I just train them?'

'Your job's with the players, Mal. I wish I could do what I used to do, but I'm not fit enough. You put a tracksuit on and you'll look like a player. I put on a tracksuit and they'll think their grandpa's dressing up for Christmas.'

'Tactics?'

'We discuss.'

'Transfers?'

'We discuss.'

'Like now? Like telling me you've already signed Ralph Brand?'

'I haven't signed him. I told you.' Joe counted to ten. 'Malcolm, you've been here five minutes. I've been here ten. We needed a forward, and Brand was a good choice – whatever you think. He's an instinctive goalscorer, and if Kevan goes we're going to be really short. If you think he's too slow, you make him faster.'

'Colin Bell's an athlete. I could make him faster. Did you ever ask yourself why Brand wants to come south?'

'He's coming because he wants to be part of something big. We can do that here, Malcolm. You and me together, son. We can really do it.'

'You've already done it. You were a great player. People will always remember you for that.'

'But I failed as a manager.' Joe held up his hand as Malcolm started to protest. 'Let's not kid ourselves. Success is winning things, and all I won was that tinpot League Cup with Villa, and when they took the team photograph with it at the start of the following season, the chairman sat in the middle with the trophy at his feet, and I was at the end of the middle row. I haven't done it as a manager, and I don't think I can by myself. Not now, after the . . . illness. That's why I want you with me. I think you've got something, son, but you're like a brilliant 17-year-old kid who can run rings round the older players on the training pitch and thinks he knows it all. He shoots his mouth off to the press about how great he's going to be, and he spends his time off the pitch with the birds and boozing in nightclubs. You need to settle down, and I can help you. I know this game. I know the people in it, and I know how they behave. You need me, Malcolm. As much as I need you. Together we can be unbeatable.'

'I fucking hope so, Joe.'

There was no mockery in Malcolm's tone, a far cry from his usual bluster, and Joe picked up on it immediately. Always intuitive, he had a fair idea what was behind Malcolm's subdued mood.

'How much do you owe?'

'There's some heavyweights after me.'

'I thought Plymouth paid off your contract.'

'They did. Sixteen hundred quid.'

'Where did it go?' asked Joe, puzzled.

Malcolm shrugged. 'I lost a bundle on a race at Kempton Park a week later. I had an inside tip, and it didn't work out. I needed the winnings to pay off a gambling . . . problem.'

'How much?'

'Two hundred and thirty quid.'

Joe whistled through his teeth. 'Why didn't you just use the Plymouth pay-off to settle with the bookies?'

Malcolm stared at him. After all these years in the game, Joe still didn't have the faintest idea what it was that made men like him gamble their wages away.

'Listen, when I was gambling professionally with Arthur Shaw . . .'

'I remember Arthur. Didn't he play for the Arsenal?'

'Yeah. We were in business as professional gamblers for two years. We made eight grand together the first year. As a player I was on 15 quid a week.'

Joe looked impressed. 'What happened?'

'We spent it. One weekend in Deauville we dropped over sixteen grand in six minutes.'

'You say it like it was a great time.'

'It was. I wish I had 16 grand to drop right now.'

Joe reached into his jacket and took out his wallet. 'Don't ever tell Norah about this. She thinks I'm hopeless with money.'

'I heard you've been subbing Tommy Lawton.'

'He's a sad case, Malcolm. Pray to God neither of us winds up like Tommy.'

'What a player, though.'

'The best centre-forward I ever played with.'

'Better than Dixie Dean?'

'Better all round. As good a header of the ball as Dixie and better with the ball on the floor.'

'I remember seeing him when he played for Notts County. He got off the ground before every defender and stayed up there longer.'

'They say he used to hang in the air. They were right.'

'He pushed off on one foot. You'd be amazed how many players have never been taught that.' Malcolm smiled as he saw Joe open his wallet and take out two five pound notes and ten singles. He slid them across the table.

'I can let you have 20 quid now, and I'll go to the bank in the morning and take out another 30 for you tomorrow.'

Malcolm folded the notes and stuffed them into his trouser pocket. 'That'll keep them off my back for a few weeks. They'll be thrilled I've taken this job. They know they'll get paid now.'

'I'm not making a habit of this, Malcolm, so don't run away with the idea that I'm a soft touch.'

'I won't. Thanks, Joe. You're a good bloke.'

'And for Christ's sake don't tell Norah.'

FOUR

The Manchester City players were as unimpressed by Mercer and Allison as the new management team was unimpressed by them. Before they saw the photograph in the evening paper of the two of them shaking hands with the Chairman outside the front entrance, they had no idea who Malcolm Allison was. Then the goalkeeper Alan Ogley pointed out that if he had been the Plymouth Argyle manager the previous season, he must have been the brains behind the penalty kick that still annoyed him whenever he thought about Trebilcock's goal.

Dave Bacuzzi grinned. 'In that case he must have been the same twat as tried to kick the fucking dressing-room door in.' There was a gathering groundswell of collective memory.

'The one Jimmy threw that bucket of water over?'

'Christ! He's a fucking madman.'

But Alan Ogley's mind was still fixed on the tactical imagination of the man who had made him look foolish. 'After the goal he came out of the dugout and stood waving his hands in the air.'

'How would you know, Magoo? You couldn't even see the fucking ball never mind the dugout.'

Alan Ogley sighed with irritation. His long-sightedness was a cause of constant amusement to the other players, but as the one who had to play in contact lenses it was much less of a laugh to him.

'Well, at least he's got a brain. Poor old Poyser didn't have one.'

'Now look here, lads.' The unmistakable sound of veteran Derek Kevan's broad Yorkshire vowels broke through the babble. 'I won't have a word said against that twat. Remember the throw-in onto Jimmy's head at the near post and me charging into the box to ram it home. I scored dozens of goals from that plan.'

'That was my idea, not his,' complained Bobby Kennedy, who had taken the throw-ins.

'He's a gobber.'

'Who, Poyser?'

'No, Allison. Always shouting.'

'You mean like Dave Ewing?'

'No, Dave's just a loudmouth when the game's on. I hear this bloke never stops.'

'I'll be glad if he shows up at all. It'll make a change after the new manager.'

The players had barely seen the manager in the three weeks they'd been doing their pre-season training. Rumours that Joe Mercer was in the building would spread around the dressing-room or the gym or the training pitch, but none of the players ever saw him. Instead, a couple of hours after the rumour had first spread another would replace it telling his frustrated charges that their new manager had not been feeling well and had gone home. For a club that was desperate to make a good start to the season with its new manager, this was not a welcome development. It seemed somehow in keeping with the way the club was being run that after relegation from the First Division in May 1963 and two unsuccessful seasons in the Second Division since then, the club's third manager in two years turned out to be seriously unwell.

The arrival of Malcolm Allison changed everything. It was like hurling a hand grenade into a building of explosives. The devastation was instantaneous. Joe, in a dark suit and open-necked shirt, stood on the touchline at Chassen Road training ground in Urmston and watched as his new coach, in fashionably skimpy shorts and a startling pink tracksuit top – a colour never previously seen on a Manchester football pitch – screamed at the players, looking to see how they would react to his methods. It was, to say the least, a mixed response, and after an intense hour and a half, a rather dejected Malcolm told the players to go and shower but to be prepared to come back and work harder after lunch.

Glyn Pardoe had just turned 19, but he was already a veteran of the club, having made his debut when he was still 15 – the club's youngest-ever player. He nodded at Joe Mercer as he trotted past him.

'Nice to see you, Boss.'

'Well done, Chris,' said Joe and smiled encouragingly at him. Glyn turned round, supposing that Chris Jones was behind him, but it was his cousin, the left-half Alan Oakes, who just raised his eyebrow slightly.

It looked like Manchester City had struck gold with this one: a very sick manager with no memory for names – just what they needed – but Malcolm quickly threw his arm round Pardoe's shoulder.

'Don't worry about him, Glyn. He knows the game, and he knows you're a good player; he'll get your name right soon enough. I hear you two are cousins.' Malcolm looked at Glyn Pardoe and Alan Oakes. 'Can't see it myself,' he said, and went back to join Mercer.

'What a big-head,' said Pardoe briefly.

'Talks a good game. Let's give him till Christmas before we write him off like all the others.'

'D'you think we'll both still be here at Christmas?'

'We might. There's plenty as won't,' observed Oakes tartly as they entered the dressing-room and he started banging the mud from his studs.

Outside, on the touchline, Malcolm began slowly, anxious not to upset the older man. Who knew if his brain had really started to go? 'You know the lad you called Chris . . .'

'Chris Jones? He's a keen lad, but I'm not sure he's going to make it.'

'That was Glyn Pardoe.'

'Was it? Are you sure, Malcolm? It can be quite tricky learning 30 new names in a day.'

'I know them all.'

'How can you be so sure?'

'On the way back to the hotel yesterday afternoon, I stopped off at a newsagents and bought all the magazines with the City players' photos in. Then I cut them out and spread them out on the table. Easiest way. It's like playing that memory game with the cards. Doesn't take long.'

'That's clever,' admitted Joe, with admiration.

'You look at the name, then you shut your eyes and think where it is on the table, then you can "see" the photograph, and you remember the player's face and his name better and faster than any other way.'

'You know, there are a fair few managers, good ones 'n' all, who couldn't remember names. When I came back from the war to Everton . . .'

'I used to hate it when it took that twat Jimmy Seed three years to remember my name when I was at Charlton.' Malcolm was in no mood for reminiscences from the other man. He was remembering his own troubles too clearly. 'I swore that when I became a coach or a manager, I'd make a point of learning all the players' names first thing. They're individuals, not a herd of cows, and if you want them to remember what you're telling them it's best they should feel you know who they are.'

Joe nodded in approval. 'I still think that was Chris Jones, though.'

At the long trestle-table with the foldaway chairs that passed for a dining room, the players were tucking into a lunch of fried eggs, baked beans and chips. They were unnaturally quiet for a group of ebullient young men who had not seen each other for two months and had much to catch up on. Normally during pre-season training they would be showing off their newly tanned bodies, and the air would ring with hurled jokes and the chattering sound of eagerly relayed gossip. The miserable summer of 1965 had put paid to the suntan comparisons, and somehow the combination of the sick manager and the would-be tyrant of a new coach, together with the realisation that they faced another long hard season as the butt of unfunny jokes from triumphant United supporters, filled them with a sense of gloom.

The players moved easily into their respective cliques – young separated from old, and extrovert sat apart from introvert. The younger players were the most responsive to the methods of the new coach. They had been part of the club's best youth side, reaching the semi-finals of the FA Youth Cup just over a year before, and they saw in a demoralised first team the chance to progress their own careers. The new manager might choose his team based only on the evidence of what he saw in pre-season training and not play all his favourites, as the old manager had mostly done. They were 18 or 19 years old, and they knew of plenty of their contemporaries who were already first-team regulars – and not just Bestie across the town. He'd played in that semi-final, too, and look how fast his career had progressed because he had a manager who believed in him. Would Mercer or Allison be like that? They fervently hoped so.

Derek Kevan was less optimistic. He knew he'd put the wind up the management with his transfer request, even though he hadn't played in the first team since the end of January because of a knee injury. He'd been a big success over the past two dire seasons, and he revelled in being the biggest fish in the small pond that was Manchester City. Forty-eight goals in fifty-seven League appearances was a fantastic striking rate whichever division you were playing in. He'd already heard from Dick Graham, his old trainer at West Bromwich Albion, who had just been appointed manager of Crystal Palace. There were already seven players on the staff there who had played with Kevan under Graham at West Bromwich, and Graham wanted Kevan to make it eight.

With a second child due shortly, Mrs Kevan was anxious to know which hospital she'd be going to when she went into labour. Her husband definitely fancied a year or two in the fleshpots of London to finish his career. He was 30, so he only had a couple of productive seasons left. If City raised his wages, it might be in his interests to hang around for a few months and see if this odd managerial combination would have an impact, but he didn't much care for the manner in which Allison had looked at him. There were only eight years between them, and he'd been scoring eight goals in fourteen appearances for England when the new coach had been forced to give up the game. He didn't need this newcomer to the coaching game to make himself look big by forcing the biggest name at the club to look foolish.

Players tend to look at managers just as subjectively as managers look at players. 'If he's scoring goals for me, I'll keep picking him,' thinks the manager. 'If he picks me, he's a good manager,' thinks the player. They can smile warmly and genuinely at each other in the wake of a hard-earned victory, but a defeat and the derision of the crowd is felt as keenly by the manager as the player who is the object of their contempt. Three or four Saturday afternoons that end like that, and the relationship between manager and player rarely recovers. Kevan wondered how long it would take Mercer and Allison to find that out, conveniently ignoring the fact that they had both in their time been on the receiving end of football's booby prizes.

'What are we going to do about Derek Kevan?' asked Joe as the players limbered up before the afternoon training session.

'Sell him and buy Wyn Davies,' came the brief reply.

'I thought you wanted Colin Bell,' smiled Joe.

'I do, but Colin's one for the future. Wyn could come in now for Kevan and do the business for us. He's younger than Kevan, he's more mobile and he's hungrier.'

'I still think you're underestimating Ralph Brand. Anyway, why are you so keen to get rid of Kevan?'

'Keep your eyes peeled,' said Malcolm shortly, then he blew his whistle and trotted over to join his players, who were coming to the end of their stretching exercises, supervised by former City players Johnny Hart and Dave Ewing.

THE WORST OF FRIENDS

'We're going to play defence against attack,' began Malcolm. There was a generally positive reaction from most of the players, who certainly responded to the increased use of the ball during pre-season. Time was they remembered under Jimmy Meadows, George Poyser's trainer (and a former City right-back, whose playing career never recovered from the knee injury he suffered in the 1955 Cup final), that they almost never saw a ball throughout pre-season. Training then was just about running and getting fit to run some more. It was believed that if players didn't see the ball during training, they would be proportionately hungrier for it on Saturday afternoons. It was a proposition rarely proved because when the ball came to them on Saturday afternoons they had no idea what to do with it.

Malcolm noticed that whenever a group of players gathered close to Kevan he would always hide himself in the middle. It was an old pro's trick. If the trainer or coach couldn't directly see you, he would be very unlikely to call on you. This defence-against-attack idea was different, and it momentarily threw Kevan. He couldn't afford to let himself be marked out of the game by some kid or reserve-team player like the eager Phil Burrows, who hadn't made it out of the stiffs, or Alf Wood, who was desperate to impress the new boss. On the other hand, he knew better than anyone that he had to reserve his energy for when it counted – between three o'clock and twenty to five on forty-odd Saturday afternoons from August to May. There was no point in hurling himself full strength into a meaningless practice during July. He wasn't surprised that Allison couldn't see that. He had suspected all along that this new coach was no better than any of the others that had littered his career.

Malcolm didn't see pre-season training as meaningless. He saw it as the time when he could spot who could be relied upon in the last twenty minutes of a vital League or Cup game on a mud heap in February, and he had doubts about Kevan for all the goals he had scored in the previous two seasons. When he had stood at the end of the tunnel and looked round the empty ground, hearing in his mind the sound of 60,000 ecstatic fans acclaiming the team that he had built, he knew there was no part in that team for the Derek Kevans of football. He wanted Manchester City to be a young team full of idealists, playing fast, skilful, exciting football that would terrify the cowards of English football and, very soon, the best teams in Europe. He had a shrewd idea how Kevan would respond to his innovations.

On two adjacent pitches, five forwards faced five defenders. Malcolm wandered between the two games, deliberately interfering at random intervals for either side and making life more difficult for both sets of players. In these imaginative five-a-sides on a full-size pitch, there was much more running to do for all the players. Malcolm carefully played balls into the gaps that the defence would inevitably create and waited for Derek Kevan to make the charging run. It rarely came, he told Joe Mercer with evident satisfaction after the session had finished and the players had gone home exhausted. There would be no nightclubbing for them during this pre-season. The best the players could do was get enough rest to be able to face the prospect of an even more intensive session on each successive day.

Joe and Malcolm faced up to the scarcity of their resources with a confidence that stemmed from the pleasure that they were each getting from dealing with problems of a specifically football nature. This wasn't about Malcolm's money or marital problems, this wasn't to do with Joe's health, this was just two football men worrying about transfers and motivating a football team.

'Kevan's not the only one. There are three or four other senior players who are cheating.'

'It's pre-season, Malcolm . . .'

'Joe, pre-season is where you tell who the cheaters are. If they can't turn it on for us during pre-season, when we've just begun and they're all starting with a blank sheet, what chance they'll do it for us when it really counts? It's not just the cheats. The whole atmosphere round this place stinks. They expect to lose and so of course they will. Sometimes I think they even *want* to lose. Maybe they enjoy losing. All I know is we've got to change the atmosphere, and the only way we'll do that is by getting rid of the players who are causing the stink.'

'Apart from Kevan, then, who else don't you fancy?'

'Not sure about Jimmy Murray, Bacuzzi and Sear both worry me, and we haven't got a centre-half.'

'Alf Wood's played there before.'

Malcolm told him how Wood had failed the test he frequently set those players whom he suspected of not being sufficiently committed.

'I like working with three or four players at a time, belting the ball straight at them or deliberately over their heads. I done that with Wood, hit it over him and watched him turn round and fetch it. Then when he passed back, I lifted my foot and let it run underneath and told him to go and get it. As he went past me, he went "Fucking hell!", and I knew we're going to have a problem with him. He's not going to make it here.'

Joe considered Malcolm's verdict, which sounded harsh on first hearing, but he knew that there was no reason for Malcolm to be prejudiced against players he didn't know, and he trusted the younger man's judgement. He nodded briefly. 'I was thinking we could try the young lad Doyle at centre-half in the friendly against Dundee. He's good in the air. I like footballing centre-halves – like Neil Franklin: what a player!'

Malcolm was not anxious to indulge Joe's nostalgia and focused on the issue at hand. 'These friendly games can be a problem if the crowd comes and sees we're just as bad now as we were last season.'

'I've had a phone call from a player I'm interested in: Mike Summerbee.'

Malcolm cocked his head. He'd never heard of the Swindon forward.

'I knew his dad, George Summerbee, and I played with his uncle at Aldershot during the war. When I was at Villa, I went to see him a couple of times. Bill Nick was interested in him before he signed Cliff Jones.'

'I'd be interested in Cliff Jones . . .'

'Swindon are down and they're offloading. Woodruff's gone to Wolves, and it looks like Ernie Hunt's going with him. Bert Head's gone, and Summerbee doesn't fancy the new manager, Danny Williams. He wants out.'

'What's he doing?'

'When he rang me, he was selling tickets for the deckchairs on the beach at Torquay.'

'No, I meant what's he doing for pre-season?'

'He's gone back to Swindon to train and get fit. I told him to put in a transfer request.'

'I know about Hunt and Woodruff, but I can't even remember Summerbee, and I was manager of Plymouth when we played them.'

'He's 22. Best years of his career ahead of him. We haven't got a right-winger, and if you're right about Murray and Kevan, we haven't got a centre-forward, either. I'm going down to Swindon next week to talk to the board.'

'Joe, if you buy both Brand and Summerbee that's our transfer budget blown.'

Joe smiled. If only the life of a manager was as easy as Malcolm thought it was. 'Look,' he explained. 'We've only got the money for one of them. We only get both of them if we sell someone. Who's your favourite for the exit door?'

'We'll get the best money for Kevan,' said Malcolm shortly.

'I talked to Raich Carter at Middlesbrough. Poor old Raich thought you must have taken a wrong turning. You were supposed to see him last Tuesday.'

'I was signing for you.'

'Yes. He knows that now. He read it in the paper.'

'I suppose you think I should have rung him.'

'Not just common politeness, Malcolm. It's how you keep your friends in a business that's notorious for losing them.'

Malcolm nodded. He knew Joe was popular throughout the game. In fact, unlike anybody else he could think of, he couldn't remember anybody ever saying a bad word about him.

'The reason I rang Raich was not just to apologise on your behalf but to talk to him about Kevan. I knew he fancied him, and he's prepared to offer cash plus Bobby Braithwaite.'

'Who's he?'

'Irish outside-left.'

'We don't need an outside-left. We've got Connor and Young to play there.'

'More to the point, we don't want a part-exchange. We need the cash so we can buy Brand and Summerbee.'

'You absolutely sure about Brand?'

'How can anyone be sure about any player in this game, but we need goals from somewhere. You can teach a defence to mark, to push up, to play offside, but you can't teach anyone to score goals. Not really. It's a God-given instinct. If Kevan and maybe Murray both go and we don't score in the first two games, the crowd'll never forgive us. They'll be on our backs and the players' backs from the start, and we'll never get the chance to show what we can do. We need goals, Malcolm.'

'The real problem with this lot is they've got no confidence. If I can instil a bit of confidence, I suspect some of the younger ones – Young, Pardoe, Ogley, Doyle – I think there's talent there. And Johnny Crossan would get into most First-Division teams.'

'You in the mood to celebrate, Mal?'

'Eh? Bit early for that. Even for me.'

THE WORST OF FRIENDS

'You got a monkey suit up here?'

'No. What's going on?'

'It's that lot on the other side of the city. They're celebrating their League Championship, and we're going to be the guests of honour.'

'What!'

'That's how the Chairman presented it to me. Five hundred guests plus the directors of Manchester City and Joe Mercer and Malcolm Allison.'

'Tell them to go and take a flying fuck.'

'Don't be like that, Mal. Matt's a good man and an old friend. You've got to celebrate your victories in this game. You don't get that many of them.'

'You don't have to encourage *me* to celebrate anything, but that lot stick in my throat. If it's the last thing I do I'll make this club number one in Manchester, and Matt Busby can kiss my fucking arse.'

'I'll be there with the Box Brownie, Malcolm.'

FIVE

Malcolm loathed them all from the moment he walked through Albert Square and into the front entrance of the Town Hall. There they were, the great and the good of Manchester, the fat and the obese, the rich and the pompous, and their ugly women with expensively coiffed hair and jewellery adorning décolletage that should have been hidden from view. Money was wasted on people like that. They didn't deserve it, and they didn't know how to spend it. And they were all there to celebrate the glory that was Manchester United and to make out that they were doing him this big fucking favour inviting him to eat their food and bow the knee before the great god Matt Busby. Well, that was fine for Joe. He and Norah seemed to be in their element. Matt and Jean's friendship clearly meant a lot to them, and he soon saw how it easily bypassed the intra-city rivalry.

Not for him. Malcolm and the United captain, Noel Cantwell, had been supportive friends as well as close teammates at West Ham seven or eight years ago, but he didn't care for the tone of voice he and the United wing-half Paddy Crerand used when they told him he'd backed a loser when he chose to go to City. United were on their way into the European Cup. City were heading for the Third Division – 'Third Division (North),' Cantwell called it patronisingly. Malcolm thought he'd never been the same since he'd lifted the FA Cup two years before, after a 3–1 upset win over Leicester City at Wembley. Well, the next time a Manchester club lifted the FA Cup it would be Manchester City, he vowed silently under his breath, even if he allowed the faintest of smiles to flit across his face as the merciless teasing continued. He'd only been in the town two weeks, and already he and his family were heartily sick of the Reds.

It had begun the very day he had arrived in Manchester. Driving to Maine Road, he passed endless games of football in the parks, on the waste grounds, on the bombsites and in the streets. Those kids with parents affluent enough to buy them a shirt close to the colour of their chosen team had invariably invested in red tops. The number of pale-blue shirts was minimal in comparison. Malcolm knew that young supporters were fundamental to the growth of a football club. There was a ritual involved in going to a football match if you went with your father or your mates that could be seductive. When they were small they went with their fathers, but as soon as they were old enough they went with their mates. If City had a decent team, they would pass on their love of the club to their own kids. That's what had happened with United when they arose from the ashes of the bombed-out Old Trafford after the war. Apart from the odd hiccup after Munich, United had been a fabulously successful club for 20 years, and the roots of their support now spread wider and deeper than just the city of Manchester. That was what Malcolm was desperate to emulate and then surpass. Meanwhile, he had to cope with the intolerable taunting of the insufferable Crerand, who was flushed with success and champagne.

'I tell you what, Mal. You'll never get 30,000 inside Maine Road again.'

'Bollocks! I'll do it before Christmas.'

'A fiver says you won't.'

'What? Before Christmas or ever?'

'Ever.'

'Right, make it a tenner and I'll take it.'

They shook hands. Malcolm kept hold of Crerand's hand and looked hard into his eyes as the United player tried to withdraw.

'I haven't come to Manchester to lick your arse, you know. I've come to take over from Manchester United.' And he let go. Crerand was a little shaken by the sudden intrusion of genuine feeling into an occasion that was essentially a self-congratulatory black-tie piss-up, but he responded with his usual bluster.

'Ten quid's going to be the gate money from your first home game,' he said in a slightly slurred Glaswegian accent, and he moved away a little unsteadily to soak up the praise that was on offer for all the United players from every quarter of the Town Hall.

It was a tough night for Malcolm. The City directors were just thrilled to have been invited to the occasion, which they saw as a celebration of Manchester football because, realistically, this was as near as they were ever going to get to one. Joe was also in his element because he was surrounded by so many old friends who were, without exception, delighted to see him back in football. Only Malcolm suffered. The worst moments were the condescension. During the endless speeches of self-congratulation, Busby and the rest of them seemed to take a perverse delight in referring to the certainty they felt that Manchester was a big enough town for there to be two Manchester teams in the First Division again and that Joe Mercer was just the manager to make sure City were soon back where they belonged.

There were loud guffaws of derision mixed with enthusiastic shouts of 'Hear hear!' and much banging of cutlery on the table. Joe beamed at all and sundry. Malcolm looked across at Noel Cantwell and then at Paddy Crerand. Their enthusiastic applause was undermined by the raucous laughter that accompanied it. Their lack of sincerity was almost tangible. Crerand was making a 'thumbs-down' gesture in the style made popular by Norman Vaughan on *Sunday Night at the London Palladium*. At that moment, Malcolm swore a bitter vow that one day, one day soon, he and his team would go to Old Trafford, the home ground of the so-called greatest team in the world, and turn them over, humiliate them so badly that the Stretford End would boo these 'gods' off the field at the end of the game. Smiling at the prospect, he joined in the applause willingly, relit his giant cigar and grinned back jovially at Crerand and Cantwell.

Unfortunately, the first time he saw his new team in action the following Saturday he experienced such a sinking feeling in his stomach that he even contemplated the prospect that Paddy Crerand and Noel Cantwell had been right, and City were more likely to be playing the following year in the Third Division than the First. In front of a few thousand initially hopeful but ultimately deeply disappointed spectators, Manchester City were beaten at home 2–1 by a very ordinary Dundee side. Nobody had a decent game, not even Johnny Crossan, the Northern Ireland international inside-forward, who Joe and Malcolm knew was head and shoulders better than anyone on the field but didn't show it that day. Neil Young, the hesitant, gangling left-winger, probably had as much talent as Crossan, but his diffident nature obscured it that afternoon. Mike Doyle, Joe's 'inspired' choice for centre-half, turned out to be exactly what Malcolm had feared: a keen youngster without the brains to function as the fulcrum of the defence – especially a defence as insecure as Manchester City's. They desperately needed a centre-half, but if Joe's transfer budget was going on Brand and Summerbee, they would have to persuade the board to stump up more cash. Having now sold Derek Kevan to Crystal Palace for £22,000, the paucity of goalscoring potential in the side made the signing of Ralph Brand a priority.

The twenty-eight-year-old Rangers forward, a Scotland international player with eight caps, made a poor impression on the desperate Malcolm when he finally arrived at Maine Road. At 5 ft 7 in. he seemed too small, and weighing only 10 st. he seemed too slight to impose himself on Second-Division defences, who would no doubt take great delight in kicking him up in the air: 'Welcome to England, my son.' Still, needs must when the devil drives, and for the next friendly, away at Tranmere, which they managed to win 3–2, Brand replaced Matt Gray, who was incensed at being made the scapegoat for the inept team display against Dundee and immediately demanded a transfer from Joe and Malcolm. They told him to put it in writing, so for the fourth time in his three seasons at Manchester City Matt Gray wrote to the directors informing them of his desire to move to another club.

The club had two goalkeepers of equal merit in the local boy Harry Dowd, who had made his debut as long ago as 1961, and Alan Ogley, the highly promising youth-team graduate signed from distant Barnsley. Joe and Malcolm could never be sure which one of them was the better player, and as a result they kept changing their minds, leaving the man who had been dropped unhappy and angry, and the man who was in possession of the first-team jersey convinced that the first time he conceded a goal he would lose his place. Unfortunately, wholehearted as both Dowd and Ogley were, neither man could be compared to Bert Trautmann, who had been such a favourite at City for 15 years and who had retired just over a year previously. Perhaps intimidated by the prospect of taking over from the great Bert, neither man had the confidence that a top-class goalkeeper required. This deficiency was symptomatic of the disease that afflicted the whole team. When they played badly, whoever was dropped felt, frequently not without good reason, that he had been made the scapegoat for the failings of others. The resulting insecurity ran through the minds of all the players, a fear which paralysed them and prevented them displaying some of the talent Malcolm had discerned on the training field.

He was frustrated to have been handed a side with two left-wingers and no right-winger. It was typical of the slapdash, thoughtless way in which the club had been run for years. Neil Young, Joe and Malcolm were both sure, was a class player with low self-esteem, who had suffered when he had first come into the senior side from having to play on the right because David Wagstaffe, a year older and a prospective England international, had made the left-wing place his own. Now young David Connor was suffering similarly. He too had graduated successfully from the youth side, which convinced both Joe and Malcolm that in Harry Godwin, the unassuming chief scout, Manchester City had a much undervalued yet vital member of staff. Godwin concurred with Joe and Malcolm's assessment that Connor was no outside-right, and Malcolm had come round to Joe's conviction that Mike Summerbee would be a more than useful acquisition, but as the days passed and no progress was being made either on the training ground or in negotiations with Swindon Town for the services of Summerbee, Malcolm was starting to get the sickly feeling in the pit of his stomach that he had first experienced after the disastrous home defeat by Dundee.

Well, at least the players were fit: of that Malcolm was quite sure. They had grumbled, then complained and finally many of them had been physically sick at the hard running and associated exercises Malcolm had demanded of them, but even they eventually realised that when a match entered its final quarter they were not going to be as tired as they used to be. If they still had running left in their legs, they could at the very least be capable of snatching an undeserved equaliser in the last five minutes. Unfortunately Ralph Brand had done more negotiating than running, and what Malcolm saw of him only substantiated his initial fears. City's much-vaunted new signing, the alleged replacement for the 25-goals-a-season Kevan, looked out of shape and slow both in training and during the friendly match at Tranmere.

The Middlesbrough game, the first League match of the new season, was only three days away when Joe and the Secretary, Walter Griffiths, drove down to Swindon to try to prise Summerbee away from Wiltshire to register his form in time for him to play in the opening match of the season. Joe was starting to look unwell again. Norah had been her usual supportive self, but the dawning realisation that he had let himself in for more of the old anxieties started to crowd in on him. He felt his breath getting shorter, and he started sweating so much he loosened his tie and opened the top button of his shirt. Walter Griffiths looked at him.

'Are you OK, Joe?'

THE WORST OF FRIENDS

'I hate long car journeys, Walter. Can we stop for lunch somewhere soon? I'd love to stretch my legs.'

Griffiths looked at his watch. It was ten past eleven. No pub or restaurant would be open. It would have to be a transport café. 'I'll find somewhere,' he said, and tried to remember the exact wording of the clause in Mercer's contract that allowed City to cancel it without cost if his health no longer permitted him to execute his duties to the club's satisfaction.

In the end, Swindon Town's desperation turned out to be greater than Manchester City's. They had demanded £45,000 for Summerbee's transfer fee, but as soon as it became clear that City's final offer of £35,000 was likely to be withdrawn if forms were not signed in time to allow Summerbee to play at Middlesbrough, an agreement was reached between the clubs. Summerbee was told to travel to Manchester to undergo the regulation medical and negotiate his own personal terms. He had still not met Joe Mercer, who returned to Manchester as soon as the deal had been agreed. Summerbee was travelling from a small West Country club that had just been relegated to a big city club who had won the FA Cup less than ten years previously. He anticipated his future earnings with relish, increasing his demands in his own mind as his sports car neared the outskirts of Manchester. By the time he arrived at Maine Road and parked his car on the forecourt, he had convinced himself that he could persuade Manchester City to pay him a minimum of £75 a week.

He ran up the stairs to the reception area, where a secretary asked him to wait in the players' room while she discovered Mr Mercer's whereabouts. The girl picked up the white telephone receiver and dialled as Summerbee opened the door on the right at the start of the long corridor. He was delighted to find a snooker table in the centre and the walls decorated with photographs of Manchester City's great players: Bert Trautmann and Frank Swift, Roy Paul and Peter Doherty, Billy Meredith and Matt Busby. He was mightily impressed. This was a big club, he thought, a significant step up from the homely, friendly, small-time Wiltshire club he was leaving. He wandered down the stairs and into the home dressing-room. He'd remembered the away dressing-room from the game he had played here six months before, but what would be his new dressing-room impressed him even more. It was bigger than both the changing-rooms at the County Ground knocked together. He wondered who he would be changing next to. He hoped it would be Johnny Crossan. Summerbee thought he could learn a lot from the Northern Ireland international.

'Oh, here you are.' The girl was slightly irritated to discover that he had moved from the room in which she had told him to wait. 'Mr Mercer's waiting to see you in the café across the road.' Summerbee took a last look round the dressing-room, which looked even bigger when it wasn't being used by 11 high-spirited footballers. Yes, this was definitely a club that could afford to pay him £75 a week. He would be a rich man in a couple of years.

His negotiations with Joe Mercer did not go quite as he had planned. Swindon Town had had the foresight to send Manchester City the details of his previous contract. Mercer had it in front of him as Summerbee joined him at the greasy-spoon café opposite the ground.

'Hello Mike,' said Joe warmly, that irresistible smile beaming all over his face. He should have been a salesman. He could sell snow to Eskimos with that smile. 'I know you were on thirty-five quid a week at Swindon, and you know we're skint, so the best I can offer you is a five-pound pay rise. How about forty quid a week?'

Summerbee mulled over the offer for two seconds.

'I'll take it,' he said, and smiled at his own pathetic attempt at negotiation. Joe smiled back. He had had no doubt his offer would be accepted, and he knew exactly what had been passing through Summerbee's mind.

'I've paid for your tea,' he added generously.

'There's no spoon,' said Summerbee. 'There must have been one once, but there's a piece of string tied to the urn and no spoon attached to it.'

Without blushing, his new manager took a spoon out of his jacket pocket and slid it across the table. Summerbee couldn't help noticing that there was a piece of string attached to it that looked very much like the short piece of string still dangling pointlessly from the hot-water urn. A spare teaspoon was a prized possession for Joe – it might be the time of Carnaby Street boutiques down south, but it was still grim up north.

SIX

In the 'Stop Press' column on the front page of the Friday late-night edition of the *Manchester Evening News* it was announced that Mike Summerbee had passed his medical examination, signed for Manchester City for a fee of £35,000 and would make his debut at Middlesbrough the following day. The medical rather took him by surprise. He was stripped to his shorts and waiting in the physio's room sitting on the treatment table when the former player and long-time physio Laurie Barnett came in.

'You Summerbee?' he asked shortly.

Mike nodded. 'I'm waiting for my medical.'

'Mr Rose said I could give it to you. He's still on his rounds at the hospital. Boss is waiting to get your forms off. Mr Griffiths has got to drive to St Annes.' Barnett cast an appraising eye over Summerbee's legs. He tapped the right one at the base of the kneecap. He grunted. Then he tapped the other one. 'Congratulations, you've passed your medical. Now fuck off and sign the papers.'

No sooner had the outside-right put pen to paper than he was summoned to meet his new coach on the Maine Road pitch. He was handed a less than spotless training shirt and pair of shorts, laced up his own boots and trotted out onto the pitch to meet the men who would be his close colleagues for the foreseeable future. But before he had time to take in his surroundings, he heard a voice bellowing 'Summerbee!' The new boy turned in the direction from which his name had been called and at that exact moment a ball caught him squarely on the side of the face. He staggered backwards for a pace or two but did not fall.

'I hope your reactions are going to be a bit sharper tomorrow,' said Malcolm Allison, looking at his stopwatch. It wasn't difficult for Summerbee to identify his new coach, flamboyantly attired as Malcolm was in a bright-pink tracksuit top. Summerbee held out his hand, which Malcolm ignored. 'Get over to that corner flag,' he said, pointing at the right corner of the ground where the main stand met the Platt Lane end. 'I want four laps of the ground – sprint the long sides, jog the short. I'm timing you.'

The one-on-one session lasted only fifty minutes, but it was the hardest fifty minutes' training that Summerbee had ever experienced. It wasn't that Malcolm was a big shouter, though he had the most stentorian of voices. It was just that his demands were remorseless, deliberately giving the new boy little time to recover between each lung-bursting exercise. When Malcolm finally brought the training session to a close he made it clear that he did so reluctantly.

'You're playing tomorrow, otherwise I'd work your bollocks off.'

'You just did,' panted Summerbee.

'You think that was hard work? Just wait till you get to Wythenshawe Park on Monday morning.' As Malcolm strode away, Summerbee almost doubled up in agony. His stomach muscles were cramping, he had no breath in his lungs and the sweat that poured down his face was streaming into his eyes, stinging them so badly he had to keep them shut while he dabbed at them ineffectually with the dirty sleeve of his training shirt. When he finally opened them again, he saw half a dozen of his new teammates smiling and laughing at him.

'Still glad you signed?'

'Hope they're paying you enough, 'cause he's obviously got it in for you.'

'Fucking teacher's pet!'

'You been shagging his wife then?'

Mike stood up again and smiled, comforted by the banter. He was familiar with this territory, and he could give as good as he got. He was going to be fine.

In Joe's office, Malcolm pronounced himself satisfied with the attitude of the newcomer. Joe let out a sigh of relief. After two weak performances by Brand in the friendly matches, Malcolm had already let him know exactly what he thought about Joe's first signing.

'I'm sorry we have to leave out Connor to accommodate Summerbee,' said Malcolm.

'We're not going to. Neil Young's just reported in with flu. I've talked to the doc and Sidney Rose thinks it won't clear up in time for the match. It might be contagious, so we're better off leaving him out and playing

Connor at outside left. At least he'll be in his proper position.'

'I want to try something, Joe.'

'What?'

'You know who Middlesbrough's key man is? The one who starts all their dangerous moves?'

'Ian Gibson.'

'I've been looking at Connor out there, and I think he's as fit as anyone. I mean, Neil Young's more talented, but Connor's definitely got something. Stickability, or persistence – I don't know what you call it. He doesn't give up, and he's a good runner.'

'You want him to man-mark Gibson?'

'I think it's worth a shot. We're away from home. A point'll be a good result.'

'A point'll be a great result.'

'We don't need to keep the home crowd entertained. A nil–nil will tell the players they can defend well. If we can nick a goal somewhere along the line, that's how we'll get up the table.'

'Have you told Connor?'

'I wanted to see what you thought first.'

Inwardly, Joe breathed another sigh of relief. He wasn't surprised that Malcolm was coming up with bold, original ideas – that was why he had wanted him at his side. The risk was that Malcolm would simply ignore him and forge a bond with the players that excluded the manager. He found it deeply comforting that Malcolm had discussed this major tactical switch with him first.

'Good idea, Mal. Let's tell the lad about it on the coach tomorrow.'

'I think we can get a draw up there. Not getting beat instils the sort of confidence into players that neither you nor I can. We can talk till we're blue in the face but if the players see they're getting through games and not giving goals away, that's how we build up their confidence.'

'I agree.' Joe just wanted to get back to Norah but Malcolm wasn't finished.

'Another thing, Joe: we have to get through the first ten games without getting beat.'

'The first ten? That's the end of October – a quarter of the season. I'd settle for tomorrow and our first match at home.'

THE WORST OF FRIENDS

The usual small group of dedicated supporters gathered in the Platt Lane car park to watch the players board the coach for the first game of the season. As the new signings, Ralph Brand and Mike Summerbee attracted the most attention. After the Fingland's coach had pulled out, two United supporters with a mischievous sense of humour walked up to Summerbee's smart sports car. Flash bugger! All they needed was to nip home and get the monkey wrench out of their dad's tool-shed. It would take no time at all for one of them to loosen the wheel nuts on the car while the other kept watch.

On the coach, the players relaxed as they always did. Peter Gardner, the friendly young local journalist who was starting his second season on the City beat, joined Harry Dowd, Vic Gomersall and David Connor at the card table. Mike Summerbee stared out of the window at the unfamiliar landscape, blissfully unaware that the two miscreants were returning with the monkey wrench to loosen the wheel nuts on his car. Malcolm sat down pointedly next to Joe at the front. He looked at his ally in the battle that lay ahead. Joe looked ill. Seriously ill. He shouldn't be on the bloody coach, thought Malcolm. They could be going home with his corpse in the luggage compartment.

'You OK?'

Joe didn't reply. He looked as though he hadn't heard. His eyes were flickering all over the coach.

'Joe?'

'What happens if we get thumped 6–0?'

Malcolm laughed scornfully. 'No chance.'

'All right, 2–0. Then we lose at home to Wolves on Wednesday, and we don't beat Bristol City on Saturday. I've already written off the game at Molyneux. In ten days' time we could be bottom of the table with one point from four games, with no crowds and the press on our backs.'

'Joe, this is crazy talk . . .'

'I've been in the game longer than you, son. I know what it does to you when it goes wrong.'

'Joe, it won't be like that. I promise you.'

'Two years, Malcolm. If that. I can't take much more than that, and I promised Norah . . . Two years and you can have it all. I know I'll have had enough by then. I might have had enough by Wednesday week.'

For a moment, Malcolm felt like a grown adult with a father who had suddenly plunged into a senile second childhood. 'Joe, it'll be fine. You go and have a drink with Raich Carter when we get there, smile and shake hands in the boardroom. I can't stand those twats. Leave the players to me. I know what to say.'

Malcolm was as good as his word. The match at Ayrsome Park ended in a 1–1 draw. Ralph Brand looked as slow as Malcolm had feared, and Summerbee looked as sharp as Joe had hoped. In fact it was Summerbee who provided the cross for Jimmy Murray's goal, which put City in the lead after an hour. They couldn't hold it, however, and Middlesbrough equalised 12 minutes from time with a free kick taken by the Wales international centre-half Mel Nurse. Before the coach left Middlesbrough, Malcolm phoned Maine Road to learn that the reserves had lost 6–0 at home to Sheffield United. The pleasure in the point away from home was soon stilled as the realisation of how far the club had to travel was made clear to both Joe and Malcolm.

As the coach pulled away from Ayresome Park, Malcolm extracted one of his favourite Montecristo cigars, lit it and watched the smoke curl up into the roof. He sat by himself, smoking and thinking about the game until the giant cigar was no more than an inch-long stub. He crushed it into the ashtray in the back of the seat in front of him and rose to his feet.

At the rear of the coach, the card school was in full swing again. Malcolm looked at his players and their various attitudes, observing the ways in which they were winding down from the frenzy of the game. Finally he went over and plumped himself down next to the thoughtful Mike Summerbee, who sat by himself in a window seat worrying about how he'd acquitted himself. Nobody had said anything to him. Was that good or bad? He thought he had done all right, but the arrival of the coach he had already learned to fear soon made him reconsider.

'We didn't pay 35,000 quid for a fucking full-back.' Summerbee's heart sank. This was obviously the beginning of another bollocking. Then the big man smiled. 'You did well today, son, but I don't want to see you in our half of the field. The only thing I want from you is to take on their left-back, beat him, get to the byline and pull the ball back accurately. If you do that, you'll scare the rest of this division. You're good enough.' And without waiting for a reply, he got up and went back to his seat next to Joe Mercer at the front of the coach.

It took Summerbee a few minutes to sort out his feelings. He had, he was sure, just been bollocked, but he felt on top of the world. He had known that Joe Mercer thought he had potential since the days when he had been a promising teenager, but after the previous day's violent training session he had felt that Malcolm Allison didn't want him at City, thought Joe had made a mistake in spending so much money on him. Now he realised that Malcolm really did rate him, and he had already decided he would go through brick walls for the man. Malcolm's coaching and smart use of psychology was on a level he had never experienced with the well-meaning but limited Bert Head at Swindon Town, and down in the depths of Wiltshire you could never be much of a football star. It wasn't that sort of county. Manchester was different.

That night he went into the Corn Exchange with Harry Dowd, Peter Gardner and Matt Gray, where he drank Mackeson and ogled the girls in their miniskirts as his companions downed Bacardi. They didn't serve Bacardi in Swindon. In fact, they weren't open to serve anything much past ten o'clock at night. He was going to enjoy his time at Maine Road. It was in this mood that he got back into his little sports car to drive back to Swindon to collect the rest of his belongings. Just outside Penkridge, the loosened wheel nuts caused the car to veer sharply across the road, where he hit a car coming the other way. Fortunately neither driver was badly hurt, but Summerbee's car was a write-off. Walter Griffiths was not pleased to be asked to drive to Penkridge on a Sunday morning to bring him back to Manchester. He wondered if that expensive room at the Grand Hotel in Aytoun Street was going to be worth the cost. He strongly suspected that Joe Mercer and Malcolm Allison were trying to cause a revolution, but if you were an *aristo* under the *ancien régime*, revolutions weren't necessarily welcome.

The other players took longer to sense that they were part of a revolution. The majority had lived through the nightmare of the previous season with a nonentity of a manager who had been sacked by Easter. They had played out their games in front of the smallest gates and most hostile crowds in the club's history. Joe Mercer might have been a great player, but he hadn't been a great manager, and he was visibly still unwell. Malcolm Allison struck most of them as a loudmouthed braggart, but they had to admit that his training regime and tactics had paid off. They had played as a team at Middlesbrough and thoroughly deserved their point.

The rejuvenated City team attracted twenty-five thousand people through the Maine Road turnstiles for Wednesday's match, and Wolves kindly donated both points courtesy of two own goals. Disappointingly the crowd dropped below 20,000 on Saturday for their second home match, but by half-time it seemed as if City's sceptics had been justified. The veteran Bristol City forward John Atyeo put the visitors ahead, and Mike Doyle unfortunately deflected a shot past Harry Dowd to send his team into the dressing-room at half-time two goals down.

It was Joe rather than Malcolm who launched into them. 'Is this who you are? A bunch of bloody softies? No soul, no heart, no brains? The crowd's down on Wednesday's because they weren't thrilled with what we did. What do you think they're going to be like for the next match here? It'll be back to Swindon. Stop smiling, Summerbee, you're on our side now. Unless you want to go back and play for Swindon in the fucking Third Division. And if I see any more of that shit in the second half the rest of you can fucking well join him.' Joe stormed out of the room and banged the door.

Malcolm rather enjoyed playing good cop to Joe's bad cop. It was a rare reversal of their assumed roles. 'He's still not well. Don't take it too bad. Mike, what did I say about taking their full-back on?'

'I can hear you, Mal, you don't have to scream at me every time I get the ball.'

'Roy, what the fuck happened with their first?'

'Sorry, Mal. I slipped.'

'Christ, Atyeo's 80 years old. He should never get past you. Mike . . .'

Mike Doyle held his hands up. 'I just sliced the clearance, Mal.'

'Well don't fucking do it again, or I'll slice your balls off.'

The referee popped his head round the door. 'All right, lads?'

'Coming, ref,' said Malcolm. The players stood up, anxious to get out of the confrontational dressing-room and back onto the pitch. Malcolm stood with his hand on the doorknob. 'I want at least a point, otherwise you're all in tomorrow morning for extra training.' He stared hard at Ralph Brand. He didn't like him. 'The Boss bought you because he told me you could score goals. Show me you know what a fucking goal is, all right?'

He opened the door and let the players file out past him, staring at each of them in turn, wondering who would have the balls to stare back at him. As he suspected, it was only the captain, Johnny Crossan, who gave him a cheeky 'thumbs up'. 'Tell the Boss not to get too upset. It's bad for his blood pressure.'

Within 30 seconds of the restart, Ralph Brand scored his first goal for his new club with a deft header. After the ritual hair ruffling and handshakes, he trotted back to the centre circle looking straight at the dugout, where Malcolm sat glaring back at him.

'More! You think one's enough? We're still fucking losing, you Scotch twat!'

The linesman bent down to talk to him. 'Moderate your language, please.'

'He is Scotch, you know,' said Malcolm reasonably, much to the amusement of the trainer, Johnny Hart, who was sitting next to him.

Emerging with a 2–2 draw, Joe and Malcolm were pleased not just that they had gone three games undefeated but also that a vital fighting spirit was emerging in the team, as evidenced by the forceful manner in which they had recovered the two-goal deficit. It was even more apparent after the return game at Wolves, where, after 20 minutes, Summerbee was unceremoniously shoved over the touchline and into the stands, splitting his head open on an iron post. The perpetrator of the 'tackle', David Woodfield, was sent off and City soon grabbed control of the game, securing a convincing 4–2 win. 'Won 2, Drawn 2, Lost 0' was a start better than Joe had dreamed of, and Malcolm was wearing the smile of a man who was desperate to say 'I told you so' to all and sundry.

By now the team was growing in confidence, and the players were beginning to realise that this man Allison was not just the voluble show-off he had first appeared. They were eager to display this new-found confidence on the pitch, and Summerbee was desperate to play in the next game, at Coventry, despite the 17 stitches in the top of his head. Malcolm was very specific with the players. 'If you see Mike in the centre, keep the ball on the ground. He's not to head anything this afternoon.'

Within five minutes, Neil Young centred from the left wing and Summerbee headed narrowly wide. He only realised what he had done when he put his hand to his forehead and found traces of blood on his fingers. He turned to look at Malcolm in the dugout. They both laughed at his idiocy, but in the macho world of competitive sport it was exactly this sort of idiocy that convinced Summerbee's new bosses he was a player who lacked nothing in courage, a judgement whose validity he was to demonstrate many times over the next ten years.

On the coach back to Manchester after an exhilarating 3–3 draw, Joe and Malcolm analysed the match, ignoring the two goals scored by Neil Young and the one by Jimmy Murray, his third in five games. 'We can't defend, Malcolm. We won't go up if we can't defend.'

'You also said we wouldn't score a goal if we sold Derek Kevan.'

'We need a centre-half. We've tried three players in five games, and they're all crap.'

'I fancy Mike England.'

'Me too, but Blackburn won't sell him for much less than £100,000.'

'How about Billy McNeill?'

'Mal, I think we should focus on players who see first-team action in the Second Division as a step up.'

'Like who?'

'George Heslop.'

'I thought Everton had already said no.'

'They turned down £15,000. They might take 25.'

'Twenty-five grand? For an Everton reserve?'

Ironically, Malcolm's words were echoed by Albert Alexander when Joe told him of his wish to return to Goodison Park with a renewed offer.

'Joe, we've just spent £60,000. I don't think I can go back to the board and ask for more money for a reserve-team centre-half. Everton seemed in no hurry to sell Hislop.'

'Mr Chairman, you asked me to get you promotion.'

'And you think this Hislop is the right man for the job?'

'Heslop. We can't defend. We won't get up with this defence.'

'As long as we score more than the opposition, does that matter? Crowds like games that finish 4–3.'

Joe was aware that directors rarely liked to put their hands in their pockets, but he was already sensing that the bloom was off the rose, and he'd been in the job for less than two months. Was it going to be Sheffield and Villa all over again, with the constant battles that just drained the life out of him?

Albert Alexander must have spotted that Joe's naturally sallow complexion had just become a shade whiter. He liked Joe. Everyone did. It was one of the reasons they had hired him despite knowing his current state of health was parlous. He softened his stance. 'You can put your case to the board at the next meeting, and I'll support you.'

In fact there was no need for Joe to argue his case to the board. A poor display at home to Carlisle that nevertheless ended in a 2–1 victory, courtesy of two Glyn Pardoe goals, was enough for the board to see the wisdom of the manager's argument. They, too, felt the stirrings of something special around Maine Road. If the team had played like they had in the previous season, the board knew that the home games against Carlisle and Wolves would have ended in defeat. They also knew that City's recovery against Bristol City had been entirely due to whatever the management had said at half-time. If City could win five points out of a possible six while playing as inconsistently as they had been, maybe Joe and Malcolm were worth backing with borrowed money.

City's new offer of £25,000 was accepted by Everton's manager, Harry Catterick, and George Heslop travelled with the team to make his debut at Norwich. However, Albert Alexander was not impressed with another exciting 3–3 draw. 'I thought we were going to start winning a lot of 1–0 games with Hislop in the team.'

'Heslop. Give him time, Chairman. Anyway, he's picked up a thigh strain. He'll miss the match at Cardiff.' Annoyed by the Chairman's impatience, Joe sought out Malcolm, who was congratulating Glyn Pardoe on his two goals. 'Malcolm, do you want to be a manager again?'

Malcolm's heart soared. Did he! 'What's happened?'

'Bloody chairmen. I hate them. They make you feel like you've held them up at gunpoint to get the transfer fee, and then we come here and draw 3–3, and he thinks I've bamboozled him because we let in three even with a new centre-half.'

'Joe, calm down. Have a drink . . .'

'I'll be all right. Look we're fifth in the League, unbeaten all season and we've scored seventeen bloody goals in seven bloody games. They scored less than 60 all last season. You'd think someone would say "well done", not "what a waste of money". It'd serve those buggers right if we lost next week.'

'Joe, you were the one that told me that directors only understand blame and they never say thanks.'

'I hate them,' muttered Joe to himself. 'Hate the lot of them.'

The Chairman was right about 4–3 victories. Crowds certainly adored them, but City's defeat at Cardiff by that score raised no smiles in the boardroom. But Joe was right, too, for City then went on a run of eleven games in which, with George Heslop as the centre of a settled defence, they conceded only four goals and gained fifteen points to establish themselves firmly as candidates for promotion that season. When Leyton Orient were thumped 5–0 at Maine Road just before Christmas, it infuriated Joe and Malcolm that a crowd of only 16,000 had bothered to turn up and see them.

'We got 34,000 to watch Norwich back in October. Where the bloody hell are they all?' asked Joe.

Malcolm wasn't too bothered. He had already pocketed his ten pounds from his bet with Paddy Crerand, who had handed over the money with an evident reluctance that only increased both Malcolm's triumph and the breadth of his smile. 'It's Christmas shopping week. Now look, Joe, I want to try something.'

'If they don't turn up for the New Year's Day match against Huddersfield, I'm going to tell the board that their promise that Manchester is made up of City supporters isn't worth a damn.'

'I'd like Glyn Pardoe to drop back to right-half and swap with Mike Doyle.'

'All right. We'll try it in training next week.'

'No. Not in training. In the match.'

'Why?'

'We're not scoring enough.'

Joe looked at him in amazement. 'We've just put five past Leyton Orient.'

'We went four out of five without a goal. And we lost at Plymouth.'

Joe grinned. 'That's what's bugging you, isn't it? Losing at Plymouth.'

Malcolm ignored the jibe. 'When we're winning is when we should experiment. The players trust us. They think anything we do'll come off. When you make changes after you've got hammered, they think we're panicking.'

'They're right.'

'Exactly. Now listen – Doyle is great in the air . . .'

'Well, just tell him to go up for corners and free kicks as usual.'

'No, usually everyone's back and looking for him. Most teams we play man-mark and don't zonal mark. If after 15 minutes Glyn goes back to right-half and Mike comes up and plays in the middle, their centre-half won't know whether to follow Glyn back into the middle of the park or stay with Doyley.'

'Well, he'll work it out after a few minutes.'

'Boss, how bright is your average footballer?'

Joe Mercer smiled. He looked at his young coach fondly. This was the reason he'd hired him. 'All right, Mal. See what happens, but if we're losing 3–0 at half-time we're going back to the original formation.'

Malcolm grinned. This was fun. This was what football was supposed to be like.

The following Saturday, City won 2–0 at Crystal Palace. Mike Doyle, moving up from right-half to swap roles with centre-forward Glyn Pardoe, scored both goals. Malcolm Allison felt as though he had invented a cure for the common cold. On New Year's Day 1966, Manchester City beat top-of-the-table Huddersfield Town 2–0 in front of 47,000 fans with Johnny Crossan joining Doyle on the scoresheet. Manchester City were now second in the table, and even Walter Griffiths found it difficult to resist the manager's blandishments when he learned that City had been drawn away at First-Division Blackpool in the third round of the FA Cup.

Walter Griffiths did not believe that he was a difficult man to please. He expected his staff to arrive at work no later than 9.00 a.m. and leave no sooner than 5 p.m. He expected all the employees of Manchester City Football Club to come to work appropriately dressed and to obey the very clear and helpful rules he had laid down for them. He expected them to observe his practice of leaving his desk at 12.30 p.m. to go into the boardroom before returning at 2.30 p.m. Between those hours he did not expect to be disturbed. Everyone knew the rules: how difficult could it be to obey them? Oh, and it was a matter of some importance to him that he was always addressed as 'Mr Griffiths', and that anyone who wished to see him in his office knocked politely on the door and waited until he called out 'Come!'

He did not like Malcolm Allison because Malcolm Allison seemed incapable of understanding any of these rules – or else he showed a flagrant disregard for them. The feeling was mutual. Malcolm Allison loathed Walter Griffiths and everything he stood for. Griffiths seemed to him, with his formal, shiny suits and his slicked-down hair with its almost centre parting, to be the archetype of every meddling old-fashioned bureaucrat in and out of football who had ever got in his way. It was with great satisfaction, then, that one afternoon after training he strode along the boardroom corridor, flashed Dorothy a large smile, ignored her anxious 'I don't think Mr Griffiths is . . .', barged into Griffiths's office without knocking and sat down, uninvited, in the chair opposite the Secretary.

'We want a decent hotel in Blackpool, Walter. None of your fucking guesthouses. Try the Norbreck Hydro or the Imperial. And make sure I have a suite. We'll need it to discuss tactics.' Having delivered his message in exactly the peremptory style he had been planning, he rose, smiled confidently at the outraged Secretary and marched out, deliberately leaving the door open. 'I think Walter would like a large glass of brandy, Dorothy,' he said with mock sincerity to the flustered secretary as he swept out into the corridor.

Malcolm didn't get his suite, but he did get a decent hotel and he introduced his players to the fleshpots of Blackpool. After all, these lads were favourites for promotion now; they were playing First-Division Blackpool in an important Cup match, so it was just as important that the players behaved like First-Division players. He could hardly complain if they were in a nightclub at 11 p.m. on the Wednesday before the big match on Saturday afternoon if he had taken them there himself and was buying the champagne. However, it was also Malcolm who was up at 7 a.m. the following morning banging on all the players' doors and tipping out of bed those who didn't respond immediately. There was a five-mile run along the beach from Thornton Cleveleys to the North Pier and back to be endured before they would be allowed the luxury of indulging in a hearty breakfast of porridge and bacon and eggs. Since Malcolm only had one lung and showed no ill effects from the previous night's entertainment, none of the players felt disposed to complain.

Joe Mercer observed his assistant's unorthodox behaviour with his usual amused tolerance. He wasn't in much of a position to argue, either, as City played out a hard-fought 1–1 draw at Bloomfield Road. Blackpool were taken back to Maine Road for a replay the following Monday night where, under a freezing January sky, Summerbee, Doyle and Crossan scored the three goals that sent a crowd of fifty-two thousand into raptures and City into the next round of the FA Cup.

Only Walter Griffiths was less than pleased. That day he had received the bill from the Blackpool nightclub to which Malcolm had taken the players. He stared at it in wonder. Over the 'Sum Owing' figure of £541 15s. was a scribbled note in what he assumed was the handwriting of Malcolm Allison, which stated 'Send to Walter Griffiths, Manchester City FC'. The Secretary drew the attention of the Chairman to the outrage. Albert Alexander read it and blinked. 'That's quite a large bill, isn't it, Walter?'

'Shall I deduct it from his wages, Chairman?'

'I don't think his wages will cover it. As I remember, we've already advanced him £500, haven't we?'

'Chairman, if we let this pass, we are in danger of setting a precedent.

THE WORST OF FRIENDS

Allison will simply regard it as an open invitation to send bills back to the club from every bar and hotel in the country.'

'We've just beaten Blackpool in front of 52,000 spectators. Do you remember the last time we had a crowd of 52,000 here?'

'The United match in 1963?'

'Very good, Walter. Nearly three years ago, and that was a relegation derby match with a lot of United supporters. We're on the way back up, you know. We asked Joe and Malcolm to get us up and bring the crowds back. That was only six months ago. I think we can let this one go.'

Walter Griffiths was clearly not convinced. 'I have bills to pay from the printers for the match programmes and from the firm that cleans the floodlights, without which we couldn't have played tonight's match. Am I to tell them we can't pay them because our trainer has decided to spend the money on champagne?'

Albert Alexander felt sorry that his long-serving Secretary was so unbending, so obsessed with protocol, that he couldn't even enjoy the pleasure of the night's triumph. 'I'll have a word with Joe. Make sure it doesn't happen again.'

'A woman arrived five minutes before kick-off and said Malcolm had promised her tickets for her and her sister. He didn't tell me anything about that.'

'Was she attractive, this woman?'

'I can't remember.'

'Walter, it's only quarter past ten now, so it was less than three hours ago.'

'Does it matter if she was attractive or not? He's got no right to go around offering tickets to all and sundry and expecting me to sort it out at the last minute.'

'I'll have a word with him myself. Make sure it doesn't happen again.'

They were words Walter Griffiths was to hear repeated many times over the next few years.

SEVEN

'Christ, look at Bell, Doc, he's fucking useless. No left foot. Can't head the thing. Fucking useless.'

'Why are you here then, Malcolm?' asked the Chelsea manager, Tommy Docherty.

'Same reason as you, Doc.'

'Oh, you're watching Colin Waldron too, are you?'

Malcolm Allison was temporarily silent. He had no idea that any manager would come to watch Bury unless it was to consider an offer for Colin Bell. 'I'm very happy with George Heslop, thanks.'

'Actually,' said Docherty after Bell had failed to control a difficult bouncing ball that had run away from him and over the touchline to give a throw-in to the opposition, 'I agree with you for once. I think Bell's overrated if this is a typical performance.'

Malcolm breathed a sigh of relief. Then panicked. Tommy Docherty was nobody's fool. He must have heard the stories about Colin Bell. Maybe he was putting out false information, like Malcolm himself was. There was no question that Chelsea could pay money that City didn't have, and players' heads were always turned by the prospect of moving to a London club. Then there was all the publicity about Peter Osgood and the rest of Docherty's fashionable young side, who were playing good football just off the King's Road, the famous Chelsea street with its trendy boutiques. If only Joe could have persuaded the board to stump up the cash after the last board meeting he wouldn't still have to come to Gigg Lane for every mid-week match to scare off scouts from other clubs.

He was desperate to sign Colin Bell. He believed in Colin Bell as strongly as he believed in himself. Bell was going to be a great player, and he was going to spend the best years of his life playing for Manchester

City. He was still only 19 years old, but he had a lung capacity that intrigued Malcolm, who of course only had half the regular complement of lungs himself. Bell frequently ran from his own penalty box into the opposition's box, picked up the ball, shot and was back in his own defence before the opposition could gather themselves for a counter-attack. He was a phenomenal athlete, and though Docherty was right that he wasn't turning it on tonight, Malcolm had seen enough of him during the past six months to be sure that Manchester City had to buy Bell whatever Bury's final demand was.

Meanwhile, in their first season in charge Malcolm and Joe welcomed both the enticing prospect of promotion and an FA Cup final at Wembley. First-Division Leicester had understandably been the favourites to progress into the quarter-finals, but Neil Young, who had scored both the City goals at Maine Road, won the replay with an expert strike under Gordon Banks's falling body, and City were through to the last eight. Unfortunately, this triumph took place on the night that Manchester United went to the Stadium of Light in Lisbon and put five goals past Benfica, George Best scoring two of them. Next day in the newspapers it was as if City's win at Filbert Street, the best victory since Malcolm and Joe had taken over, didn't exist. All the newspapers wanted to write about was Manchester United and, in particular, George Best, the new Fifth Beatle, or 'El Beatle' as the headline writers christened him after he was photographed wearing one of those stupid Mexican-type sombreros. Well, if it was hats the press were interested in, Malcolm'd give them bloody hats . . .

Malcolm's loathing of Manchester United was more intense, more personal and, in a way, more bitter than that of Mike Doyle, who loved to proclaim his hatred of the traditional enemy. Doyle was just a Manchester kid who preferred blue to red. Malcolm's anger at Manchester United was a more intense feeling, a conviction that the world was an unfair place and that it was made unfair by Manchester United and their acolytes. More and more he was building himself up for the day that he would go to Old Trafford and show those insufferable, pompous fools that Manchester City were the best team in Manchester. His son Mark had already suffered the taunts of United bullies in the playground and brought home tales of suffering that no father could listen to without wishing he could make everything better for his child. Fortunately for Malcolm, he was in a position to do something about it. The day City went to Old Trafford and won would be the day he would feel fulfilled as a father as well as a coach. He knew he lacked some of the traditional virtues expected of a father, but he lacked nothing as a coach.

The week after the victory at Leicester, as deadline day for the season's transfers approached, Joe finally managed to convince Bury to settle for £42,500 and, to Malcolm's intense relief, Colin Bell became a Manchester City player.

'I hope you're right, Mal,' said an anxious Joe after he told him that the deal was done.

'I am. Anyway, he'll score more for us than Ralph Brand.'

Joe grinned sheepishly. He had to admit that Malcolm's initial reservations about the Scottish inside-forward had been proved right: a mere two goals provided a poor return on his outlay of twenty-five thousand pounds. Brand had been injured in October and had played only three or four games in the first team since recovering, as the indefatigable David Connor had proved his worth in yet another position.

Malcolm lit an enormous cigar and talked to anyone who would listen about the incipient greatness of Colin Bell. Everyone was impressed with the build-up, and much was expected of him in his debut match away at Derby County. Being a shy and quiet young man, Bell made little impression in the dressing-room, but his new teammates had heard what their now greatly respected coach had been saying about him and were looking forward as much as the fans to seeing him do it on the pitch in front of them.

Unfortunately, Bell started poorly at Derby. The ball seemed to run away from him whenever he tried to control it, and passes to colleagues never seemed to find their target. Malcolm could sense that the travelling support was unimpressed with its first sight of their would-be new hero, and the nerves of the debutant were starting to transfer themselves to the bench, where even Malcolm had begun to wonder whether the step up to a big club was having a negative effect on the lad. He really wasn't looking forward to having to bluster his way past a sceptical Joe at the end of the game.

Then the Derby full-back, Ron Webster, took an enormous swing at a loose ball to clear his lines and Colin Bell, the nearest City player to him, turned his back on it. Unfortunately for the defender, he didn't get the necessary elevation on his kick and the ball smacked into Bell's backside, whence it looped in a gentle arc over the goalkeeper and into the Derby net. Allison climbed out of the dugout and saluted the genius of Colin Bell's bottom. He turned to a relieved Joe Mercer and said simply, 'I told you he was a great player.' Joe laughed.

At the end of the game, a 2–1 victory against a poor Derby side, Joe was quick to put his arm round the debutant who had done little other than get his backside in the way of a hard-driven clearance. 'That's going to be the first of many goals you'll score for this club.' Bell looked at his new manager, grateful for the confidence he was showing but only too aware that he hadn't exactly distinguished himself in his new colours. 'But you're dropped next week.' Bell looked up, shocked at the brevity of the statement and the harshness of what he thought was a premature sentence. But his manager was smiling. 'It's the sixth round against Everton, and you're cup tied.' Bell grinned back. They were both relieved he would have a few more days to help him integrate into the side.

Sixty-three thousand fans crammed into Maine Road to witness a tense, scrappy nil–nil draw, and a further sixty thousand filled Goodison Park for a replay which lasted one hundred and twenty minutes yet failed to produce a goal. On both occasions City acquitted themselves well, but Malcolm constantly bemoaned the loss of Colin Bell. 'If we can hold a team like Everton scoreless for 210 minutes as we are, we'd have fucking murdered them if Colin Bell had played,' he said afterwards, when Joe came back from his glad-handing. Joe had been a distinguished half-back for Everton before the war, and though he left for Arsenal somewhat disgruntled, feeling himself prematurely written off, he enjoyed the warmth of the welcome that he'd always received at his home-town club. He tried to convince Malcolm that City had performed heroically, and he reminded his assistant that they were still only ninety minutes from a semi-final, that promotion had always been their primary aim, and that the rest of the football world had already sat up and taken notice of what they had achieved at Maine Road in less than nine months.

'Mal, this is a happy night. The players are happy, the directors are happy, the fans are happy, I'm happy, even your good friend the Secretary is happy.'

'Really?'

'As happy as he can be till he finds something to complain about.'

'We need more striking power, Joe. No one's impressed just by good defending. To strike fear into opposing teams we've got to have two or three players who score regularly and two or three more who can score from the midfield.'

'Derek Kevan's not doing much at Palace. We could get him back for three bob.'

'I'm serious, Joe. I know we're doing well, but all I can see are the cracks.'

'One step at a time, Mal. Promotion is what we want. Then the board can be convinced to release more money.'

'Don't kid yourself. This board will never release money. Not money like we want. They're small-minded. They've spent so long penny-pinching they have no idea what it's like to write out a cheque for a hundred grand and get the best players in the land.'

'Last I heard, the Secretary couldn't afford to write out a cheque to pay the printer's bill.'

'We've had one hundred and twenty thousand through the turnstiles for the last two home Cup ties. Are you telling me they can't find us the money we need to buy who we want?'

'Who is it you want, Mal? What's bugging you?'

'I'm pissed off we couldn't have Bell *and* Wyn Davies.'

'Jesus! We had to hold the Chairman upside down and shake the money out of his trouser pockets just to pay Bury. There was no chance we'd ever have been able to get Davies as well.'

'I have such plans for this club, Joe.'

'I know you do, son, but Rome wasn't built in a day.'

'Might have been if I'd been the emperor.'

Malcolm was way ahead of Joe in his thinking. Malcolm believed they were up the day they signed Colin Bell. Joe and the nervous supporters who could scarcely believe the speed at which their club had been seemingly transformed didn't believe they were up until Colin Bell headed the only goal of the game at Rotherham and they were mathematically certain of starting the following season back in the First Division. It was a goal that Colin Bell treasured as much as the supporters because whatever the words Malcolm had used to bolster his waning self-confidence, he knew he hadn't convinced anyone in the games he'd played after his transfer. But the scintillating Cup run, which had ended in a 2–0 defeat by Everton in the second replay, plus a stirring promotion campaign, which had culminated in the Second-Division Championship trophy, proved more than sufficient for City's supporters, who always hoped for the best but, in recent years, had grown used to expecting the worst.

THE WORST OF FRIENDS

At the ensuing celebration at the Town Hall, hosted by the appropriately named lord mayor, Mrs Nellie Beer OBE, JP, Albert Alexander approached the hulking figure of his assistant manager and tried to impart even more good news. 'Malcolm, the board have decided to grant you a bonus of £400.'

Malcolm was not impressed by the board's munificent gesture. He could lose 400 quid at a casino or at a racetrack in a matter of minutes. Was this really what the board considered his value to the club had been?

Unfazed by the display of Malcolm's less than overwhelming gratitude, the Chairman's good tidings knew no bounds. 'We're giving Joe an extra 600 and Walter 400.' Malcolm had by now moved up through the gears from irritation to outrage. Was the Secretary really considered to have been as influential in Manchester City's startling ascendancy to glory as Malcolm had been? He stared at the Chairman, whose beaming countenance was eventually replaced by a look of concern. What on earth was this extraordinary man thinking, wondered Alexander. Is he somehow displeased that we've decided to give him another £400? Four hundred pounds was about two months' salary, for heaven's sake.

'Yes,' said Malcolm as cuttingly as he could. 'That's a good idea. The Secretary certainly booked us into some nice hotels.' He puffed cigar smoke over the Chairman's bald head and said artfully, 'You know we're going to have to sign a player or two to cope with the demands of the First Division.'

'Nobody too expensive I hope,' smiled the Chairman ingratiatingly.

'I don't want the club to waste its money paying me when we need every penny for the transfer kitty.' Albert Alexander began to mellow towards this eminently reasonable young man. 'Why don't you just pay off my overdraft at the bank and we'll call it quits?'

'How much is the overdraft?'

'Oh, I don't know the exact figure. Maybe a few quid.'

'All right, Malcolm, that sounds fine.' They shook hands and each wandered away: Malcolm to find Joe and complain some more, Albert to tell the good news to Walter Griffiths.

The Secretary paled when he heard what his Chairman had agreed to. 'How much is his overdraft?'

'"A few quid," he said.'

'And you believed him?' Griffiths was astounded at Alexander's naivety.

'I know bank managers, Walter. Nobody would lend a spendthrift like Malcolm Allison more than 50 quid at the most.' It was two months before Albert Alexander could bring himself to sign the cheque for six hundred and fifty-two pounds that cleared Malcolm Allison's overdraft and left him with a balance of nil.

Joe had taken Norah outside the dining room and was sitting on a bench in the expansive Alfred Waterhouse-designed foyer uncomplainingly signing autographs for the waitresses. When he had signed everything, including the plaster cast of a youngster's broken arm, he smiled fondly at his wife, who was pouring coffee from a large silver pot into two china cups. 'I've got more good news for you, love.'

'You told me about the £600.'

'This is more than money. This is fame.'

'A newspaper column?'

'Oh, much more than a newspaper column.' He waited until the blank look on his wife's face indicated that she had no idea what he was talking about. 'I'm going to be a television star.'

'Joe! You're going to be on the *Black and White Minstrel Show*!'

Joe laughed. He loved Norah. It was impossible to impress her. 'Some bloke rang up from the BBC today to say they were going to have a panel of experts to analyse the World Cup matches and did I want to be on it?'

'What did you say?'

'I said I'd have to speak to my wife first. See if she'd let me stay out that late at night.'

'Get away with you.' She pushed his arm playfully, then handed him his coffee.

'I said I'd do it. It'll be first-class travel and a hotel in London the night they want me on.'

'How much are they paying you?'

Joe looked blank. 'I forgot to ask.'

'Joe!'

'Well, whatever it is,' he said with irrefutable logic, 'it'll be more than the nowt they'd have paid me if they hadn't asked me in the first place.'

'Hello, Norah.' Malcolm smiled as engagingly as he could at Joe's wife, considering the emotions that were still swirling around inside him. 'Do you know the club wants to pay that twat of a Secretary the same bonus as me! After all I've done for this fucking team.' He caught himself immediately. 'Sorry, Norah,' he apologised, and then saw that

Joe was looking at him with that half-smile playing around his mouth. He paused briefly. 'After all *we've* done,' he corrected himself.

Joe got to his feet and steered Malcolm into a quiet corner. 'Mal,' cautioned Joe. 'It's not worth getting yourself all worked up like this. We've won the Championship in our first season together. We've got a young team that could set the First Division alight. Just think of the glory ahead. Then we'll both get the money. What's the point of making waves now?'

After Joe had calmed Malcolm down and returned to Norah, he finished his coffee and turned to his wife with quiet satisfaction. 'Still wish I hadn't taken the job?'

'Joe, you know I only ever wanted you to be happy.'

'I know. But I am, Norah. I'm as happy as I've ever been since I stopped playing.'

'You had good times at Sheffield. And at Villa, and look how quickly they turned around.'

'Norah, love, please, there's nothing about the dark side of the game you can tell me. We both know what it's like. Ever since I talked to the board last July I've felt as though something was calling me. Not just back to the game but here, to City. It's like we were destined for each other.'

'You're talking like the two of you are lovers.'

'In a way, that's just what we are.'

'That's the first time I've ever heard you talk about a board of directors like that.'

'I get the feeling they trust me. They can sense what's going on around here, and they're as excited as I am.'

'Directors, Joe?'

'They want more of what we've given them this year. Why wouldn't they? You've seen the smiles on the faces around the ground. We did that. Me and Malcolm and the players.'

Norah considered her husband's palpable happiness and wondered if she dared to puncture his balloon of content. 'And how do you think Malcolm feels about all this?'

'We just talked about the future. How exciting it is.'

'No, I mean about you. The two of you. How your partnership is going to continue.'

Now it was Joe's turn to look bewildered. 'We're going on as before. We've got something going here. I wish I'd had Mal at Sheffield or Villa. I'd never have been relegated, never got ill. It's the perfect partnership. I told you I was going to delegate more this time, and I've done it, haven't I?'

Norah looked away. She wished fervently that her husband had learned by now how to protect himself, but he hadn't, not really, and she knew that her job, as it had always been, was to see dangers that he couldn't or wouldn't. Her instincts had been aroused by Malcolm's emotional behaviour. She thought – no, she knew – that it couldn't last. Malcolm seemed to her to be emotionally volatile, and though for the moment everything seemed to be fine on the surface, she couldn't see how the partnership could carry on like this – so lovey-dovey. This wasn't the brutal, heartless business of football she had experienced down the years with Joe, but what she could see was how happy her husband was. She could hardly deny that the Mercer–Allison partnership was, for the moment, working.

Joe was sensitive to his wife's moods and he caught her anxiety immediately. 'What? Tell me.'

'Nothing, Joe. I'm happy because you're happy. I'm happy because I haven't seen you looking as well as this for ten years. I don't know why the doctors didn't prescribe winning the Second-Division Championship years ago. It seems to cure almost everything.' They both laughed and Norah tried to bury her fears. Joe saw the tension leaving her face, and he relaxed as well.

He got to his feet and held out his hand to help her up. Two of his players, their ties askew, their shirt buttons undone and clearly the worse for the alcohol they had imbibed, were leaving the Town Hall with their wives or girlfriends. At least he assumed that they were their wives or girlfriends, but knowing the behaviour of players as he did, the chances were that their wives or girlfriends were sitting chatting to each other elsewhere in the building and these were two random sexy young women who found virile footballers attractive enough to disappear with them into a hotel room for half an hour. Times were changing. That sort of thing happened only occasionally in his day and, in any case, never to him. He always ascribed it to his infamous bandy legs. Still, this was no time for a moral witch-hunt, no time indeed to do anything other than smile indulgently at them. There was plenty of time for players' excesses before the start of pre-season training in July. He would be on television by then, passing judgement on the best footballers in the world. Malcolm would be only too pleased to have sole charge of the players. It would be good for him to spread his wings. It might make him a little less angry at the world.

THE WORST OF FRIENDS

1965–66: MANAGER JOE MERCER

1	AUG	21	(A)	MIDDLESBROUGH	D	1–1	MURRAY	17,982
2		25	(H)	WOLVES	W	2–1	OPP OWN-GOALS 2	25,572
3		28	(H)	BRISTOL C	D	2–2	BRAND, OPP OWN-GOAL	19,349
4		30	(A)	WOLVES	W	4–2	DOYLE, CROSSAN, MURRAY OPP OWN-GOAL	22,799
5	SEP	4	(A)	COVENTRY C	D	3–3	YOUNG 2, MURRAY	29,403
6		11	(H)	CARLISLE U	W	2–1	PARDOE 2	22,891
7		15	(A)	NORWICH C	D	3–3	PARDOE 2, CROSSAN	16,381
8		18	(A)	CARDIFF C	L	3–4	MURRAY, PARDOE, GRAY	11,520
9		25	(H)	DERBY C	W	1–0	MURRAY	20,834
10	OCT	2	(A)	SOUTHAMPTON	W	1–0	YOUNG	21,504
11		9	(A)	HUDDERSFIELD T	D	0–0		31,876
12		16	(H)	CRYSTAL P	W	3–1	PARDOE 2, YOUNG	24,765
13		23	(H)	PRESTON NE	W	3–0	YOUNG 2, BRAND	25,117
14		27	(H)	NORWICH C	D	0–0		34,091
15		30	(H)	CHARLTON A	D	0–0		23,102
16	NOV	6	(A)	PLYMOUTH A	L	0–1		15,954
17		13	(H)	PORTSMOUTH	W	3–1	MURRAY 2, PARDOE	22,106
18		20	(H)	BOLTON W	L	0–1		22,968
19		27	(H)	IPSWICH T	W	2–1	CROSSAN 2	19,416
20	DEC	4	(A)	BIRMINGHAM C	L	1–3	SUMMERBEE	10,442
21		11	(H)	LEYTON O	W	5–0	YOUNG 3, SUMMERBEE, CROSSAN	16,202
22		18	(A)	CRYSTAL P	W	2–0	DOYLE 2	12,847
23	JAN	1	(H)	HUDDERSFIELD T	W	2–0	DOYLE, CROSSAN	47,171
24		8	(A)	PORTSMOUTH	D	2–2	DOYLE, SUMMERBEE	17,352
25		12	(H)	ROTHERHAM U	W	3–1	DOYLE 2, CROSSAN	25,526
26		15	(H)	PRESTON NE	D	0–0		26,668
27		29	(H)	MIDDLESBROUGH	W	3–1	SUMMERBEE 2, YOUNG	25,278
28	FEB	5	(A)	BRISTOL C	D	1–1	YOUNG	25,723
29		19	(H)	COVENTRY C	W	1–0	CROSSAN	40,190
30		26	(A)	CARLISLE U	W	2–1	SUMMERBEE, PARDOE	9,000
31	MAR	12	(H)	CARDIFF C	D	2–2	CONNOR, YOUNG	29,642
32		19	(A)	DERBY C	W	2–1	BELL, YOUNG	22,533
33	APR	2	(H)	PLYMOUTH A	D	1–1	CROSSAN	24,087
34		8	(H)	BURY	W	1–0	SUMMERBEE	43,104
35		12	(A)	BURY	L	1–2	SUMMERBEE	21,437
36		16	(H)	BOLTON W	W	4–1	KENNEDY, SEAR, CROSSAN, CONNOR	29,459
37		23	(A)	IPSWICH T	D	1–1	CROSSAN	15,995
38		30	(H)	BIRMINGHAM C	W	3–1	BELL, YOUNG, CROSSAN	28,409
39	MAY	4	(A)	ROTHERHAM U	W	1–0	BELL	11,376
40		7	(A)	LEYTON O	D	2–2	BELL, OPP OWN-GOAL	6,109
41		13	(A)	CHARLTON A	W	3–2	OAKES, CROSSAN, CONNOR	13,687
42		18	(H)	SOUTHAMPTON	D	0–0		34,653

FINAL LEAGUE POSITION: 1ST IN DIVISION TWO

FA CUP

3	JAN	22	(A)	BLACKPOOL	D	1–1
R		24	(H)	BLACKPOOL	W	3–1
4	FEB	12	(H)	GRIMSBY T	W	2–0
5	MAR	5	(H)	LEICESTER C	D	2–2
R		9	(A)	LEICESTER C	W	1–0
6		26	(H)	EVERTON	D	0–0
R		29	(A)	EVERTON	D	0–0
2R	APR	5	(N)	EVERTON	L	0–2

LEAGUE CUP

2	SEP	22	(H)	LEICESTER C	W	3–1
3	OCT	13	(H)	COVENTRY C	L	2–3

EIGHT

It happened to him the first time at the traffic-lights on Wilbraham Road. A Ford Zephyr drew up alongside his car, and a man leaned out of the window and shouted 'Joe! Joe!' He stared straight ahead. Being approached by strange men at traffic-lights was not a new experience. It had happened to him quite frequently at Sheffield and while driving through Birmingham when Villa were experiencing the dark times. The best thing, he had learned painfully, was to ignore everything hurled at him and never to engage in conversation with these lunatics because you could never win. They were opinionated, bigoted and unwilling to listen, so there was simply no point. However, the red traffic-light at the junction of Wilbraham Road and Withington Road seemed to last for ever, and the tone of the man's voice wasn't the same as the angry voices that had vilified him so dreadfully at Villa. He decided to risk a sideways glance. The man was grinning at him. Joe rolled down the side window of his 1964 Rover 2000.

'I thought you were great on t' telly, Joe. Even my missus thought so, and she knows bugger all about football.'

'You a City fan, then?'

The smile was wiped off the man's face as if by an unseen hand. 'You must be fucking joking. I'm a Red.' The lights turned to green and the Ford Zephyr roared away, revealing a back box on the exhaust that clearly needed changing urgently. Joe rolled his window up and drove on into town, where he was due to meet Norah at Kendals for lunch. He parked his car at the bottom of Bridge Street and then walked back up the hill towards Manchester's biggest department store.

Mostly he found Manchester folk friendly but not intrusive: a perfect combination. Since the beginning of the season and the dawning realisation that City were progressing upwards rather than sliding down towards the Third Division, he had seen a lot of smiles and heard many shouts of 'Good luck, Joe!' but that was about the extent of it, apart from the ubiquitous autograph seekers who bothered him in restaurants. Mostly, though, they went after the players, and he could live a private life in Manchester without any significant restrictions on his movements.

It took him half an hour to walk the 500 yards from the bottom of Bridge Street to the entrance of Kendals on Deansgate. Everybody he met wanted to stop and talk about his appearances on the World Cup panel. He'd never known anything like it. He'd always been able to make people smile with the occasional humorous observation, but from the way people talked to him now it seemed like he was the best comedian on the BBC. They seemed to find it hilarious that he pronounced the name of Brazil's most famous player as 'Peely'. 'Hey, Joe, Hancock's finished. You should take his place,' was one comment he reported to Norah with a laugh. Norah marvelled at the look of him – whereas he had been sallow only a few months before, he now seemed to be bursting with health and vigour. When he had been grimacing, he was now smiling broadly. His mouth had always curved in a natural *U* shape like the painted face of a clown, but now there was no inner sadness that the smile was trying to mask. He was a naturally happy and contented man.

Ten days before the end of July, Malcolm sat at home with Beth and watched Joe and David Coleman pontificating on the powerful Argentina side and the difficulties they would likely provide for England when they met them at Wembley on Saturday afternoon. In particular, Joe admired their captain, the tall, uncompromising, dark-haired Antonio Rattín, whose aggression reminded him of the old Arsenal half-back Wilf Copping. 'I love the way he can even con the referee. It's Rattín who controls the game.'

Much as he liked Joe, Malcolm couldn't help thinking that comparing Rattín to Wilf Copping was going to confuse a lot of the viewers at home, who would never have heard of a player whose career had effectively finished at the outbreak of the war. It was typical of Joe, always harking back to the time when he was a player. Malcolm made a point of never talking about 'in my day' to players who would never have heard of the men he'd played with and who wouldn't have cared even if they had. The next match, the next opponents were the only ones worth mentioning.

Stuck in the house on the couch watching television, Malcolm seethed with impatience. This World Cup tournament was driving him crazy. Alf Ramsey had produced a dull, functional, uninspiring side with none of the verve Malcolm considered so important to the creation of a winning team, yet the country was lapping it up. It said it all that Joe was becoming a national hero by talking about the pre-war days. He, Malcolm, was the man of the future. He should be the one on the telly. He would tell the viewers what they needed to hear: that Alf was ruining English football. Malcolm was the man destined to be the manager who would win the World Cup for England, not this dull, frightened, cautious man – although there was a chance Alf might actually do it because, apart from Portugal, there was no team that Malcolm had seen that was likely to give England a real game.

'I'm going to get fish and chips,' he said to Beth, and walked out banging the front door behind him. He walked briskly towards the Rose & Crown, ordered a double brandy at the bar and looked around at the clientele. In the far corner sat an attractive woman with long, straight, blonde hair, wearing a fashionable shift dress with a hemline short enough to reveal her long bare legs. Next to her was a short, rather dumpy plain girl. He was always intrigued at how often a pretty girl would have a plain girl as her best friend. Presumably she thought the plain girl wouldn't be much in the way of competition and that the comparison would make her look even more attractive. Conversely, the plain girl was more likely to receive male attention in the company of a pretty friend than ever she would by herself. Malcolm looked at himself in the mirror behind the bar and saw a handsome man as fit and as charismatic as he had ever been. He took his drink and sat down next to the two women. 'Hello, girls, been watching the match?'

'We came here to get away from the match.'

'Me too.'

'Oh, don't you like football either?'

'Can't stand it,' said Malcolm.

'What do you do then?'

'I'm a photographer – colour magazines and that.'

'So do you come from London?'

'Just outside: Bexleyheath,' confirmed Malcolm, and wondered how long it would take him to separate the blonde woman from her friend and how long from that point it would take him to get her into bed. In the event, he achieved both ambitions in less than the ninety minutes that it would normally take England to scrape a goal, though he was aided by the fact that the pretty girl's parents were away in Blackpool for the wakes week holiday, and she lived only two streets from the Rose & Crown.

It was 10.30 the following morning when Malcolm opened the front door, wondering as he did so exactly how he would explain to his wife his absence since the previous evening when he'd gone out with the avowed intention of buying fish and chips. Certainly, it hadn't been the first time in their tempestuous marriage that he had disappeared without explanation, and Beth was by now unsurprised by almost any manifestation of Malcolm's erratic behaviour. He thought, with some justification, that she knew perfectly well that his dismay at the way England were playing combined with his liking for a drink or two might have led him to an all-night bender, but you could never be entirely sure with women. As a rule, he mused philosophically, they tended to be more tolerant of drunken rampages than casual infidelities committed only a few streets away.

Beth was coming down the stairs as Malcolm walked in through the door. She stood and looked at her errant husband and noted that he had returned empty-handed as well as 13 hours late. 'Malcolm,' she complained testily, 'where the hell are the fish and chips?' Malcolm smiled. That's why he had married Beth. He was a rotten father to their four children, he knew, but at least they had the comfort of knowing they couldn't have had a better mother.

During the quarter-final on Saturday afternoon, when Antonio Rattín was sent off after 35 minutes Malcolm expected England to pour through the holes his expulsion was bound to create. But the Argentina players covered so heroically that in the end they were unlucky to lose to a near-post header by Geoff Hurst 12 minutes from time – a tactic familiar to teams that had played against West Ham but which took the Argentinians by surprise. Joe, meanwhile, was at his beloved Goodison Park watching North Korea race into a three-goal lead against the heavily fancied Portugal team. But with the help of four goals from Eusebio, Portugal finally booked their place for the semi-final against England with a 5–3 victory, and every time the television gave the score from Liverpool Malcolm was more and more convinced that the only way to win football games was to attack teams. Defensive caution was the bane of modern coaches. He knew he was the man to take England to new heights after Ramsey had been 'found out'.

His arrangement with Joe was that the old man would have another year in charge at Manchester City before handing over to his assistant. Malcolm was perfectly content with this because he suspected that it might be a bit of a struggle in the top division for the first season, but if Joe went in 12 months' time, as he had always promised, the players would be ready, after a first season of consolidation, for a push for real honours. Once that happened, it would only be a matter of time before Malcolm would be in prime position to succeed Alf Ramsey as England manager, maybe even in time for the 1970 World Cup if results started to turn against the national team.

By now Malcolm understood Joe, understood his little vanities, how he could be manipulated into doing exactly what Malcolm had wanted. They had agreed that they needed a right-back once promotion had been secured. Dave Bacuzzi had started the 1965–66 season at Manchester City in that position but had been replaced by Bobby Kennedy, who was really a half-back. Malcolm was sure that Kennedy would be unable to live with the speedy wingers of the First Division, such as Peter Thompson of Liverpool. He was also sure that his original judgement on Bacuzzi – that he was one of the old pros he'd rather see moved out of the club – had been accurate. The left-back Cliff Sear was another who fell into that category, so a new full-back became a priority. Malcolm considered eight players, three of them full internationals, but was not convinced by any of them. Finally, ten days before pre-season training started, he made up his mind. 'I know the perfect man,' he said to Joe.

'Go on.'

'Tony Book.'

'Who?'

'Played for me at Plymouth and at Bath. He's a real athlete. Recovers like lightning. Nobody'll get past him twice, believe me. Don't you remember – he marked Neil Young out of the game when they beat us at Home Park?'

'I'll think about it.'

Malcolm knew exactly what Joe's 'I'll think about it' meant. He'd go home and ring up his old mates who hadn't played for years – men like Stan Matthews and Tommy Lawton – and ask them. He was prepared for the inevitable response next day.

'This chap you want – Book – he's 31 years old! We can't be doing with someone that age.'

'How old were you, Joe, when you left Everton?'

'Thirty-two.' Joe could see where this conversation was going, and he knew he'd been caught out.

'And how many years did you play for Arsenal?'

'Seven.'

Malcolm was reeling him in now. 'And what did you win at the Arsenal?'

'Everything.' Joe was smiling as well, now. It was a fair trap he'd fallen into.

'He's like a whippet, Joe, looks after himself really well, complete professional, and because he's not a kid I think he's captaincy material.'

'Crossan's a good captain.'

'If anything happened to Crossan.'

'How much did you pay to take him from Bath to Plymouth?'

'Not much. Two or three thousand.'

'I'm not paying more than 15 grand for him, Mal. D'you think Plymouth'll go for it?'

'Not from me, but they might from you, Joe.'

Malcolm was right: Plymouth eventually did, although it took £17,000 to persuade them. By now Joe was starting to trust Malcolm's hunches, though it never stopped him from grumbling. He couldn't believe the sums of money clubs nowadays demanded for ordinary players. Why, Plymouth wanted more for the unknown Tony Book than Arsenal had paid Wolverhampton Wanderers for Bryn Jones! The £14,000 that changed hands for Jones was a world-record fee, but that had been 30 years before, and life, even Joe recognised, had moved on since then. He remembered that particular transfer because Jones had been broken under the intense pressure that such a high figure had created, and Joe had been wary of paying large transfer fees ever since then. Still, Joe liked the look of the leathery-faced, polite former bricklayer Tony Book when he met him and noted that he was as thin as a rake, just as he had been himself in his playing days. Carrying no extra weight at 31 meant there was a good chance Book's frame would stay like that for the rest of his playing days, and that would enable him to keep up with wingers. The days of the full-back who was expected to remain resolutely in his own half and simply bundle the opposing winger into touch whenever he approached were long gone, buried for ever by the success of the overlapping full-backs Ray Wilson and George Cohen in England's recent World Cup triumph.

The City players were ebullient when they met for pre-season training, in marked contrast to the downcast mood that had prevailed a year earlier. Even the normally reticent Alan Oakes demonstrated an unexpectedly extrovert side to his character.

'Can't wait for the season to start, Mal.'

'Why's that?'

'I want to go to places like Highbury and Anfield and Old Trafford and really show them what we're made of.'

'You'll need to be fit,' warned Malcolm, delighted that Oakes was digging an enormous hole for himself.

'We were the fittest side in the Second Division.'

'You're not in the Second Division now, son.'

'Your training methods worked last year.'

'And they'll work this year.'

'So no problem.'

'Not if you can take training twice as hard as last year.'

Oakes started to smile, but Malcolm looked at him implacably. 'You can't work us twice as hard as last year. It's not possible.'

'Just wait and see me try.'

Oakes backed away, running to tell the other players exactly what Malcolm had wanted them to know. It would be so much more powerful coming as a rumour from another player. They really would be on their toes now.

Initially Malcolm's murderous pre-season training seemed to pay off as City hit the First-Division running flat out. A first-day draw away at Southampton was followed on Wednesday by an invigorating and thoroughly deserved 2–1 win over Liverpool, the League Champions of the previous season. A week after their return to the First Division, a solitary goal by Alan Oakes proved good enough to beat Sunderland at Maine Road, and Manchester City were top of the League with five points out of a possible six. Joe was hard-pressed to stop Malcolm from telling the world that City were going to do the double. Everything that Malcolm believed in was being affirmed. If you attacked teams you would win more games than you lost, and in players like Book, Bell, Oakes and Summerbee he had players who would grace any team in the land. City's stunning start prompted the press to proclaim to its readers that Malcolm Allison was a coach of genius. It was an accolade that Malcolm went to great lengths to ensure was heard loud and clear by the board of directors. His only concern was that Joe didn't seem to be joining in the celebrations.

'Mal, for God's sake, we're only three matches into the season.'

'Who was it that told me to celebrate my victories?'

'I meant when you've won a trophy, not a 1–0 home win against Sunderland.'

Malcolm was determined to press home the advantage granted them by the current League table. 'Have you got Crossan's revised contract sorted out?'

'Not yet.'

'Why not?'

'Not the right time.'

Malcolm was frustrated and let Joe know it. 'It's never the right time.'

'Malcolm, let me handle the directors.'

'They're just a bunch of butchers and bakers who know fuck all about football. Why are you so worried about them?'

'Because they know nothing – that's what makes them dangerous.'

Malcolm shook his head and walked away. He simply couldn't understand why Joe didn't just tell the directors what he wanted and make sure they gave it to him. It seemed to him that with City riding high on success delivered to these fools by himself and Joe, they should be able to demand anything of these men and get their way. But Joe was from the old school, which seemed terrified of Establishment figures. He wasn't particularly combative with anyone, yet he was always wary of middle-class authority figures, who were the sort of people that became directors of football clubs.

It was as if everything that had happened in Britain over the past four or five years had passed Joe by. Centuries of social deference had been destroyed. Who could now take politicians at face value after the sordid details of the Profumo Affair and the huge popularity of *That Was the Week That Was*? The country had tossed the Tories out of Downing Street and twice elected a Labour government under that well-known Huddersfield Town supporter Harold Wilson. There was an explosion of music and fashion, which had clearly made very little impact on the middle-aged, provincial Joe and Norah. Girls who had flirted with footballers in the '50s now had the confidence to go to bed with them in the '60s. It was a different country from the one scarred by years of post-war austerity and national service. Malcolm was far more tuned into what was happening in the country at large, and maybe that was why he couldn't stand what he regarded as Joe's obsequiousness in front of directors.

Football was changing, too, but the men who ran it appeared not to notice. England had won the World Cup playing crap football, but at least they'd won it, and it was now perceived by everyone as being sexy. The country had celebrated the World Cup win with more enthusiasm than it had shown since VE Day. *Match of the Day* moved from the niche channel of BBC2 to the traditional national channel of BBC1. Women who knew nothing about the game knew who Bobby Moore was and found him attractive, with his long legs and tiny white shorts. The game was no longer the preserve of working-class men; television exposure had opened up the game to all classes and both sexes. Conversely, players didn't just appear on TV during games; players such as Moore, Hurst and Peters could be found doing adverts as well.

Football now meant fame and fortune, and was part of a world that cared about *Coronation Street* and Sean Connery as James Bond. This was a world Malcolm moved in easily, but one that Joe Mercer and the City directors found alien and slightly frightening. That was why Malcolm now felt ready to take over the club. There would still be room for Joe. He knew how much Joe gave to their partnership, and he was always grateful for Joe's understanding and his ability to calm things down after Malcolm's natural exuberance had caused some kind of explosion. He just felt so constricted by his position as the coach when he knew perfectly well that it was to him the players always turned first. Joe might have been their favourite uncle, but Malcolm was their father and mother.

In the event, Joe's caution, as ever, proved entirely justified. After the heady triumphs of the two early home wins, City lost their next three games, conceding ten goals, and they would be going into the first derby match against Manchester United with diminished confidence. And it wasn't only the players who now lacked confidence. The defeats had hit Malcolm hard, too. He was so sure they were moving in the right direction, thinking that though they might not win the First Division this year, they might the next. Only they couldn't if they were back in the Second Division next season. Busby and United would sense City's vulnerability. He wished he could postpone the derby match until he had steadied the ship again. Malcolm confided his anxieties to the Boss. 'We can't let United stuff us.'

'I remember a derby match once when I was at Everton. Liverpool were the second team in the city . . .'

'Joe, United, this week, now, 1966.'

'I thought we done all right against the Arsenal. It was a good point.'

'Booky's going to have to continue as sweeper, and the rest of the team will have to mark man to man.'

'How's Crossan doing?'

'I talked to the physio. He's not going to make it.'

'Where's Pardoe going to play?'

'We give him the number 10 shirt, but he sticks to Law like Connor sticks to Charlton.'

'What about Bestie?' asked Joe.

Malcolm shrugged. The final member of United's trio of superstars was one too many to take care of with any guarantee of success. 'That should be Booky, but he's going to have sweep up behind so it'll have to be Bobby Kennedy.' Malcolm understood why the boss looked anxious. 'What's worrying me is how are we ever going to score?'

Joe looked pained, as if his assistant was deliberately adding to their troubles. 'Nil–nil'll do me.'

'Me too. And the fans. But we're going to have to be lucky.'

They weren't lucky, and a single goal by Denis Law gave United victory. Despite the fact that it wasn't the hammering City had feared, it was a subdued coach that drove away from Old Trafford through ranks of exultant United fans banging on the windows, happily reminding Malcolm of who had won the game, in case he had forgotten. After the match, Matt Busby had been formally courteous to Malcolm and as jovial as ever with Joe, but Malcolm still couldn't warm to the great man, who attracted more reverence than anyone else in the city of Manchester. Today had not been the day that he had been dreaming about, but it was coming. One day, one day . . . Still, the truth was that Malcolm was disappointed with the team and disappointed with himself. What had happened to the swashbuckling football he had promised the players and the fans? It had only been three weeks since he had been telling the world how Manchester City were going to sweep aside all before them this season. Now everyone at the club seemed to be panicking lest they slip into the relegation zone. Well, it was a season of readjustment to the demands of top-flight football, of consolidation, of feeling that they belonged in the same division as United and Liverpool and Leeds.

When they entertained high-flying Chelsea at Maine Road, the gulf in class between the two sides was made embarrassingly obvious as the Londoners won 4–1 with disconcerting ease. The Kippax abused Peter

Osgood throughout the game, chanting 'Osgood No Good', but Chelsea's star forward showed his disdain by calmly scoring the final goal and then giving a two-fingered salute back to the Kippax, which reacted with predictable fury. The City players had tried their best, but they were simply unable to match the skill and composure of their opponents.

'I've got an idea,' said Malcolm to Joe after training the following Monday morning.

'Well, I'm glad one of us has,' smiled the older man, 'because we can't go on like this.'

'Connor's out, Kennedy's out, and we haven't got a left-back.'

'I was thinking of bringing Cliff Sear back,' said Joe with no great enthusiasm.

'I want to make Glyn Pardoe a full-back.'

'Well, he's played everywhere else on the field . . .'

'No,' interrupted Malcolm excitedly. 'I mean permanently.'

'Why? He's right-footed.'

'Something Summerbee said to me. Said he was the best tackler in the club.'

'On the other side of the park maybe,' said Joe, doubtfully.

'He's thoughtful, Glyn. He knows when to go in and when to back off and harass. If the right-winger tries to go past on the outside, Glyn's shrewd enough positionally to jockey him into an area where he can't hurt us, and if he tries to go inside it'll be the winger's left foot against Glyn's right. Besides, he's good enough with his left peg to clear his lines down the wing with it.'

Joe admired Malcolm's ability to think laterally, even if at least half of his ideas were hopelessly impractical. 'Let's try it in training tomorrow.'

'I already did.'

'And?'

'You can see for yourself in the morning, but I wouldn't even be talking about it to you if it hadn't worked.'

Malcolm was right. Joe saw exactly what he had been talking about. Glyn Pardoe, who had started off as a centre-forward, looked as though he had found his natural position at the age of twenty, after four years of first-team football. Even though the following Saturday brought yet another home defeat, this time 2–1 at the hands of high-flying Tottenham Hotspur, the performance was a vast improvement on the Chelsea catastrophe.

THE WORST OF FRIENDS

The Tottenham manager Bill Nicholson offered his condolences. 'You'll be all right, Joe,' he said in Joe's office while the players were in the bath.

'We're going to have to start picking up points, Bill. Can't do it with plucky performances.'

'You've got a winner in Malcolm.'

'I know. Christ! I wish I'd had him with me at Villa. He's great.'

'Just a word of advice.'

'Oh?' Joe's eyes narrowed. Bill Nick was famously taciturn and not in the habit of handing out words of advice.

'Watch your back.'

'Eh? With Malcolm? You must be joking.'

'He's not like Eddie. Eddie's happy to be my number two. Malcolm's ambitious.'

'For the team. Like me. We're both ambitious.'

'Just be careful, all right?'

Eddie Baily stuck his head around the door. 'Coach is leaving, Boss.'

'I'm coming.' The Yorkshireman got to his feet and looked at his old friend. 'Don't forget what I said, Joe. Not today, not tomorrow, but one day . . .'

NINE

I t was a hard winter. They fought like tigers – quite literally in Mike Summerbee's case, having been sent off at Newcastle – but good results proved elusive. Malcolm's stentorian voice, which was audible to linesmen even when there were 50,000 excitable fans in the ground, got him into trouble with the Football Association, too. In December he served a 28-day touchline ban, which frustrated both Malcolm and Joe, although Summerbee was relieved not to have 'Take him on, take him on!' constantly bellowed at him from the dugout for a few matches. In the stand, Malcolm seethed with the injustice. He loathed the Football Association and its Disciplinary Committees as much as he loathed football club directors, and for much the same reason: they were constituted by tired, old, probably impotent men in shiny suits who thought Winston Churchill was still the prime minister. In the confines of the directors' box he had to restrain his usual explosive vocabulary, and at the end of each half he simply flew down the stairs to the dressing-room to evacuate the torrent of abuse and invective that had been boiling away inside him for the past 45 minutes.

It didn't help that without his touchline presence it seemed as though City had lost the ability to score a goal. As the team continued to struggle to score goals throughout February and March, Malcolm spent every night of the week watching other teams' matches, desperate to find someone who would spark his forward line into life. Johnny Crossan, who had been such a mainstay of City during the first season and a half, had unaccountably lost his form. Joe and Malcolm had dropped him for the derby match, but restored him for the next game. However, the indignity of being dropped failed to act as the motivation they had hoped for, though he retained his place in the side till the end of the season. There wasn't much money around, so Malcolm knew there was no point wasting his time watching First-Division games. If he was going to unearth a catalyst for the forward line, the player would have to come from the lower divisions. He quite fancied a left-winger from Doncaster Rovers called Tony Coleman. He mentioned the name to Joe and was astonished to get such an emotional reaction.

'Tony Coleman? Mal, are you crazy? The lad's a lunatic.'

'Nothing I can't handle.'

'He's been kicked out of the club by Preston and Stoke.'

'I know.'

'They said he was unmanageable.'

'Not by me.'

'Tommy Jones had him at Bangor. He said not to touch him.'

'Joe, I saw him play for Bangor at Altrincham. He was fantastic. We could have had him for three grand then.'

'Nobody came in for him because they all know he's a lunatic.'

'He's reformed a bit, I think, since that spell in non-League.'

'Reformed? When Doncaster signed him, he flattened the ref in his first match back.'

'He's got spirit.'

'He's got some kind of mental disorder if you ask me. First time I came across him was at Lilleshall.'

'Oh, not the bed thing . . .'

'He threw a bed out of a third-floor window! What sort of a nutcase does that?'

'What does that matter? Joe, I've seen him three times in the last two weeks, and he destroys defences . . .'

'And I know how.'

'He'll give us width and balance on the left. We can bring Neil Young inside. Coleman will give us Young's goals back.'

Joe could see the sense in that. Young had been top scorer in the first season, with fourteen goals, but had disappointed in the First Division, having only scored three times all year. It took three more conversations for Malcolm to get his way, but just before the transfer deadline day in March, entirely against his better judgement, Joe signed Tony Coleman from Doncaster Rovers for twelve thousand pounds.

If Malcolm was planning ahead for the next season in the First Division, Joe was much more concerned that they might not even be there. Blackpool had always seemed likely to finish bottom, but there were a number of clubs who could be relegated with them: Aston

Villa, Newcastle, Southampton, Fulham and Sunderland, as well as Manchester City. On April Fool's Day, City travelled over the Pennines to Bramall Lane, where they fought tenaciously as ever. But six minutes before the break, Sheffield United's Mick Jones headed the ball past Alan Ogley and once again City went into the dressing-room a goal down, knowing that their goalscoring record was so poor that defeat was virtually ensured. Joe was incensed. All his old anxieties seemed to grab him by the throat. He and Malcolm and the players had worked so hard, but fate seemed to be against them. There was a strong possibility that if things continued this way he would be relegated for the third time in his career as a manager. The loss of face, the professional implications and the potential medical consequences overwhelmed him. He stormed into the dressing-room and rounded on Alan Ogley, who was carefully adjusting his contact lenses. 'What the fuck did you do that for?'

Ogley was astounded. Joe rarely swore, and certainly never at him. Why was he suddenly being picked out as the baddie? 'Do what, Boss?'

'Let Jones get to the ball first. It was your cross.'

'It was outside the six-yard box, and I could see George was going for it.'

'*You* should have gone for it. Good goalkeepers come out for crosses, they don't wait on their goal lines for the centre-half to clear. It's your fault we're a goal down.'

'Look, Joe, I'll handle it.' Malcolm put a restraining hand on the shoulder of the furious manager, but Joe just shrugged it off.

The unfortunate Ogley was as incensed as his manager. 'I've made about ten great fucking saves because we've got a crap defence and an attack that can't score, and this is all *my* fault?' Ogley pulled his goalkeeping jersey over his head, dropped his shorts and stamped off towards the showers.

'Great,' yelled Joe. 'Best place for you.'

There was total silence in the dressing-room. Malcolm followed Ogley into the showers. The goalkeeper was clearly very upset. The coach put his arm around him. 'You shouldn't have done that, son.'

'You heard him! You saw what I did out there!'

'He was wrong. But he's the manager and you're the player.'

'I don't want to play for that bastard ever again.'

'If you don't get your kit on again right now, you'll never play for anyone again.'

'Mal! You said I played well and he was in the wrong.'

'You've got ten teammates out there who are relying on you. What are they going to think if you're sat in here and I have to stick Doyley in goal?' Even in his emotional state, Ogley saw the sense in what Malcolm was saying. 'Get dressed and apologise. I'll see what I can do.'

They went back into the dressing-room, but Joe had already left. The players sympathised with Ogley, but they knew he had crossed some kind of a line. So did he. Malcolm accompanied Ogley down the tunnel and onto the pitch. 'Go and prove him wrong, son,' he said and ducked into the dugout.

Ogley hurled himself around heroically in the second half, but City's inability to score continued to haunt them. There were no further goals, and at full-time the players tramped wearily back into the dressing-room. Malcolm was already focusing his players' minds on the quarter-final tie at Elland Road the following week. They'd had a good Cup run, and it would do everyone good to let go of the enervating struggle for League survival and think about the prospect of travelling down Empire Way towards the twin towers of Wembley on Cup final Saturday.

Meanwhile, Ogley prepared himself to say something to the manager. He didn't know what. His career so far had not prepared him for the confrontation he had just had. He was the politest of young men, always calling the manager 'Boss' and the Chairman 'Sir'. What had happened at half-time had been entirely out of character. Ogley was hoping that Joe would start a conversation that might allow him to make some kind of apology, but he wasn't exactly looking forward to it so he was both relieved and worried that the manager didn't come into the dressing-room. Had he caused him to have a heart attack? Where was he?

In fact, Joe was talking to Peter Gardner of the *Manchester Evening News*. 'Same side next week if there's no injuries?' asked Gardner.

'No. I'm going to bring Harry Dowd back.'

Gardner was surprised. He couldn't see what Ogley had done wrong to be ruled out a full week before the next match. 'Is Ogley injured?'

'He's tired. He needs a rest, and we've got Harry, who's raring to go.'

'Does he know who you're playing?'

Joe smiled. Harry Dowd's ignorance about the teams they were due to face was legendary. 'He'll know soon enough when Lorimer starts shooting at him.'

Joe sat in his usual seat at the front of the coach on the journey back along the Snake Pass. Alan Ogley sat quietly by himself, staring out of the window as the coach slowly climbed the steep hills of the A57. He was a Yorkshire lad himself – born and raised in Barnsley, his dad was a miner in the South Yorkshire coalfields. Ogley had left home three years earlier as a nervous schoolboy international to be apprenticed to the great Bert Trautmann in Manchester. It had quickly become his home, and he felt he belonged at City. But now, for the first time in three years, he wasn't looking forward to returning to Lancashire. He comforted himself with the knowledge that he had played really well at Sheffield – aside from letting in the goal for which Joe had reprimanded him so severely – and would surely be in the team for the cup tie at Leeds. But still . . .

It was only when he picked up the early edition of the *Manchester Evening News* after training on Monday lunchtime that he found out he was going to be dropped. He raced up the stairs and, after knocking once on the manager's door (old habits died hard), stormed into Joe's office. 'You've dropped me!'

Joe was implacable. 'You need a rest.'

'I don't need a rest, Boss. I need to play in the sixth round of the Cup at Leeds.'

'I've picked Harry. It'll do you good to play in the stiffs for a bit. Get your confidence back.'

'There's nowt wrong with my confidence. Till you dropped me. For what? For letting in 15 goals in 17 games?'

'You're playing in the reserves on Saturday.' The unsmiling Mercer was clearly not to be moved.

Ogley slammed the door behind him. He went back into the dressing-room, where he picked up his coat and car keys, unaware that the room had fallen silent as he had entered it. The other players looked at him, waiting for some clue as to what had transpired 'upstairs', but Ogley simply walked out without a word. The traumatised goalkeeper was unlocking his car when he heard the sound of his coach's voice. 'Magoo! Magoo!' Malcolm was running towards him.

'The bastard's dropped me, Mal. After all that!'

'I know . . .'

'If I can't play in the sixth round of the Cup, I'm not fucking staying here and playing in the stiffs!'

'No, you're not.' Malcolm put both hands on the goalkeeper's shoulders. His whole body seemed to be trembling with emotion. 'You won't be playing in the reserves. You're coming with us on the coach. You're in no state to play football.'

'Thanks, Mal.'

'Go home, talk to Diane, come in tomorrow and I'll work on a few things with you.'

'You've got a quarter-final to prepare for, Mal.'

'Did you hear what I just said?'

Ogley nodded dumbly.

'Then fuck off home and do it. And be here at ten in the morning.'

Alan Ogley got into his car, then sat there with the ignition off for ten minutes as he thought about what had just happened. In his opinion Malcolm Allison was the greatest coach who had ever walked the earth. He would do anything that man asked of him.

Malcolm walked back to the dressing-room wondering how best to approach the subject with Joe before concluding that there was no point. Ogley was clearly in no emotional state to play in goal at Leeds whatever the outcome of his discussion with Joe. As Malcolm sat down with Joe to discuss the team and tactics for Saturday, he thought about confronting him with how ineptly the older man had handled his goalkeeper, but decided no good would come of it, not just now. Joe could be as stubborn as a mule, and the decision to play Dowd rather than Ogley had been made and would not be unmade. Instead he decided to air something he'd been thinking about for some weeks.

'Joe. Let's surprise them.'

'By winning, you mean?'

Malcolm ignored the flippant remark. 'What are Leeds expecting? We pull everyone behind the ball and try to hit them on the break.'

'Why not? We're the away side and bringing them back to Maine Road would be a good result for us.'

'Let's go for it.'

'Go for what?'

'Attack them. Tell Summerbee and Young to stay in their half of the field. It'll stop Bremner surging forward.'

'I've got my eyes shut at the thought of Neil Young taking on Bremner and Hunter.'

'He's a big boy, Joe. He'll have to look after himself. Best thing he can do to avoid getting kicked is to score. Anyway, Summerbee and Coleman won't be intimidated, that's for sure.'

'I think Summerbee's actually looking forward to kicking the Leeds lads.' Joe smiled. He loved Summerbee's whole-hearted commitment which verged on the homicidal on occasions. 'What about Tony Book? Are we still playing him as sweeper?'

'No. That's what Leeds'll think we'll be doing. He can play as a normal right-back and mark Eddie Gray.'

'You're right, Mal, you're absolutely right.' Joe was full of enthusiasm for the bold plan. 'It works, doesn't it? You and me, like this.'

Malcolm was smiling, too, his mind whirring with delight at the prospect of shocking Leeds and Don Revie, a side and a manager he grudgingly admired but did not greatly like. 'Let's tell the team on Friday. I don't want them to think too much about it. I just want them to play by instinct. It's so difficult in the League; I want them to be free to express themselves, play the sort of football we've seen them do on the training ground.'

Joe was almost chortling with delight. 'Leeds won't be expecting anything like this.'

'If they're kicking the ball off their own goal line they won't have the time to put our defence under pressure.'

'What happens if we go three goals down in the first twenty minutes?'

'Joe, why do you always think so negatively? This game is our chance to show the football world that we're not a bunch of cloggers.'

'Summerbee and Coleman are two of the best cloggers I've ever seen!' Joe was smiling again.

Malcolm ploughed on remorselessly. 'I mean I feel this side is capable of so much. We haven't scratched the surface of what those players can do. We're not a great defensive side – though we've got better over the season – but we are potentially a great attacking side.'

'Even though we've barely scored all season?'

'That's my fault. I was so anxious to consolidate, to make sure we didn't go straight back down again.'

'That's me, too,' admitted Joe.

'But now this is the perfect chance to do exactly what nobody's expecting, not even the players.'

Joe was silent for a moment. Then the smile cracked open across that much-loved face. 'Malcolm, sometimes I wish to God you'd keep your trap shut. But not today. I think it's a bloody brilliant idea.'

On Saturday, the Fingland's coach headed back over the moors again, this time on the A62 to Leeds. Malcolm looked at his players and was delighted to see that the tension that had been so much in evidence during their recent run of poor League results wasn't there. That tension had gripped them so strongly that it had mentally paralysed them. Today, there was plenty of healthy laughter on the coach. Tony Coleman had got hold of a pornographic magazine, which he was showing with great delight to Alan Oakes. 'Look, Shagger, that's how they do it outside Winsford.'

'Piss off, TC.'

'I'll bet there's not a bird with tits like that in the whole of Cheshire.'

'How would you know?'

''Cause I've had the lot,' grinned Coleman.

The game went almost entirely to Malcolm's plan. From the kick-off City surged down the field, the whole forward line looking menacing as they kept possession and shot frequently when they got the ball, and chased back and harried constantly when they lost it. Leeds' keeper Sprake did well to save shots from Young, Bell and Summerbee, and when the City players went back into the dressing-room at half-time with the game still scoreless, Malcolm was bursting with pride at the way they had played. 'They're all cowards,' he yelled. 'You can murder them. One goal and you're away. You're doing everything right.' Joe was a little more restrained but he, too, had nothing but words of praise for his players. It was a revelation to sit in the directors' box and watch his team pour forward in such numbers, outclassing the powerful Leeds team. He thought City desperately unlucky not to have been at least two goals ahead by half-time. Colin Bell had, unaccountably, missed two good chances, whereas Leeds had scarcely mustered a shot on the City goal.

Joe and Malcolm sent them out again full of the prospect of an FA Cup semi-final and maybe even a first-ever appearance at Wembley. What a story that would make! Unfortunately, five minutes into the second half Leeds were awarded a corner and their centre-half, Jack Charlton, came loping forward looking like nothing so much as a giraffe. Instead of hanging back around the edge of the area or the penalty box and timing his run towards goal, as most tall attackers tended to do at corners, Charlton went up to stand on the goal line directly in front of Harry Dowd. Dowd, at 5 ft 9 in., was nearly six inches shorter than the England international, and as the players jostled for position it became apparent that Charlton's sole purpose was to block the City goalkeeper from getting to the ball. When Eddie Gray swung in the cross, Charlton simply allowed the ball to glance off his head into the net as Dowd frantically tried to get his hands to it. To the City players it seemed a blatant case of obstruction, but the referee pointed immediately to the centre spot and waved away all their protests.

In the dugout, Malcolm was going berserk. In the directors' box, Joe was feeling exactly the same emotions and expressed them forcefully to Albert Alexander, who shared the torment of both his manager and his coach. It was difficult to express their emotions openly as they were technically guests of the Leeds directors, who were sitting only a few seats away. Long years in the game, a history of bitterness and fulminating helplessly at bad refereeing decisions never stopped football men from feeling the full fury of righteous indignation every time a particularly poor decision went against them. The fans, the players, the coach, the manager and the Chairman were as one as the City players, with hunched shoulders, made their way angrily to the centre circle.

City launched further waves of attacks, but with the security of the one-goal lead the Leeds defence was confident enough to repel them, and the familiar feeling of helplessness at City's inability to score overcame both the players and their supporters. They never gave up, and Bell missed another clear chance as they came desperately close to snatching a fully deserved equaliser, but Leeds held out for a 1–0 win that took them into the semi-finals of the FA Cup and sent City back across the Pennines with only the prospect of the fight against relegation to accompany them.

The sense of grievance and injustice helped to soften the blow of their departure from the Cup. Reporters were astonished to see City's attacking capabilities on display, which few of them had suspected even existed. Despite losing, Malcolm was nearly a contented man. Almost everything he had tried had come off: the purchases of Book, Bell and Coleman; Book's move to sweeper and back to right-back again once Malcolm and Joe thought the defence confident enough to manage without the extra defender; the new attacking spirit that had lifted the team and their supporters and made the rest of the division sit up and take notice. It was time to knock their eyes out with a purchase that would solidify the defence for years to come.

They had both heard that Leicester City were willing to sell Gordon Banks. His young understudy, Peter Shilton, had been displaying such outstanding form that the club felt confident enough to cash in on the commercial value of the England international goalkeeper. 'How much do you think Leicester want?' asked Joe with his usual anxiety. Every transfer discussion went through this particular hoop: it was as if Joe were spending his own money. It was an attitude Malcolm never understood. Later that day, Joe came down to the training ground and watched Harry Dowd and Alan Ogley in action. He knew Malcolm was right when he said every great team needs a great goalkeeper, though he couldn't help remembering that United had won the Championship with Pat Dunne in goal two years before. Of course, Busby had subsequently snapped up Alex Stepney as soon as he became available, which probably validated Malcolm's belief in the primacy of a top-class goalkeeper. It was clear to Joe that neither Dowd nor Ogley could hold a light to Gordon Banks: he still hadn't forgiven Ogley for that display of temperament in the dressing-room at half-time during the Sheffield United game, and Dowd, bless him, always gave his best and was a great club servant, but he was never going to be Gordon Banks.

Malcolm came jogging over to him. 'Did you speak to Matt Gillies about Banks?'

'Yeah. He wants fifty thousand.'

'Great. When will he sign?'

'I've offered forty.'

'What?'

'I'm not going to give him what he wants just because he asks for it. You'll learn, Mal, that's not the way we do business.'

'We could win the Championship with Banks.'

'Matt'll come back to us with forty-five, and I'll settle at forty-two or three. That's good business.'

'Not if he fucking goes somewhere else it's not.' Malcolm walked away in a rage. He could see Banks slipping through their fingers for the want of a measly ten grand.

Two days later he was talking to the local football writers about Saturday's game when one of them asked if he'd heard that Gordon Banks had signed for Stoke. The natural tan that Malcolm's face showed even in Manchester's spring sunshine seemed to drain from his cheeks. He couldn't believe they'd lost the best goalkeeper in the country. Banks would have saved them ten points a year: the difference between a mid-table finish and winning the Championship. He felt sick and angry and bitter all at the same time. Joe's legendary meanness was going to keep the club at ground level while Malcolm believed it could soar.

If Joe was embarrassed by losing Banks he didn't show it and, ironically, the last half-dozen matches of the season seemed to justify his actions. Gradually, the disappointment of the defeat at Leeds in the Cup wore off, and City finished the season in fifteenth place in the League, ten points clear of the relegation zone. City had slogged their guts out to ensure that they remained in the First Division, while United had cruised their way to victory, clinching the Championship in style with a memorable 6–1 win away at West Ham. To Malcolm it was a shame City had to have a close season. He would have liked pre-season to start the following day because now he felt certain he was close to having the team that would dethrone Manchester United. He knew Busby was obsessed with winning the European Cup, and the odds were against United winning the League again next year: no English side had won the Championship in successive seasons since Wolverhampton Wanderers nearly a decade ago. Whenever the derby match was scheduled next season, he knew they would be ready for it. There would be no more spineless timidity in the bear pit of Old Trafford.

Joe drank a glass of champagne with him as they toasted the successes of the season of consolidation. Joe, too, had been thrilled by the new attacking force he had seen his side display. 'You're right, Mal. I think we're ready to take on the world.'

'We still need a goalkeeper.' There was a short pause. Joe knew that Malcolm had not forgiven him for the Banks transfer fiasco. Malcolm took advantage of his temporary embarrassment. 'Plus a centre-forward. One who can score goals in the First Division. Not Ralph Brand.'

'Not now, Malcolm,' groaned Joe. 'Let's have a holiday first.'

'Let's get what we can for Brand, and I think we've seen the best of Crossan. Put those two together and we'll have enough to go to the board and ask them to cough up for Wyn Davies or Francis Lee.'

'Let's see how next season starts. They're playing so well. "When in doubt do nowt", as Stanley Baldwin used to say.'

'Who?'

'Stanley Baldwin.'

'Who did he play for?'

'He was a Worcester lad, as I remember.'

'Non-League, then?' They smiled at each other. It was the sort of conversation that amused them both. 'Seriously, Joe, this isn't the time to be complacent. It's a time to keep making changes.'

'I agree with you, Mal.'

THE WORST OF FRIENDS

Malcolm waited for Joe to say something about their own relationship. After all, the two years were up. He'd sat on the coach at the beginning of that first season and heard Joe say, 'Two years. That's all. Just give me two years, then you can have it.' Well, he'd done his part: he'd faithfully played out the number-two role, advised Joe, harassed him into changes he didn't have the courage to make by himself, cheered him up when he was down, and supported him over the Ogley business and picked up the pieces. He knew perfectly well that it was a partnership of equals, that Joe brought qualities of knowledge and experience to the partnership that he didn't possess, but he was ready to fly solo now. His gamble at Leeds had proved it to the players, to the directors and to the media. So when was Joe going to let him take off? Malcolm looked across at his friend and partner, who was smiling and pouring a glass of champagne for Albert Alexander, who had come into the office to join them. And then it hit him. Joe wasn't going to watch him take off solo, because Joe had no intention of getting out of the pilot's seat himself. No intention at all.

THE WORST OF FRIENDS

1966-67: MANAGER JOE MERCER

1	AUG	20	(A)	SOUTHAMPTON	D	1-1	SUMMERBEE	19,900
2		24	(H)	LIVERPOOL	W	2-1	BELL, MURRAY	50,320
3		27	(H)	SUNDERLAND	W	1-0	OAKES	34,948
4		30	(A)	LIVERPOOL	L	2-3	MURRAY, GRAY	51,645
5	SEP	3	(A)	ASTON VILLA	L	0-3		15,118
6		7	(H)	WEST HAM U	L	1-4	BELL	31,079
7		10	(H)	ARSENAL	D	1-1	PARDOE	27,948
8		17	(A)	MANCHESTER U	L	0-1		62,500
9		24	(A)	BLACKPOOL	W	1-0	CROSSAN	25,761
10	OCT	1	(H)	CHELSEA	L	1-4	YOUNG	31,989
11		8	(H)	TOTTENHAM H	L	1-2	SUMMERBEE	32,551
12		15	(A)	NEWCASTLE U	L	0-2		16,510
13		29	(A)	BURNLEY	W	3-2	CROSSAN 2, BELL	25,996
14	NOV	5	(H)	NEWCASTLE U	D	1-1	YOUNG	26,137
15		12	(A)	STOKE C	W	1-0	SUMMERBEE	27,803
16		19	(H)	EVERTON	W	1-0	BELL	39,572
17		26	(A)	FULHAM	L	1-4	YOUNG	14,579
18	DEC	3	(H)	NOTTINGHAM F	D	1-1	KENNEDY	24,013
19		10	(A)	WEST BROM A	W	3-0	PARDOE, JONES, CROSSAN	16,908
20		17	(H)	SOUTHAMPTON	D	1-1	BELL	20,104
21		27	(A)	SHEFFIELD W	L	0-1		34,005
22		31	(A)	SUNDERLAND	L	0-1		28,826
23	JAN	2	(H)	SHEFFIELD W	D	0-0		32,198
24		14	(A)	ARSENAL	L	0-1		22,392
25		21	(H)	MANCHESTER U	D	1-1	OPP OWN-GOAL	63,000
26	FEB	4	(H)	BLACKPOOL	W	1-0	BELL	27,840
27		11	(A)	CHELSEA	D	0-0		28,633
28		25	(A)	TOTTENHAM H	D	1-1	CONNOR	33,822
29	MAR	4	(H)	BURNLEY	W	1-0	BELL	32,692
30		18	(A)	LEEDS U	D	0-0		34,366
31		24	(H)	LEICESTER C	L	1-3	CROSSAN	35,396
32		25	(H)	WEST BROM A	D	2-2	HINCE 2	22,780
33		28	(A)	LEICESTER C	L	1-2	JONES	17,361
34	APR	1	(A)	SHEFFIELD U	L	0-1		16,976
35		12	(H)	STOKE C	W	3-1	BELL 3	22,714
36		19	(A)	ASTON VILLA	D	1-1	SUMMERBEE	21,817
37		22	(H)	FULHAM	W	3-0	OAKES, BELL, CROSSAN	22,752
38		29	(A)	EVERTON	D	1-1	COLEMAN	33,239
39	MAY	2	(A)	NOTTINGHAM F	L	0-2		32,000
40		6	(H)	SHEFFIELD U	D	1-1	CROSSAN	21,267
41		8	(H)	LEEDS U	W	2-1	CROSSAN, YOUNG	24,316
42		13	(A)	WEST HAM U	D	1-1	BELL	17,186

FINAL LEAGUE POSITION: 15TH IN DIVISION ONE

FA CUP

3	JAN	28	(H)	LEICESTER C	W	2-1
4	FEB	18	(A)	CARDIFF C	D	1-1
R		22	(H)	CARDIFF C	W	3-1
5	MAR	11	(H)	IPSWICH T	D	1-1
R		14	(A)	IPSWICH T	W	3-0
6	APR	8	(A)	LEEDS U	L	0-1

LEAGUE CUP

2	SEP	14	(H)	BOLTON W	W	3-1
3	OCT	5	(A)	WEST BROM A	L	2-4

TEN

W hat ended as a dream started as a nightmare at the Victoria Ground in Stoke at the end of August. It was hot, it was ugly and it was a total shambles. Summerbee spent most of the match in a kicking contest with the Stoke defender Bill Bentley and was lucky not to get sent off. The constant threat of violence transmitted itself to the crowd, which turned ugly. Fighting broke out on the terraces behind one of the goals and two men with blood streaming down their faces were led away by the St John Ambulancemen. David Connor was playing centre-forward and Mike Doyle at inside-left, much to Malcolm's dismay. He had wanted to bring in Paul Hince at outside-right and for Summerbee to move into the middle, but Joe had overruled him because he wanted the team that had lost 3–2 at Southampton to have another chance. Coleman was injured, the team was unbalanced and lacking focus, and Stoke took full advantage of a wretched display to score three times without reply.

Malcolm was seething with frustration. None of this would have happened if he'd been in charge or if Joe had listened to him. Joe was losing it. Malcolm had known it at the end of the previous season, but he'd swallowed his pride, unwilling to upset the players, whom he knew loved Joe. It was players that won you trophies, he repeated to himself, but he was determined that there should be no repeat of this spineless surrender, which he had hoped he had eliminated the previous year.

The City supporters felt much the way Malcolm did – except that they blamed him for the inept display. On his melancholy way up the tunnel, one of their number, with only a blue scarf draped over his otherwise naked torso, leaned over the wall and spat at Malcolm. It was a direct hit. It took a moment for Malcolm to realise what had happened, as the warm spittle dripped slowly from the side of his face. The drunken lout, his face red with the effects of sun, alcohol and a three-goal drubbing, yelled at the coach: 'Allison, you fucking arsehole, you'll drag this club down . . .' Before he could finish the sentence Malcolm had lost his temper, identified him and was about to climb into the stand to take his revenge when he was restrained by Stoke officials. Still furious, he wiped off the spittle and stormed off towards the dressing-room to have it out with Joe, only to find the manager coming out of it with a huge smile on his face.

'You know what, Mal? For the match against Southampton on Wednesday, why don't we move Mike Summerbee to centre-forward and bring Paul Hince in on the right wing?'

Malcolm smiled. It was hard to stay cross with Joe for long, though the memory of that awful afternoon in Stoke proved a useful source of motivation as the extraordinary season unfolded.

In Wednesday's match, after three draws and a defeat in the last four matches against Southampton, the revamped City team secured a thumping victory with both Bell and Young scoring twice. Just to prove it wasn't a fluke, they took on Nottingham Forest, who had finished as runners-up to United in May, and beat them by a far more convincing margin than the final scoreline of 2–0 suggested. Summerbee thrived on the crosses by Coleman and Hince, who gave John Winfield such a torrid time that Forest's experienced defender was sent off for yet another reckless hack at the speeding winger. An injury to Roy Cheetham earlier in the week had allowed Mike Doyle to move back into the right-half slot and, finally, he looked at home there.

After some violent exertions during training in Wythenshawe Park on Monday morning, Malcolm drove back to the ground to talk with Joe. 'We need Francis Lee, Joe. You know he wants to leave Bolton.'

'We don't need anyone else. You saw how they played on Saturday. We've got it right.'

'We're short of a goalscorer.'

'Young's got his touch back. Three in the last three games.'

'You think Neil Young is going to do it for you when you're two goals down at Anfield?' Joe paused, and Malcolm took advantage of it to hammer his point home. 'I love Youngy. He's as talented as anyone in that team, but he can't tackle and he doesn't scare defenders. Plus we need a penalty taker.'

'We haven't got the money.'

'Have you asked?'

Joe paused. 'How much do you think?'

'He's 23 years old. He'll have the best years of his career here. He's worth 60 grand.'

'They'll never go for it.'

'Talk to the Chairman.'

'I'll talk to Bill Ridding. Maybe I can get the price down.'

Malcolm walked out of the room. He'd made his point logically and calmly, but Joe's instinctive penny-pinching was still driving him crazy. He'd already lost Banks. Lee was the missing piece of the jigsaw. Yet ironically it was the excellent performance of the City team over the next month that prevented him from pressing his case. They won five games in a row, scoring sixteen goals. Young Stan Bowles made a sensational debut, scoring four goals in his first two games. Then they went back to Highbury, another ground where the crowd adored Joe, where Harry Dowd broke a finger and they lost to a John Radford goal.

After the Banks debacle Malcolm had continued scouting for a goalkeeper who could make the first-team place his own. If Dowd was out that meant Joe would have to restore Alan Ogley, which he was reluctant to do. Instead they decided to take the plunge and buy Ken Mulhearn from Stockport County, who wanted Ogley in part-exchange. Ogley was initially reluctant to go. Malcolm sympathised with Ogley's plight, but he could be just as ruthless as Joe. He now knew the extent of Ogley's talents and though he didn't know the extent of Mulhearn's he was ready to gamble, particularly now that he had convinced Joe that Mulhearn was available at a bargain price. He tried his best to smooth Ogley's way to Edgeley Park, but the desperate goalkeeper was having none of it.

'Put me in the team against United on Saturday,' pleaded Ogley. 'I'll show you how good I am.'

'Jimmy Meadows wants you at Stockport.'

'I want to stay and fight for my place.'

'Jimmy rates you. Always has.'

'I don't want to drop down the divisions.'

'The money's good. Jimmy said they'll go up to £60 a week, and you won't have to move house.'

'I played blinders for you last season, Mal.'

'What about the goal you gave away at Southampton last month?'

'Jesus, Mal. One goal and I'm out?'

'Suppose you stayed. We want Mulhearn, and he gets a run in the team and does well, and Harry's finger gets mended and he's in the reserves. What sort of life are you and Diane going to have?'

'I've been here since I left school.'

'Change of club, change of luck.'

'I've never wanted to do anything but keep goal for Manchester City since the first day I got here.'

'Magoo, it's best. Best for you, best all round.'

Ogley knew he was beaten. He could fight Joe if Malcolm was backing him, or even Malcolm if the Boss was backing him, but he was only a player and he couldn't take on the two most powerful men at the club. It was a hard decision to accept. He had given his heart and soul to Manchester City. His dad, an underpaid, overworked miner in the Barnsley coalfields, had turned down a bribe from Don Revie worth five grand because he knew his son wanted to go to Manchester City, not Leeds United. He felt he was letting everyone down now, dropping into the Third Division. It was Malcolm's words that eventually calmed him. Plenty of players had fought their way back from disappointment before. He wasn't injured, and he had great faith in his own ability – as did Jimmy Meadows, now to be his manager once more. He'd show them all. He'd be back!

When Ken Mulhearn walked into the home dressing-room that Saturday afternoon he looked positively anaemic. Despite being prescribed sleeping pills, he had scarcely slept for more than an hour a night all week. His restless antics had sent Mrs Mulhearn back to her mother's house until the first match was over. When Malcolm walked into the dressing-room two hours before kick-off, he found his new goalkeeper fully changed and nervously trying on his gloves. The colour had drained from his face so much that it looked as though he was wearing some kind of white make-up.

'Are you OK?' Malcolm asked.

'Bit nervous.'

'It's just another game of football, Ken.'

'No, it isn't. Last game I played was in front of about 3,000. Doyley says there'll be 63,000 out there.'

'Ken, we've bought you to play in games like this. This is what you've always wanted, isn't it?'

Ken Mulhearn wasn't at all sure that this was what he had always wanted.

Malcolm ushered him into Peter Blakey's physiotherapy room, where he made Mulhearn lie down on the treatment table. Malcolm turned out the lights and locked the door. He was so concerned about the state Mulhearn was in that he would have dropped him and played Alan Ogley – if he hadn't just sold him to Stockport County. The other players certainly didn't need to see that their new goalkeeper had been paralysed by nerves.

Half an hour later, Malcolm unlocked the door, turned on the light and released his new signing from captivity. He handed Mulhearn a telegram. 'You'd better open it. I hope it's not from your wife saying she's left you.'

'She has as it so happens,' said Mulhearn, ripping open the buff envelope. 'She's gone back to live with her family till I get over me nerves.' He read the short lines on the telegram paper with amazement. 'Bloody 'ell!'

'Who's it from then?'

'The Mayor of Stockport wishing me all the best.'

They both laughed, which seemed to release some of the tension, and Mulhearn went out to make his debut in the biggest match of the season so far. Manchester United were always the yardstick against which other sides measured themselves. The desire to beat them had turned into a raging obsession for Malcolm. City would never have a better chance to do it, given their home form since the start of the season. United would not be looking forward to having to beat back the hordes of blue attackers, and they'd know that one day they would be unable to do so and City would sweep past them. Today was that day. As the team prepared to trot out of the tunnel, Tony Book, the captain, made a point of going over to Mulhearn, who still looked as though he was about to throw up. 'Don't worry, son. We're so good you won't touch the ball all game. OK?'

Mulhearn smiled, grateful for the comforting words, but unconvinced that a forward line of Manchester United's capability would be unable to breach the City defence and threaten him at least once in a while.

Yet the opening exchanges seemed to bear out Book's promise. Colin Bell scored after five minutes and Malcolm started to relax, convinced that City had been playing so well at home that this would be the day he finally put United in their place. City's superiority, however, did not last, and United gradually took control of the game. Though Book marshalled Best particularly well, Bobby Charlton grabbed hold of the midfield and looked increasingly menacing. Eventually the pressure told, and Charlton scored twice to send United in at half-time in the lead. Malcolm was as infected by the frantic atmosphere as the crowd and urged City to respond when they came back onto the pitch. The tackles got wilder and the crowd bayed for blood. Brian Kidd and Stan Bowles, two teenagers from Collyhurst, took their commitment to the cause beyond the legal limit and punches were exchanged. Book and Crerand sprinted over to separate the incensed combatants and, on behalf of the two young players, successfully begged the referee for leniency.

In the dressing-room at the end of the game, Joe grabbed the half-naked Bowles and pushed him up against the wall. 'No player of mine behaves like that. I don't know why you weren't sent off.'

'Tony Book asked the ref . . .'

'Shut up. I won't stand for it, do you hear me?'

The other players stood and watched the entertainment, relieved that they could probably postpone the inevitable post-mortem till Monday morning. It was going to be a tough weekend anyway – all those United supporters all over town reminding them who had won yet again.

'He's a dirty bugger, Kidd, always has been,' Bowles protested.

'You're going to apologise.'

'I did. Ref made us.'

'I mean officially, tomorrow, in front of the cameras.'

'What cameras?'

'Don't worry about that. I'll arrange the cameras. If you do that once more you'll never play in one of my teams again, do you understand?'

Next day a sheepish Stan Bowles and Brian Kidd stared bemusedly at the press photographers standing in front of Kidd's parents' house. Joe, like Matt Busby, had always known the value of hard tackling and fierce physical commitment, but both managers also believed strongly in the spirit of the game, and this kind of free-for-all exchange of punches was something that neither of them was prepared to tolerate. With a bit of luck, this kind of ritual humiliation would be enough to harness Stan Bowles's undoubted talent and keep him on the straight and narrow.

Meanwhile, Malcolm was in the social club at Burnden Park talking to Francis Lee and Peter James, Lee's partner in the waste-paper business that they ran together. 'You remember that penalty you scored against Bath in the third round of the Cup when I was manager there?' Malcolm asked.

'Course,' said Lee.

'I liked the way you took it. Last few minutes, 1–0 down to a non-League side – bit of pressure there.'

'No problem. I'd scored every penalty I'd taken, but running up to hit it I heard Bryan Edwards say, "He's due to miss one, you know." So I just belted it.'

'You want to come to City?'

'Wolves and Stoke have come in for me.'

'I can make you a player.'

'What?'

'You've won nothing. I'll guarantee you'll win something with us, and you'll play for England.' Malcolm made a strategic retreat to the Gents and left Lee to talk it over with his business partner.

'What a fucking big-head.'

'Just what you need,' smiled his friend.

On the day that Francis Lee was told that Bolton Wanderers had accepted an offer for him from another club, he drove to Burnden Park, where the manager, Bill Ridding, with whom he had fallen out quite spectacularly, told him to get into his car and follow him to the location where he would meet his new manager. It was only when he started to follow Ridding's car that he glanced at his petrol gauge and saw that it was hovering on empty. There was no chance Lee would make it to Wolverhampton or Stoke, so he was grateful when Ridding's car headed east rather than south and they made their way to Manchester. Lee liked Joe Mercer, though he reserved judgement on the coach until after his first game for his new club, which was won comfortably 2–0.

The lads told him he'd be suffering after his Monday training session at Wythenshawe Park, but Lee was an old pro now and was wise to the wind-ups. All right, Saturday was his first match for nearly a month because of the fuss surrounding his transfer, but he knew he still retained his basic fitness. And as far as he was concerned there wasn't much new under the sun when it came to training. The opening was a reasonably tough two-and-a-half-mile warm-up followed by extremely tough sprinting – four hundred and forty yards in sixty-five seconds, two hundred and twenty yards in thirty seconds and one hundred and fifty yards in fifteen seconds. First time round he managed it well, the second time was more difficult and the third time he failed. Then the hard work started – a cross-country run for three miles interspersed with heavy sprinting before repeats of the four hundred and forty, two hundred and twenty, and one hundred and fifty yards torture. The session ended with everyone completing four sets of one hundred and fifty-yard sprints. 'Welcome to Manchester City,' grinned Mike Summerbee as Francis Lee reacquainted himself with that morning's breakfast. The newcomer realised he had entered Malcolm Allison territory. It was a world he didn't even know existed. It hurt, but it was worth it. Until Boxing Day, City went on an unbeaten run of 11 games, when the goals flowed and it was a joy to go to work.

It wasn't just the new boy who was exhilarated by the wave of success they were riding. Everyone at the club felt it. Malcolm saw the team he had dreamed about taking shape and growing up before his eyes. The board of directors couldn't believe the speed at which the club had begun its rise – not just to solvency but also to prosperity. Albert Alexander noted wryly how quick the directors were to congratulate themselves on the perspicacity of their choice of managers. The supporters couldn't wait to see the next match, and the players couldn't wait to play in it. The apogee of City's sensational run came in December when, on an ice-bound pitch, the team played Tottenham Hotspur off the park and won 4–1 in front of the *Match of the Day* cameras.

In fact it had only been the presence of the cameras that had ensured that the match went ahead. In similar situations the referee would usually have called off the game because the pitch was clearly unfit, but the crowd had gathered and there was great reluctance to cause distress to the BBC television schedules. As soon as it was confirmed that the match was to be played, Mike Summerbee carefully took the leather cover off his studs to expose the nails that would give his boots a better grip on the icy surface. Malcolm saw what he was doing and nodded his head in approval. He knew that victory was going to the team that paid the least attention to the hazards of the icy pitch. 'Don't think about the ice. It's just there to be run over. Think about the ball and think about how long it's going to take Cyril fucking Knowles and Mike fucking England to turn round out there!'

Despite the extra preparation, Greaves put Tottenham ahead early on, but Bell equalised before half-time. The City players, aided by their extra-long studs, which gave them a grip on the icy turf that the Spurs players couldn't match, ran their opponents ragged in the second half: Summerbee outjumped England to score beyond Jennings with a superb header, Neil Young hit both posts before finding the net and Coleman completed City's scoring.

Joe revelled in the praise, particularly from his former Everton colleague Dixie Dean, who told Joe that Manchester City would be champions by the end of the year and that Mike Summerbee would play for England. Summerbee's move to centre-forward had remained Malcolm's most significant tactical move. He not only scored regularly but also had the strength to hold the ball up when it was cleared from defence, as well as being skilful enough to bring his wingers and inside-forwards into play. Goals simply poured from the team, and the fact that the defence was still prone to moments of aberration didn't matter because the forwards knew they could always outscore their opponents.

City's seemingly unstoppable winning streak came to an end at The Hawthorns on Boxing Day. Stan Bowles replaced Colin Bell, who had been injured in the home match against Stoke the previous Saturday. Unfortunately, however, Stan had taken the Christmas spirit way beyond the level accepted as normal by professional footballers and was in no condition to play a vital First-Division match at high intensity like the other 21 players. He played as though he were still lying on the sofa watching television. Lee and Summerbee dragged City back into the game after they had gone two goals down, but a fifteen-minute delay in the second half due to a collapsed goalpost seemed to inspire West Bromwich. Five minutes from full-time, Mulhearn hesitated, Jeff Astle scored and the game was lost.

In the dressing-room, Malcolm seized on Stan Bowles and berated him fiercely for his lack of professionalism. Bowles really annoyed Malcolm. He knew that the young lad was as gifted as anyone on the team, yet the boy showed no inclination to learn from the coach. Bowles came under the influence of only one member of the senior squad – a man whom even Malcolm had to admit was not the best mentor for him: Tony Coleman. Bowles didn't play in the first team again for 12 months. Neither Malcolm nor Joe took kindly to being let down by such a blatant lack of professionalism.

Joe in particular hated anything that looked amateurish. At Nottingham Forest in January, City were awarded a penalty, which Francis Lee prepared to take. As he placed the ball on the spot and turned to walk back to the edge of the area, where he would commence his run up, Tony Coleman came sprinting past him and blasted the ball past a surprised Peter Grummit into the Forest goal.

Lee was incensed. 'What the fuck do you think you're playing at?' he roared.

'Look where the fucking ball is,' replied the smiling Scouser.

Lee was even less impressed two weeks later, when Coleman failed badly in an attempted repeat performance. This time the penalty came in a third-round FA Cup tie at home to Reading. It was 15 minutes from time, and the score was a disappointing nil–nil. Again, as Lee was on his way out of the penalty area preparing to take the kick, Coleman burst past him and hammered the ball with his trusty left foot – but this time it went about 25 feet over the bar and into the top of the Platt Lane Stand.

'You twat, you've done it again! What the fuck do you think you're doing?' screamed Lee.

'I just fancied it,' replied the unabashed winger.

'Well, you won't fancy it so much when you get back in the dressing-room.'

Lee was right. Joe Mercer tore into him. This was exactly the sort of irresponsible behaviour he had feared Coleman would display and one of the reasons he had resisted Malcolm's blandishments for so long. 'We've got a really difficult replay at Reading now thanks to you.'

'We'll win it, Boss. No problem.'

'We could have won it today if you'd let Francis take the kick.'

'We'll hammer them down there.'

'I've a good mind to hammer you. Look at your teammates. You've let them down. You've let the fans down. And you've let me down.'

Still Coleman couldn't find the words for an apology. 'We'll win the replay. We can't play as bad again.'

Although Joe couldn't excuse Coleman's behaviour, he was proved right on both counts. With a sterling performance, City won the replay 7–0. Joe Mercer was hugging himself with the pleasure his team gave him that night, but he had no intention of apologising to Coleman, who cheekily told him that if it hadn't been for him Joe would never have seen how well his team could play.

The League Championship now distilled itself into a race for the title between four teams: City, United, Leeds and Liverpool. Throughout the second half of the season, the team in fourth place was never more than three or four points away from the team at the top. How they performed against each other would be critical. Before Easter, City were due to play both Leeds and Manchester United in the space of four days. The Leeds match would be City's first appearance on *Match of the Day* since the sublime display of the 'ballet on ice', as the game against Spurs had come to be known. Joe and Malcolm were aware of television's power to shape unformed minds and also that City were an attractive antidote to the deeply unattractive side Don Revie had nurtured at Elland Road. It would be a pleasure to go there and humiliate them for the delectation of the Saturday-night viewing audience. But as it turned out, City showed nothing of their much-vaunted attacking skills and went down to a two-goal defeat that could have been worse, given the overwhelming possession that Leeds had.

The rearranged derby match at Old Trafford, which had been postponed in the snow and ice of January, now began to fill City's supporters with alarm. United were already through to the semi-finals of the European Cup, where they were due to meet old rivals Real Madrid, and they were two points clear of City at the top of the League. If United won, moving four points clear of City, they would be favourites to retain their title and do the double over City. And those defeats would hurt all the more for happening in City's best season for at least 12 years.

During the days leading up to the game, Malcolm dropped into the Fletcher's Arms in Denton to talk to the landlord, a voluble City supporter called Ian Niven. There had been a long-standing agreement amongst public-house licensees not to encourage the discussion of politics, religion or football: the three topics on which feelings ran high. Niven decided to ignore the tradition and turned the Fletcher's Arms into a shrine to Manchester City, with framed photographs of his heroes decorating the walls. He had hired Mike Doyle's wife, Cheryl, to serve behind the bar, and gradually more and more of the City players began to visit the Denton pub until one day the great figure of Malcolm Allison himself walked in.

It had been clear to Niven from listening carefully to the comments of the players that they revered Malcolm. He was the greatest coach any of them had experienced, his knowledge of psychology and advanced training methods marking him out as the leader of his field. This final derby match of the season gripped the city's thousands of football supporters as each team sought desperately to establish primacy in the race for the Championship. United could no longer adopt the air of contemptuous superiority that had so incensed Malcolm when he had first arrived in Manchester. They were taking City seriously now.

Malcolm himself, particularly after the bad defeat by Leeds on the Saturday, was starting to worry that his team had hit some kind of wall whenever they played the best teams. It was all very well to beat Sheffield United 5–2 or Leicester 6–0, but they had lost to both Leeds and United, although they had fought back well to snatch an equaliser in front of a packed Anfield. He was not, however, prepared to admit as much to anyone, and when Niven started to talk about the prospects for the match Malcolm cleared all such doubts from his mind.

'What do you think the score's going to be, Malcolm?'

'3–1.'

'To us?' Niven, who was always supremely confident about City's future performances, even when they flew in the face of reality, was surprised by the certainty of Malcolm's reaction. He decided that a grand gesture was called for. 'If you win, you're invited back here.'

'Me or the whole team?' asked Malcolm.

'Everyone – you, the players, Joe, the directors, everyone.'

'Plus their wives?'

'Plus their wives and girlfriends.'

'And you're paying?'

'I'm paying.'

'Champagne?'

'Champagne. Much as you want.'

'We're coming. Just so you know, Alan Oakes and Glyn Pardoe don't drink.'

'Free lemonade on tap. But only if you win.'

'Get the champagne on ice.'

Niven was outside the ground with a ticket waiting for the late arrival of a friend when the game kicked off on Wednesday at 7.30 p.m. Within 40 seconds he heard the telltale deafening roar that signalled a home goal, and his heart sank.

Inside Old Trafford, Tony Book had got the ball trapped under his feet, and before he could get it clear George Best had robbed him of it, swept into the penalty area and thumped it past the helpless Mulhearn. As far as the United faithful were concerned, normal public service had been restored. As far as City supporters were concerned, it was looking ominous.

'Now,' thought Malcolm in the dugout, 'now they can relax. The worst has happened.' He stood up and clapped his hands as his players looked nervously at him, wondering what his reaction would be. He gesticulated towards the United goal at the open end. 'Take them on!' he bellowed. 'Attack them!'

Gradually City realised that the United defence panicked under pressure like any other defence, and the best way to stop Best getting hold of the ball was to keep possession of it themselves. Colin Bell grew in stature as the game progressed, and he and Mike Doyle seized control of the middle of the field from Stiles, Crerand and Sadler. After 20 minutes and another lung-bursting run, Bell sent the ball past Stepney into the top of the net, and by half-time City were well on top, even if the score did not reflect their superiority.

Joe and Malcolm urged them not to lose the impetus when the second half began. The players, who had listened to their exhortations all season, trusted their manager and coach implicitly when they told them that the game was theirs for the taking. Malcolm felt that victory was so close he could taste it. He urged the players on. 'This is an old side you're playing. They're going to tire. They don't like the game played at your pace, not theirs. They want to slow it down. You've got to keep it up.'

As they trotted out of the dressing-room to the acclaim of the crowd, Malcolm seized Colin Bell. 'This is your night. What you do in the next 45 minutes could make you a hero for all time in this city. They're shit scared of you. Make them pay.' Bell nodded and ran off to join his teammates, who felt as though it was the start of the first, not the second, half. Those agonising Monday mornings at Wythenshawe Park were beginning to pay off. The players felt full of running, and United simply couldn't catch the ubiquitous Bell. After fifteen minutes Tony Coleman sent over a free kick, and George Heslop, whose lumbering presence at set pieces over the past two and half years had rarely caused problems to the opposition, this time managed to get his head to the ball. It bounced agonisingly slowly towards the corner of the United net. Stepney on the goal line went scrambling after it. For 64,000 people, time seemed to stop as it took seemingly for ever for the ball finally to cross the line and nestle in the corner, despite Stepney's frantic efforts to catch up with it.

In the stand, Joe rose to his feet and looked around the ground. Though most City supporters were packed into the open end to his right, there were many thousands of them dotted all over the ground, wherever they had been able to gain admittance. They felt no circumspection about revealing their identities on this night of naked passion. Joe felt what Malcolm was feeling, what all their supporters were feeling: some invisible scales were being tipped in their favour. This result, if they hung on, meant far more than the two points that were technically at stake. This was about the emergence of half a city from the shadows of mediocrity and embarrassment.

United were not, however, unduly perturbed by the scoreline. City had taken the lead in September and lost it. What bothered Bobby Charlton was that he couldn't get into the game. The role he usually played had been taken by Colin Bell. The 21-year-old Bell came from Hesleden, a village in County Durham, not far from where the Charlton brothers had grown up. It had been more than ten years since Bobby had emerged to conquer Manchester, and to his intense frustration it looked as though his place was being usurped by another young lad from the north-east who had the youth to make the most of his talent.

In the dugout, Malcolm was aware that Bell's performance validated every thought he had ever had about the game. Malcolm knew a great player when he saw one in the Second Division, he knew how to make ordinary players great and he knew how to foster team spirit that could produce a comeback such as the one he had seen this night. Above all, everyone could now see that his belief in attacking-football was true: that an attacking team would always win against a team that thought first about defence. It was, Malcolm couldn't help feeling, a philosophy that Matt Busby himself had subscribed to. And now Busby was sitting in the stand with his trilby hat on watching his team of League Champions being humiliated on their home ground by the team he had so condescended to at the dinner that celebrated their 1965 League Championship.

As these thoughts flashed through Malcolm's mind, Colin Bell slipped the ball past Francis Burns and set off towards the United goal. Burns turned and chased the player who had given the whole United side a torrid time that night. If he couldn't tackle Bell fairly he'd make sure he hurt him, but by this time Bell had already carried the ball into the penalty area. As Alex Stepney advanced to narrow the angle, Burns hurled himself at Bell and brought him down from behind. Bell fell badly, holding his knee in pain, and the referee blew his whistle, pointing to the penalty spot in dramatic fashion – though in truth nobody in the ground was surprised by the decision. Malcolm climbed out of the dugout screaming vengeance on the perpetrator of the foul. In the stand, Joe Mercer got to his feet, equally outraged. Matt Busby sat a few seats away next to his Chairman, his shoulders hunched, the acrid taste of a derby defeat in his mouth. He knew the result even if the game had lost its best player, who was now being stretchered off. As Bell was carried carefully into the dressing-room, Francis Lee placed the ball on the spot and, with a warning glance at Tony Coleman, turned round, ran up and blasted it past Stepney to seal the victory.

The remaining few minutes were just a formality. United were beaten and broken in spirit. City kept the ball with ease, playing it to each other as if they were engaged in a practice exercise on the training pitch.

United knew they had lost the battle but not the war. Even after tonight's defeat, they were level on points at the top of the table along with City and Leeds, and they had the attractive prospect of a European Cup semi-final to come. Leeds and City had not won League titles in recent memory. United had, and they knew how to do it. There was no way that City could avoid dropping points in the nine matches that were still to be played.

Meanwhile, Sidney Rose examined Bell's knee and told Joe, Malcolm and the player that he would be out for three or four weeks. It was the only blemish on a perfect night.

Matt Busby, hurting inside though he must have been, came to the City dressing-room and congratulated Joe and Malcolm on their team's stunning performance. He shook Malcolm's hand and looked him in the eye. 'If I had you as my coach,' he said slowly, in his well-known Scottish burr, 'I would be able to go on managing till I was 70.' Malcolm wondered if Joe had heard, but Joe was surrounded by admirers. On a night like this, the winning dressing-room was where everyone wanted to be.

After the press boys had reluctantly left the dressing-room and the players had emerged from the showers and were starting to dress, their shirts sticking to their backs as their bodies refused to cool down, Malcolm addressed his troops for the last time that night. 'Remember tonight. Remember what you've done here. I said you could beat them. I said you could fucking murder them. And you have. But this isn't the only time you'll do it. This town belongs to you. You can come back here year after year and beat them over and over again. They know what you can do, and they're frightened of you. Now you know you can win the League.'

The party began as soon as Ian Niven got back to the Fletcher's Arms. Chief scout Harry Godwin started playing the incongruous baby grand piano and alternated with Marge Thomas, who came over from the pub nearest to City's ground, the Lord Lyon on Claremont Road, to join in the celebrations. When Malcolm arrived, Ian saluted him. 'This was the greatest night of my life.'

'Told you, didn't I?' grinned Malcolm.

'The only thing you didn't tell me was that United would score after less than a minute.'

'I thought the team needed waking up, so I arranged it that way.'

'Or the names and times of the goalscorers.'

'That's 'cause you never asked me. Now, where's the champagne?' Malcolm's question was accompanied by a loud pop and a mighty cheer. Francis Lee and Mike Summerbee were firing champagne corks at each other across the room.

The press came to interview them, to praise them and to drink with them. Malcolm seemed to be lighting a new Montecristo every ten minutes. Colin Bell was photographed cradling a celebratory glass of lemonade, though when the pictures appeared in the newspapers they cropped the sight of his plaster-cast leg, which was stretched out on a low table in front of him. Joe and Norah stopped by briefly, Joe's face wreathed in smiles. Asked if City would now win the Championship, Joe prevaricated, pointing out they were in a three-way tie at the top along with United and Leeds, with Liverpool two points behind but with a game in hand. Any one of those four clubs could win it, and tonight's result was just one of forty-two League games.

They asked Malcolm the same question. He smiled broadly and told them what they wanted to hear. 'This side can be the greatest team in the history of football. There's no limit to what they can achieve. You just saw the first of many games we'll play like that in the future. Not only can we win it, we *will* win it, because we fear no one and the others are frightened of us – and that includes Manchester United.'

It was Malcolm's words that dominated the back pages of all the papers the next day. He was so plausible that Joe's slightly calmer view of the situation was lost in the rush to admire the new contenders. City hadn't been realistic potential champions for 30 years. Once more the contrast in the personalities of Mercer and Allison benefited the team, who were grounded by Joe's cautious realism even as Malcolm was lifting their heads towards the heavens. Joe wanted to believe that Malcolm was right and that they were going to win the title, but he also thought it was important that the players kept their feet on the ground, particularly because Manchester United had just beaten Stoke 4–2 as City were losing at Leicester. Conversely, Malcolm knew only too well football's capacity for destroying dreams but felt that the players needed to believe they were going to win the Championship so they could shrug off the temporary disappointment of dropped points and go into the next game still believing they would emerge victorious. Despite the contradictory positions the manager and the coach adopted, the players had absolute trust in them.

It was just as well. Nerves and fatigue were starting to attack them. Bell returned after three weeks out with the injury sustained at the end of the derby match, but even that was insufficient for City to recover the panache they had displayed on that memorable night at Old Trafford at the end of March. A fortunate own-goal victory at home to Sheffield Wednesday was not the form of prospective champions. The following Monday, City and United were both due to play rearranged fixtures against the winners of Saturday's two FA Cup semi-finals. United, with the second leg of the European Cup semi-final in Madrid to come, went down to a stunning 6–3 defeat at West Brom. When the half-time score from The Hawthorns went up at Maine Road, the crowd awoke from its collective slumber. City had never looked like scoring against Everton, but this remarkable change in the atmosphere stimulated them to a vital 2–0 victory. It was their last home game of the season, but it meant that if they won the last two matches at Tottenham and Newcastle, none of the other teams could catch them because of their superior goal average.

'How do you feel, Joe?' asked the assembled football reporters.

'I feel like we have to climb Everest and K2 in a week,' he replied cheerfully.

It had been years since he had been involved in a title race like this. The hypertension that had so nearly brought a premature close to Joe's managerial career was replaced by a different kind of tension altogether. Now he was feeling the strain of losing something precious that was within his grasp. Norah was fearful that this kind of tension was as bad as the kind that arose from bad results and supporters' abuse. Malcolm, however, suffered few such anxieties and knew exactly what Joe needed: a slap-up dinner at the recently opened Piccadilly Hotel, which had replaced the now rather staid Midland Hotel as Manchester's most prestigious hostelry. And Walter Griffiths could hardly refuse to pay the bill if it had Joe's name on it.

Joe carefully took out his reading glasses and placed them on his nose as he opened the menu and studied it. The prices swam before his eyes as the waiter hovered, pen poised over the pad.

'Bloody hell, Mal. These prices are a bit steep.'

'Forget the prices, Joe. This is my treat,' he lied glibly.

'Twelve and six for a steak!'

'You can pay more in London.'

'Christ! They even charge extra for the vegetables.'

THE WORST OF FRIENDS

'Joe!' A note of irritation was creeping into Malcolm's voice. 'It's OK, really. Just order whatever you want. We'll have a couple of bottles of wine, I think. Any preference?' he asked with a smile, knowing that Joe didn't know one vintage from another.

'I think I'd better just have an omelette.'

'Do you want the steak?'

'Well . . .'

'Two fillet steaks, medium rare, with baked potatoes and peas. Tell the wine waiter I need a few minutes.' The waiter finished writing and withdrew silently.

'Are you sure, Mal?'

But Malcolm didn't want to continue this particular conversation. It had lost all appeal for him. Besides, they had come to talk about tactics for the game at White Hart Lane on Saturday. Joe was worried about it. In his view, any side with Jennings, Mullery, England, Greaves and Gilzean could not be underestimated, particularly on their own ground. Malcolm didn't see it that way. 'We stuffed them here.'

'Because Spurs couldn't stand up in the snow and ice.'

'We're a better side.'

'We were a better side at Leicester and Chelsea and we lost,' said Joe.

Malcolm was in no mood to listen to any of Joe's negative thoughts. 'I think Dave Mackay is vulnerable.'

'There I agree with you.'

Malcolm seized eagerly on the first point of concord. 'Good. I want Francis Lee to pull Knowles out wide on the right and Summerbee to do the same to Mike England.'

'What happens if England doesn't follow him and allows Summerbee to be picked up by Mullery?' asked Joe.

'He won't. He knows how vital Summerbee is to the way we play. And as soon as he's out of the middle, Colin Bell can have a free run at Dave Mackay. He'll slaughter the old man.'

It was May already. The cricket season had started and England cricket supporters were once again nervously weighing up their chances of regaining the Ashes. As the Fingland's coach turned off the High Road in Tottenham into the small, crowded car park at White Hart Lane, the players noticed that their supporters were all dressed in short sleeves, T-shirts and summer dresses. They looked like a crowd preparing to go on holiday. For the players, there was still business to be done. They had not slogged their way through the wind and rain, the snow, the ice and the mud of an English football season to lose their concentration now. There would be time enough for relaxation in eight days, particularly if they concluded the season with the two victories their supporters yearned for as much as they did.

In the bright sunshine of a warm afternoon in early summer, Colin Bell destroyed the exposed Mackay exactly as Malcolm had known he would, scoring twice as City went in at half-time three goals up, with the game effectively won. At the same time United won 6–0 at home to Newcastle, which left the United players and their supporters depressed, because if that was the standard of opposition City were going to face the following week, United could beat Sunderland and still be unable to stop the Championship from ending up at Maine Road. They could only hope that City's players would wilt under the pressure of their elevation to title favourites. If results went against them, they could lose the title to either United or Liverpool. City had to win, and the pressure was unrelenting.

They pretended all through that excruciating final week of the season that they didn't feel it.

'If they score six, we'll score eight!' boasted Mike Summerbee, whose fitness, along with that of Colin Bell, was in doubt after each had sustained an injury during the triumph at Tottenham.

'What do you think?' asked Joe nervously of Peter Blakey, the team's physiotherapist, as his centre-forward lay on the treatment table in some discomfort just three days before the most vital match in the club's history since the Cup final in 1956.

'Boss, I'll play this fucking game on crutches if I have to,' said Summerbee.

'Mike, this way!' called a photographer. The press had been all over Maine Road since the start of the week, only adding to the sense of occasion and the consequent nerves. Now they, too, were in the treatment room.

'What is this, Boss?' asked Summerbee in mock alarm as the photographers' cameras clicked. 'Has there been an accident or something?'

Joe smiled. He'd signed Summerbee because he thought he was a good player, but Mike's infectious humour was a blessing that week as the nerves tightened for everyone at the club.

'I'm worried about Bell,' said Joe to Malcolm the following morning. It was their last full day in Manchester. After lunch on Friday they would begin the journey to the north-east. 'If this was the start of the season, I wouldn't think about playing him on Saturday.'

'He's a hypochondriac,' said Malcolm shortly.

'He's injured, Mal.'

'Leave him to me. He won't be injured when I've finished with him.'

'Everyone wants to kick him up in the air. He's not a hypochondriac. You think he was pulling a fast one when Francis Burns chopped him down?'

'I'll handle him. He'll play.'

Summerbee and Bell were both selected for the game against Newcastle, but the nerves had now got to everyone. As the coach made its way into St James' Park, the players were astonished to see it was more like Cup final day than an away League match. There must have been 20,000 fans from Manchester in blue-and-white scarves who had made the trip. It was going to be the biggest day of all their lives. Not one of them entertained the prospect that the result would be anything other than a win for Manchester City.

Albert Alexander was the Chairman of the prospective League champions, but he felt exactly like the fans. He was 76 years old and his association with the club stretched back over 50 years, but today he was like a child. Neither he nor the directors could quite believe the speed at which the club had been transformed. Joe tried to smile his way through the pre-match formalities, but he was as agitated as the players and the fans. Only Malcolm was impervious. He believed it was his destiny to win the League and what was happening was simply the logical consequence of a phenomenon whose force was irresistible.

When Summerbee opened the scoring after 12 minutes, Joe thought it would calm the players down and they would go on to dominate the game as they had at Tottenham the previous week, but within a couple of minutes George Heslop had failed to cut out a Newcastle attack and 'Pop' Robson had equalised. Twenty-five thousand Newcastle fans celebrated wildly. The awful possibility of failure crept into the minds of the players and their manager. A desperate goal-line clearance by Book kept out a Wyn Davies header that had beaten Mulhearn. The fluent, devastating City of the previous week was nowhere to be seen.

Five minutes before half-time, Neil Young volleyed City back into a slightly fortuitous lead. If they could only hold on till half-time, Joe and Malcolm would tell them what to do. But they couldn't. Three minutes later, George Heslop, who was having a nightmare in the most important game of the season, cleared the ball straight to Jim Iley, who slipped it to Jackie Sinclair, and the winger hammered it high into the net beyond Mulhearn. A goal by Young that would have calmed all their nerves was disallowed by the referee for no reason anyone could discern. There was no point in arguing. The game continued at its breathless pace, but when the whistle went for half-time Newcastle were still deservedly on level terms.

At half-time, Joe and Malcolm strode angrily to the dressing-room.

'What the fuck's going on out there, Joe?'

'What's happened to the defence? They're a bunch of useless statues.'

'I'm going to give them a right bollocking. They're fucking it up.'

Malcolm opened the door to the dressing-room and saw, for the first time that season, 11 players struck almost dumb with nervous tension. Even Summerbee, Lee and Coleman, the most extrovert of them all, were quiet. Joe looked at Malcolm and shook his head. Malcolm went over to Neil Young. 'Fantastic goal, son. Give me two more, all right?' Young smiled in relief.

Joe was with George Heslop. 'Come on, George. You can't let Wyn Davies run at you like that. You're giving him too much space. All of you, close down quicker. Oakie, look for MacNamee coming up for corners and free kicks. George'll have his hands full with Davies.'

The quiet words of comfort and encouragement had an immediate impact. City kicked off the second half and instantly found the composure that they had been lacking earlier. It took only four minutes before three or four slick passes created a chance for the lethal finish from the left foot of Neil Young, which put City back in front. Joe started to breathe more easily. Malcolm had no doubts. City wouldn't sit back and hold the 3–2 lead; that wasn't the way he'd coached them. As they pressed forward in search of the killer goal that would give them a winning two-goal advantage, Bell slipped the ball past a static Newcastle defence to find Lee on yet another of his surging runs cutting in from the right wing. Willie McFaul came out of his goal to smother the danger but Lee was too quick for him, and he lifted the ball past the goalkeeper into the net for the vital two-goal lead.

Lee finished his run on the wall behind the goal, both hands raised in the air as his worshippers on the terraces acclaimed him. Now City started to play as they usually could, free of that crippling tension, and Lee scored again only for it to be chalked off. In the dugout, Malcolm swore. That was the second time the ref had wiped out a perfectly good goal – it should have been 6–2 by now, he thought. Yet Newcastle never stopped giving as good as they got. What the fuck are they doing? wondered Malcolm. They've got fuck all to play for. Robson clearly didn't think so, as he skipped away from Pardoe down the right wing and centred. Heslop was marking Davies, but nobody had gone with MacNamee, who rose unchallenged to head past Mulhearn. Joe Mercer thought his heart had stopped. Malcolm climbed out of the dugout and roared at Alan Oakes. 'Oakie! Oakie! What the fuck did I tell you?!' Johnny Hart pulled him back inside again. City were on the verge of winning the Championship. United were losing 1–2 to Sunderland at Old Trafford. It would be just like Mal to get himself sent off again at this moment of supreme triumph.

For a further seven agonising minutes, play continued as Joe Mercer and twenty thousand City supporters stared and screamed at the referee, urging him to blow his whistle, even though they knew from the plethora of transistor radios in the ground that United's defeat had guaranteed them the title. At last the whistle sounded, and the Manchester fans raced onto the pitch as the players sprinted to find a way through them and get back to the dressing-room. It was over. The loudspeakers belted out Cliff Richard's recent number-one hit 'Congratulations', and the Newcastle supporters generously slipped away from their own ground to allow the Manchester fans to begin their celebrations.

The second half seemed to have lasted since before Christmas, but it was over now and Manchester City, the no-hopers from the wrong side of town, had won the First-Division Championship. Joe and Malcolm had done it just three years after taking over a team that had no supporters, a ground that was crumbling before their eyes and a squad of players who thought that if they weren't going to be in the Second Division at the end of that first season it would be because they were in the Third.

The dressing-room was utter bedlam, the atmosphere of excitement punctuated by the periodic explosion of champagne corks. Lee and Summerbee were jumping in and out of the bath like children on holiday let loose in a hotel swimming pool. All of them were being congratulated or embraced by what seemed like a hundred well-wishers, relatives, friends, directors, pressmen and complete strangers.

Malcolm and Joe stared at each other. They were drained with the emotion that had been expended, not merely since the start of the match or the beginning of this last week of mounting tension, but since the season had begun back in August with those two bad defeats in the first three matches. It was impossible to say now whose smile was larger or whose heart was beating more fiercely. What they had done together defied the imagination. Malcolm knew how much Joe had contributed, and Joe knew how much this was Malcolm's triumph. What they felt for each other at that moment they could neither of them express. It was love.

THE WORST OF FRIENDS

1967-68: MANAGER JOE MERCER

1	AUG	19	(H)	LIVERPOOL	D	0–0			49,343
2		23	(A)	SOUTHAMPTON	L	2–3	BELL, COLEMAN		23,675
3		26	(A)	STOKE C	L	0–3			22,426
4		30	(H)	SOUTHAMPTON	W	4–2	BELL 2, YOUNG 2		22,002
5	SEP	2	(H)	NOTTINGHAM F	W	2–0	SUMMERBEE, COLEMAN		29,547
6		6	(H)	NEWCASTLE U	W	2–0	HINCE, YOUNG		29,978
7		9	(A)	COVENTRY C	W	3–0	HINCE, BELL, SUMMERBEE		34,578
8		16	(H)	SHEFFIELD U	W	5–2	BOWLES 2, SUMMERBEE, YOUNG, BELL		31,922
9		23	(A)	ARSENAL	L	0–1			41,567
10		30	(H)	MANCHESTER U	L	1–2	BELL		62,942
11	OCT	7	(A)	SUNDERLAND	L	0–1			27,885
12		14	(H)	WOLVES	W	2–0	YOUNG, DOYLE		36,476
13		21	(A)	FULHAM	W	4–2	SUMMERBEE 2, LEE, YOUNG		22,108
14		28	(H)	LEEDS U	W	1–0	BELL		39,713
15	NOV	4	(A)	EVERTON	D	1–1	CONNOR		47,144
16		11	(H)	LEICESTER C	W	6–0	YOUNG 2, LEE 2, DOYLE, OAKES		29,039
17		18	(A)	WEST HAM U	W	3–2	LEE 2, SUMMERBEE		25,595
18		25	(H)	BURNLEY	W	4–2	COLEMAN 2, SUMMERBEE, YOUNG		37,098
19	DEC	2	(A)	SHEFFIELD W	D	1–1	OAKES		38,207
20		9	(H)	TOTTENHAM H	W	4–1	SUMMERBEE, COLEMAN, YOUNG, BELL		35,792
21		16	(A)	LIVERPOOL	D	1–1	LEE		53,268
22		23	(H)	STOKE C	W	4–2	LEE 2, YOUNG, COLEMAN		40,121
23		26	(A)	WEST BROM A	L	2–3	SUMMERBEE, LEE		44,897
24		30	(H)	WEST BROM A	L	0–2			45,754
25	JAN	6	(A)	NOTTINGHAM F	W	3–0	SUMMERBEE, YOUNG, COLEMAN		39,581
26		20	(A)	SHEFFIELD U	W	3–0	DOYLE, BELL, LEE		32,142
27	FEB	3	(H)	ARSENAL	D	1–1	LEE		42,392
28		24	(H)	SUNDERLAND	W	1–0	LEE		28,624
29	MAR	2	(A)	BURNLEY	W	1–0	LEE		23,486
30		9	(H)	COVENTRY C	W	3–1	BELL, SUMMERBEE, YOUNG		33,310
31		16	(H)	FULHAM	W	5–1	YOUNG 2, SUMMERBEE, BELL, LEE		30,773
32		23	(A)	LEEDS U	L	0–2			51,818
33		27	(A)	MANCHESTER U	W	3–1	HESLOP, LEE, BELL		63,400
34	APR	6	(A)	LEICESTER C	L	0–1			24,925
35		12	(H)	CHELSEA	W	1–0	DOYLE		47,132
36		13	(A)	WEST HAM U	W	3–0	YOUNG 2, DOYLE		38,754
37		16	(A)	CHELSEA	L	0–1			37,171
38		20	(A)	WOLVES	D	0–0			36,622
39		25	(H)	SHEFFIELD W	W	1–0	OPP OWN-GOAL		32,999
40		29	(H)	EVERTON	W	2–0	BOOK, COLEMAN		37,776
41	MAY	4	(A)	TOTTENHAM H	W	3–1	BELL 2, SUMMERBEE		51,242
42		11	(A)	NEWCASTLE U	W	4–3	YOUNG 2, SUMMERBEE, LEE		46,300

FINAL LEAGUE POSITION: 1ST IN DIVISION ONE

FA CUP

3	JAN	27	(H)	READING	D	0–0
R		31	(A)	READING	W	7–0
4	FEB	17	(H)	LEICESTER C	D	0–0
R		19	(A)	LEICESTER C	L	3–4

LEAGUE CUP

2	SEP	13	(H)	LEICESTER C	W	4–0
3	OCT	11	(H)	BLACKPOOL	D	1–1
R		18	(A)	BLACKPOOL	W	2–0
4	NOV	1	(A)	FULHAM	L	2–3

ELEVEN

Malcolm loved North America. He had spent an enjoyable summer in Toronto in 1964 before assuming the reins at Plymouth, and he gravitated naturally to the expansive nature of big-city nightlife in America. The grin he usually wore when surrounded by champagne, cigars and attractive women seemed permanently etched on his face. He was a coach, the assistant manager of one of the top teams in the English Football League and a few months short of his forty-first birthday, but he still felt like a player with all of a player's attendant irresponsibility.

At the friendly match with Bury, arranged for the Tuesday night following the Championship triumph on Tyneside in order to parade the Championship trophy to the fans, he had come on as a substitute for George Heslop to the acclaim of the crowd. They adored him, and he basked in their adoration. At a press conference with Joe and Tony Book, the manager had spoken of the need for caution when playing in Europe, of the pragmatic necessity of tempering the buccaneering attacking style that had won them the League Championship and so many admirers. Joe thought they ought to get past the first two rounds of the European Cup. The assistant manager, on the other hand, had talked volubly of winning the European Cup and 'terrifying the cowards of Europe'. According to Malcolm, City would be the first team to play on Mars. He was living the dream he had had as a player but had never been able to indulge. Indulgence was to play a significant role in the tour of North America.

He had always known he and Joe were different animals, but rarely had there been a more public demonstration of it. Joe would by far have preferred to be playing in the back garden in Chorlton with Susan, his two-year-old granddaughter, driving Norah down country lanes in Cheshire or playing golf in the uncertain Manchester weather. Deprived of these attractions, he ended up spending most of his time with Albert Alexander. The Chairman, Malcolm recognised, had some virtues, but he doubted that one of them was that he would make the perfect holiday companion.

The players went off in their parties of twos and threes, but Malcolm wanted total freedom from the men who surrounded him at work every day. In Chicago he disappeared for two days. Joe wondered aloud to Albert Alexander, not entirely jokingly, if Al Capone had got him. Malcolm showed up on the third day with a large smile and a firm reluctance to answer questions on his activities over the previous 48 hours. He was, however, clutching that summer's bestselling book: *The Master Game* by a biochemist called Robert S. de Ropp. It would rarely leave his side for the rest of the trip as he absorbed the author's belief that life games reflect life aims. The games men chose, Malcolm read, indicated not only their type but also their level of inner development.

Joe thought it was so much American gobbledegook, but he could see that Malcolm was taking it all very seriously. Joe wasn't stupid. He knew that Malcolm's temperament was different from his own and that the wild Malcolm as opposed to the inveterate-planning Malcolm would get him into trouble of one sort or another during this trip. Malcolm clearly couldn't handle money, he wasn't very good at sorting out the hangers-on that are the bane of football men with integrity, and he was dangerously addicted to the glamour of life on the edge. After the astonishing success of the three years they had worked together, Joe wasn't going to start acting as if he was surprised by Malcolm's outlandish behaviour or his predilection for characters of dubious propriety. It was unfortunate for his family that as a husband and father Malcolm should behave so much like Tony Coleman and Stan Bowles, but Beth and the children could hardly be surprised by his behaviour in America given Malcolm's domestic track record over the years.

In Atlanta, Malcolm answered questions at a local radio station, and at a party later that night he was introduced to the wife of the station's owner. She was slim, elegant and well dressed, and knew exactly the impact of her sexual allure on men. She took one look at the tall, powerful, charismatic figure of the English soccer guy and made a play for him. The attraction was mutual and overwhelming. It was an evening that neither of them was ever likely to forget, and in the morning the conversation took, for Malcolm, an unpredictable turn.

'Do you like Atlanta, honey?' she asked, her smile as dazzling as it had been the previous night, when it had been enhanced by the consumption of Atlanta's famous mint juleps.

'Seems like a nice town,' he replied, unsure where the conversation was heading.

'I'm a rich woman, you know.'

'It doesn't surprise me,' said Malcolm, looking around at the tasteful and expensively decorated bedroom, with its view into a walled garden heavy with the blossom of peach trees and jacarandas.

'My husband's impotent.'

'That doesn't surprise me either.'

'Huh?'

Malcolm shook his head. It wasn't worth going into.

'He's crazy about me.'

'Why not, you're a very attractive woman,' he said as he traced a line from the nape of her neck to the small of her back.

'If I asked him to divorce me he'd do it just like that.' She snapped her fingers to indicate the speed of the legal process.

'Why would you want a divorce? You're sitting pretty.' He waved a hand to indicate the luxury at her disposal, while remembering that he had spent all the dollars Walter Griffiths had given him and would need to borrow money to get back to the team hotel. He got out of bed and padded over to the peach-coloured en suite bathroom. She followed and admired his firm, broad, smooth back as he splashed cold water onto his face. As he wiped himself with a towel he felt her arms circle his chest, and she crushed her breasts against his back. It was a delicious feeling. He dropped the towel on the floor, turned and took her in his arms again.

She broke off the embrace to whisper the words of seduction she thought he would wish to hear. 'With a divorce settlement I'd be worth over five . . . hundred . . . thousand . . . dollars.' For heightened dramatic effect, she left a suitable pause after each figure. Most men, she believed, not unreasonably, would find their ardour increased by such words breathed directly into their ear. Malcolm's response was to wonder briefly what that was in English money and whether it would buy Wyn Davies from Newcastle and Gordon Banks from Stoke. When he thought of how Joe had caused them to miss out on Gordon Banks for a measly ten grand he became incensed all over again, and he started to calculate how many points they would drop the next season because

THE WORST OF FRIENDS

Ken Mulhearn was too indecisive in leaving his line for crosses coming into the area outside the six-yard box.

She looked down with evident disappointment. 'Oh honey, you've retreated into your shell.' Her hand and mouth were soon busy, driving thoughts of transfers and team selection out of Malcolm's head. When she had restored his interest, she held onto her prize and smiled at him. 'Why don't you give up that soccer team and come and live with me in Atlanta? You'd fit right in here, honey.'

'I'm a football manager from London. How would I fit in here?'

'Well, you're real attractive and you have this great accent. You could ask for anything and people would just give you what you want. What is it you want, honey?'

She was on her knees in front of him now with her mouth wide open and her eyes twinkling. Malcolm thought for a moment. 'I'd like twenty dollars.'

'Twenty bucks? What for?'

'I need a cab to get back to the hotel.'

The tour of New York, Atlanta, Chicago, San Francisco, Los Angeles and Mexico City had sounded exotic and exciting when it was being planned in the Manchester spring, but the reality of campaigning in the heat of the American summer after such a long and gruelling, if ultimately successful, season at home began to take its toll. The nine matches in America produced one win, four draws and a humiliating four defeats. The crowds were disappointingly small, the pitches were the size of school football fields and the players were taken back to their own schooldays when for one match they were forced to use the public toilets to change in. Their opponents were rarely the welcoming, naive college players they were expecting. Instead they were either the hardbitten Scottish players of Dunfermline, who were also on a tour of North America, or ex-European professionals who for one reason or another had been exiled from their own countries and who looked forward to kicking and spitting at the champions of the English Football League.

Every game brought an injury, some of them serious; those sustained by Neil Young and Stan Horne were so bad that they eventually had to be sent home. The deep gash in Young's leg required 48 stitches, which were only inserted after Johnny Hart had returned to the team headquarters and gathered sufficient money to pay the hospital bill. The

National Health Service suddenly acquired new respect from many of the City party, who had to confront the American healthcare system at first hand.

The touring party was badly depleted. Alan Oakes had been excused for domestic reasons, Colin Bell and Mike Summerbee had been called up by England, and Mike Doyle only arrived from an England Under-23 tour in time to play in two of the nine matches. He was sent off in the first and injured in the second. City used all the squad players they had brought with them, but eventually Malcolm himself was required to play and Harry Dowd, the reserve goalkeeper, was used as an outfield player. When they arrived in Mexico City, their hosts were so incensed to find that only three of the side that had won at Newcastle were going to play that they angrily cancelled the game and City were forced to fly back across the border.

In addition, the attractions of America in that long, hot, troubled summer of 1968 were greatly diminished by the urban tensions that arose from a country suffering from two serious social problems. One was the widespread disenchantment with the continuing and increasingly unpopular war in Vietnam, and the other was the fallout from the progressively more violent civil rights movement, exacerbated by the recent murder of Dr Martin Luther King in Memphis, Tennessee, which had happened in early April, two days before the 1–0 defeat at Filbert Street.

The players could not ignore this general atmosphere of violence as something that just happened on television. On two occasions they experienced it at first hand. George Heslop, Bobby Kennedy and Neil Young had been sitting quietly in a pizza restaurant on Broadway when a row broke out, and a man at a table ten feet away drew a gun and shot his girlfriend. Even Stan Bowles and Tony Coleman were brought up short when one of their predictable disagreements was peremptorily ended by a cop trying to arrest the inebriated players, who fired two shots from his hand gun into the pavement in front of them. No referee had ever commanded their immediate attention more quickly.

On the evening of 5 June, Joe Mercer retired to his room to watch television as his players and his assistant manager got ready to disappear from the hotel for their evening's entertainment, not without plenty of the now-traditional warnings from the manager and Chairman. Joe was horrified to discover, flicking through the channels, that all the networks were showing the scenes of a terrible shooting in the Ambassador Hotel in Los Angeles. Eventually he realised that JFK's younger brother Bobby had been assassinated. It had happened only minutes after he had appeared in front of the television cameras and his election troops to thank them for their efforts in helping him to win the Democratic primary in California and promising to go on to win the presidential nomination at the convention in Chicago in August. Joe picked up the phone and dialled the room number of Albert Alexander. It was impossible he hadn't seen the news. It was on every channel. It seemed from the thickness in his voice that Albert had been asleep when Joe rang him. 'Chairman, have you seen the news?'

'No. What's happened?'

'They've shot Bobby Kennedy.'

'I thought he said he was going to the pictures with George Heslop?'

'What?'

'Didn't you tell him to stay out of trouble?'

'What? Oh . . .'

Joe wished fervently he had never agreed to the tour in the first place, and was relieved when the plane landed at Ringway Airport after a trip of some twenty thousand miles through three countries in thirty-two days. Now all he had to worry about was the seven serious injuries the team had sustained and the fact that pre-season training started in three weeks' time. He was also delighted to be back in the temperate climate of a Manchester summer after the heat and humidity that had bothered him and Walter Griffiths, who had struggled to cut his normal smartly dressed figure.

Ill fortune with injuries continued to haunt the club after their return. Pre-season training began as usual in the second week of July, and within days Tony Book snapped his Achilles tendon, a significant injury that threatened to keep him out of action until the New Year. The players displayed a tetchiness that had never before been apparent, and Malcolm shared their feelings. Three years ago he had suffered through the official Manchester United celebration of their League Championship triumph and had sworn to take his revenge. Now the City equivalent at the end of July had failed to satisfy him, and it was one celebration too many for the players, who did not enjoy looking at five hundred Manchester dignitaries enjoying their drinks when they had been forbidden alcohol. When the dancing started at 8.30 p.m. and the band struck up the ubiquitous 'Congratulations', they'd had enough. Having seen sufficient

POW movies, they knew that their best chance of escaping undetected was to disappear quietly in small groups.

Joe was deep in conversation with the lord mayor, Alderman Harold Stockdale, when Walter Griffiths came up to him, apologised to the Lord Mayor and took Joe to one side. 'The players have left,' Griffiths hissed.

'Left?'

'All of them. Without permission.'

'I can't believe it.'

'Guess who's gone with them.'

'Don't tell me.'

'Your assistant manager.'

'Now I can believe it.'

'It's an outrage.'

'I agree. Get Johnny Hart and Dave Ewing over here.' Joe returned to speak briefly to the lord mayor, telling him that the players were under orders to be in bed early during pre-season training, and since they didn't wish to draw attention to themselves or to be thought rude, they had slipped away quietly.

Joe's impressive excuse was somewhat compromised when a doorman told a reporter from the *Daily Mirror* that Malcolm Allison had organised the taxis that had taken them all to the Cabaret Club. At 9.30 p.m., an hour after Malcolm had led the escape party, Johnny Hart rang to tell Joe that the players were all on their way home because Malcolm had assured him that they would all be leaving in a few minutes. The manager was understandably infuriated when his attention was drawn to the splash story in the following morning's *Daily Mirror*, which clearly stated that the players had been drinking in the nightclub until after midnight. Joe let them all know how badly he felt let down and how they had disgraced the title of League Champions. Malcolm said nothing. Johnny Hart felt like a fool for having taken Malcolm's word, but he said nothing either.

They still knew when to play 'good cop/bad cop'. Chris Jones, who had graduated through the City youth team to become a loyal servant and willing enthusiast, was deemed not to have made the grade for the first team. When Joe and Malcolm decided to add Bobby Owen to the squad after the friendly against Bury in the week after the win against Newcastle, Jones's days at Maine Road were effectively numbered. The former youth-team centre-forward had run his heart out for the cause on the ill-fated American trip, so when he saw the newcomer from Bury at pre-season training he was incensed and demanded an interview with the manager.

'Have you bought him to replace me?' Jones demanded.

Joe squirmed uncomfortably. He knew this was part of the job, but he didn't like it. He knew that Jones's departure was inevitable, but he wasn't looking forward to being the one who pushed him out the door. 'The squad needs strengthening.'

'Play me. I'll score you the goals. I've scored buckets of them.'

'For the reserves.'

'So play me in the first team.'

Joe said nothing. Chris was increasingly anxious. He didn't want to leave the club he'd always loved, but he wasn't getting the assurances he needed.

Joe offered the carrot he'd been keeping back. 'I've had a phone call from Danny Williams at Swindon. He's interested in you.'

'Are you putting me on the list?'

'I think you should stay and fight for your place, if that's the way you feel.'

'Do you want me to stay?'

'Yes.'

'I don't think Malcolm does. He won't even look at me in training.'

'I'm the manager. I decide who stays and who goes.'

Jones went outside to get into his car and drive over to training, his mind buzzing. What did the Boss mean? Did he mean he'd turned down Swindon? How serious was the offer in the first place? If Swindon fancied him maybe that would flush out Malcolm.

'Jonesy!' Malcolm came running over to him. 'You coming to Wythenshawe Park?'

Jones nodded. Malcolm opened the passenger door and slid in. Jones started the car and drove towards Platt Lane. It wasn't often he had Malcolm as a passenger. 'What did the Boss say?'

'He said I should stay and fight for my place.'

Malcolm was silent for a moment, then spoke. 'We've had an offer for you from Swindon.'

Now it was Chris Jones's turn to be quiet.

'I think you should take it.' Malcolm's tone was so decisive that Jones's heart sank. What was the point of the Boss's assurance now? 'I've bought Owen and I'm going to play him,' said Malcolm.

'The Boss said I should stay. He said I'm good enough to play in the first team.'

'I think you should take the offer from Swindon,' said Malcolm, and the remaining ten minutes of the journey passed in silence. It was the last time Malcolm Allison ever spoke to him. The following week, Chris Jones signed for Swindon Town. It broke his heart to do so. For as long as he could remember, the summit of his ambition had been to play centre-forward for Manchester City. The dream was over. In the FA Charity Shield match against West Bromwich Albion the week before the season started, City won 6–1, with Bobby Owen scoring twice.

Jones left for Swindon Town as his contemporary John Clay went to Macclesfield Town. Clay had been as skilful as Jones had been enthusiastic, but they became bit-part players as the first-team bandwagon rolled on. Clay had spent six years at the club and played just one full game of first-team football: the 0–2 home defeat by West Brom the previous season. He had been unlucky with injuries, but his fate was sealed when Joe Mercer came to a reserve-team game to check on his progress, along with Stan Bowles and Paul Hince, for possible restoration to the first team. Clay and Hince had developed a system whereby whichever of them felt in need of a rest hung about on the right wing and got his breath back, while the other went in search of the ball. Dave Ewing, who was deputed to look after the reserves, had long since turned a blind eye to the malingering because he liked the lads, and who cared anyway? It was only the reserves.

Joe soon noticed what was going on, and as the players came off at half-time he seized Clay and Hince and took them into the treatment room. Both of them knew what was coming. 'You're a disgrace,' raged the manager. 'Both of you. A disgrace to the club. You're cheating the supporters. They don't pay their money to watch you two cheats loafing about like that. I pick the team. You stick to your positions. Understand? What?'

During the reprimand, Clay had noticed that the manager was wearing two ties: a brown one and a green one, one on top of the other. Hince saw what Clay had spotted. They couldn't control themselves. The harder they tried the more impossible it became, and the laughter escaped from them like air leaking out of a tyre. Joe, unaware of what they were laughing at, left the room, slamming the door behind him. Neither Hince nor Clay played in the first team again, and within six months they were out of the club. Joe was no kid's soft touch.

The overwhelming victory in the Charity Shield proved a false dawn. Joe and Malcolm were mystified when they went nine League games without a win and were knocked out of the League Cup by Blackpool. Neither of them knew exactly what was wrong, apart from the obvious absence of Tony Book, nor how to fix it. In the defeat at Liverpool, Malcolm was out of the dugout in a flash as Tommy Smith introduced Bobby Owen to the reality of the First Division by chopping him down in typically brutal fashion. Malcolm's list of obscenities impressed the Anfield crowd but not the referee or the linesman. When Smith went after Mike Summerbee and left the centre-forward, who knew exactly how to look after himself in such close-quarters combat, rolling on the ground in agony, Malcolm was on his feet again. This time the torrent of abuse directed at the phlegmatic Liverpool defender didn't stop until the referee raced across and publicly sent the outraged coach from the touchline into the stand.

When the heat of anger had cooled, Joe tried to instil some restraint into Malcolm. 'Mal, you're not helping me or the team or yourself.'

'Bollocks! The players love to see me all fired up. At least they know one of us'll defend them.'

Joe stared at him. Malcolm finally had the grace to look away. 'You're getting a reputation with the FA.'

'That load of cunts! You fucking hate them as much as I do.'

'They're going to get you off the touchline permanently if you don't curb your tongue.'

'I'll shut up when they start protecting skilful players like Summerbee from thugs like Smith.'

'If you want to be a manager you're going to have to learn to be a bit cleverer, son.'

Now it was Malcolm's turn to stare at Joe, who quickly realised his mistake, and it was his turn to look away.

The attempt to retain the League title was effectively over by the end of September and – infinitely more devastating to them – so was their attempt to emulate Manchester United by winning the European Cup. They had been drawn against the unknown Turkish side Fenerbahçe, whom neither Joe nor Malcolm had bothered to watch before the Turks arrived at Maine Road for a ritual slaughter in the middle of September. The match followed the predictable pattern of waves of blue shirts pouring down on the opponents' goal, but unlike the previous season, when such attacking moves had produced a cascade of goals, the ball simply wouldn't go into the net. City rattled the woodwork; the

Fenerbahçe goalkeeper, the 21-year-old Simsel Yavuz, pulled off a series of outstanding saves; and the City forwards simply missed chance after chance. Most of them seemed to fall to Mike Summerbee, who hadn't put a foot right all season, and when he missed what by common consent was an open goal, for the first time in his life he heard the sound of booing at Maine Road directed at him.

Joe and Malcolm were shaken but not devastated by the scoreless draw. A goal away from home would mean that Fenerbahçe would have to score twice, and City couldn't possibly play as badly again. A 4–0 win away at Sunderland and an even more impressive 3–1 win over top-of-the-table Leeds United told relieved supporters that the old City was back, and they set off for Istanbul in good heart – particularly Summerbee, who had been married the day before. They flew into Istanbul the day before the game, visited the National Stadium and noted the bumpy state of the pitch, but apart from that there didn't seem to be anything to worry about unduly.

The large Hilton Hotel where they were staying was perched high on a hill, and from it they could see both the National Stadium and the Bosphorus.

'Look,' said Joe to Tony Coleman, 'you can see Europe and Asia from here.'

The left-winger was unimpressed. 'You can see Birkenhead and Liverpool from the Liver Building.'

Coleman lost a little of his fabled mischievous sense of humour when he was woken twice in the night by someone hammering on the door. By the time he had grabbed something to cover himself with and opened the door, there was nobody to be seen. Most of the other players reported similar nocturnal interruptions, and nobody had managed to sleep through the night undisturbed.

Next day, as Tony Book drew the curtains of his room, he couldn't help noticing a crowd of people making their way towards the National Stadium. He looked at his watch. It was just before 10 a.m. By the time the coach carrying the nervous City players arrived at the ground it was clear that it had been full for hours, the crowd was in a state of fervent excitement and the pitch was ringed by armed Turkish soldiers.

'Bugger me,' said Francis Lee. 'This is a bit different from playing at Barnsley.'

In the dressing-room, Joe tried to release some of the tension that he could see was building up in the players, as it had at Newcastle. Joe looked at Ken Mulhearn. The goalkeeper looked as nervous as he had been before his first match against United, 12 months before. 'Now listen, lads, you have to score, 'cause if it's nil–nil they toss a coin to decide who goes through to the next round, and I'm crap at tossing.'

'Let TC do it,' came the familiar voice of Francis Lee. 'He tosses himself off all the time.' There was a roar of laughter that sent them out in a better state of mind, but their arrival on the pitch was greeted by an outburst of sustained hostility from the fanatical crowd such as they had never experienced even at Old Trafford. Firecrackers exploded, flares illuminated the night sky over the Bosphorus and the noise made by the many klaxon horns in constant use was so overwhelming that the Manchester players could scarcely make themselves heard to each other at a distance of more than six yards.

Fortunately they chose the most successful method of quietening the crowd when after 12 minutes Coleman seized on a pass from Lee, rounded the goalkeeper and slipped the ball into the empty net for the lead and the precious away goal. Joe and Malcolm were faced with the same dilemma they had confronted at half-time at Newcastle. Did they calm them down or fire them up? They opted for what had worked on Tyneside, but it was the wrong option. A minute into the second half, the substitute Abdullah controlled a cross, which either Mulhearn or Heslop should have cut out, and equalised.

If the 1–1 scoreline became the result it was still good enough to take City through to the second round, but Joe and Malcolm knew their players and they could see that they had lost confidence in each other. That intangible spirit that tells those 11 men that they will not lose, that someone will score even against the odds they were facing, was nowhere to be seen. The players who had frozen at Newcastle – Heslop and Mulhearn, in particular – were similarly afflicted again, and this time the forwards were not good enough to rescue them. Malcolm thought fleetingly of the confidence a goalkeeper like Gordon Banks would give to the whole team, but his bitterness at Joe's failure to complete that vital bit of business was stilled as he saw Fenerbahçe launch yet another attack down the wing. David Connor was no Tony Book, and he was unable to prevent Can from crossing. Again Mulhearn failed to come for the ball, and it bobbled about in the City penalty box until Ogun scrambled it into the City net.

The crowd erupted. Joe had only been a year old when Johnny Turk had annihilated the Allied forces at Gallipoli, but he couldn't help thinking of the massacre as the rampant Turks played out the remaining ten minutes of the match to the sounds of triumph. There was no chance that his team would snatch an undeserved draw. They had been well beaten. The crowd gathered menacingly on the touchline, and when the referee blew for full-time they invaded the pitch. The riot police, armed with batons, of which they made indiscriminate use, had been stationed there ostensibly to prevent precisely that occurrence. They managed only with difficulty to escort the City players off the pitch and into the tunnel without further injury.

Rockets were launched and fires were started on the terraces. This was presumably the foreigners' equivalent of going to the pub and getting drunk, their way of celebrating a famous victory their newspapers would claim was the most important in the history of the country. Malcolm, with a heavy heart, made his way back to the dressing-room, well aware that tomorrow's papers would be full of references to his boast that he would terrify the cowards of Europe. Joe knew that even his restrained promise that City would reach the third round at least would invite some public ridicule. He couldn't remember a result as bad as this one, and it brought back many of the feelings of despair and depression he thought he had conquered. City were out of the European Cup at the first hurdle, and all they had to look forward to now was Manchester United's increasingly impressive defence of their European title.

Malcolm didn't deal with the inevitable mocking headlines and the snide comments very well. He drank, he gambled money he never had in the first place and increasingly he found himself waking up in strange beds. By now, however, his reputation for being broke was starting to precede him into restaurants, bars and nightclubs, his preferred locations of rest and relaxation. He had been unable to resist the temptation to buy good champagne even when he didn't have the means to pay for it. He liked it, the ladies liked it, he liked the ladies and after two bottles of the good stuff the ladies invariably liked him exactly the same way that he liked them. He found the Cotton Bar at the recently opened state-of-the-art five-star Piccadilly Hotel to be a particularly effective location for talking attractive, if impressionable, women into bed. There was a model called Barbara whose resistance he felt would not last too long. He was right.

One evening, things were going particularly well and they were both in the mood by 10.30 p.m. He picked up the bill with nonchalance and wandered over to the bar to pay it as Barbara disappeared into the Ladies to repair her make-up. He chatted briefly to Ben the barman, a United supporter, which always fuelled the banter. Unfortunately the name Fenerbahçe now cropped up in their conversations far too frequently for his liking.

'We're having a new cocktail named after you, Mal.'

'Yeah? What's that then?'

'We're calling it the Fenerbahçe.'

'Yeah?' he said as he opened his cheque book and began to write. 'Why?'

''Cause it tastes like shite,' crowed Ben with barely suppressed laughter.

Malcolm smiled calmly and carefully tore out the cheque made out to the hotel for the full amount on the bill. 'Here,' said Malcolm evenly, 'I've added a ten-bob tip for you. Make sure the stingy bastards cough it up.'

'Will do, Mal. Thanks,' he said gratefully. 'That bird of yours, she looks fab,' he added admiringly.

'She is, she's a model,' replied Malcolm and walked towards the lift where he met Barbara coming out of the Ladies just as Ben's boss came into the bar from his office, recognising the departing back of Malcolm Allison. His eyes narrowed in alarm and he walked briskly to the bar.

'Did Allison leave without paying?' he asked Ben.

'No.'

'Thank God!' said the manager. 'What did he have?'

'Two bottles of Dom Pérignon.'

'And he paid in cash?' he asked, his heart sinking, for he knew perfectly well what the answer would be.

'No. But he added a tip for me. Ten bob!' said Ben and held up the cheque, beaming.

The manager stared at it and then exploded. 'A cheque! You took a bloody cheque?' and he raced towards the exit. 'Mr Allison! Mr Allison!' he called urgently. He arrived in the lobby just in time to see the lift doors closing on a smiling Malcolm Allison, his camel-hair coat draped round his shoulders like a cloak, a cigar in his left hand and his right arm around the waist of a very attractive young woman with blonde hair, wearing a simple shift dress with a very short hemline.

'Night, Luigi,' he called out through the closed doors.

Furious but impotent, the manager returned to the bar. 'No cheques! Don't ever take a bloody cheque from that man.'

'He's the assistant manager of City.'

'He could be the assistant manager of the Bank of England, but he hasn't got any money. Give me that.' The frustrated Luigi snatched the bill and wandered back into his office. Ben watched him go with his ten-bob tip and vowed to exact revenge on Malcolm somehow at the next derby match. In his office, Luigi took a clean envelope from the top drawer of his desk and slipped Malcolm's bill into it. He took out a sheet of hotel notepaper and began to write slowly: 'Dear Mr Griffiths, I am sorry that I have to write to you once again on the matter of a bill which has been left unpaid by Malcolm Allison . . .'

Malcolm's small temporary triumphs in the bars and clubs of Manchester paled into insignificance that autumn as City's results failed to improve in the League. Mike Summerbee, whose performances the previous season had been such a significant feature in the Championship victory, seemed to be in a slump that neither he nor Joe could correct. They called Summerbee over after training.

'How do you feel?' asked Joe, who was as concerned as the player and the coach.

'Sharp. I feel really sharp out there,' replied Summerbee.

'What's different off the pitch then?'

'I got married.'

'Diet, lifestyle?' asked Malcolm, knowing that Joe wasn't as convinced as he was as to the supreme importance of the science of football.

'Different but better. Tina makes me a good breakfast before I come out, and there's always a good dinner waiting for me when I get back.'

'You're shagging too much then.' Malcolm's analysis was brutal but brief.

'I'm not,' replied Summerbee indignantly.

'Why not?' asked Joe. 'You're a newly wed.'

They all laughed, but Summerbee's performances failed to improve and the team's results were infuriatingly inconsistent. It was the inconsistency that bothered Malcolm more than anything. He couldn't attribute everything to Tony Book's absence. Why didn't the referees and linesmen protect his players better?

Southampton came to Maine Road determined to kick everything that moved. Centre-half John McGrath brutally hacked down Mike Summerbee, and in the melee that followed punched Francis Lee in the face. One down at half-time, the players were seething.

'That cunt Hollywood . . .' complained Summerbee, who loathed the Southampton defender as much as anyone he had ever played against. 'Did you see what he did to TC?'

Tony Coleman was on the treatment table having a gash in his leg cleaned up by Peter Blakey.

'When he kicked me into the Kippax I thought the crowd was going to come on and sort him out,' grinned Coleman.

'I wish they had,' said Summerbee, who was still livid. 'This lot are animals.'

In the second half, City had two strong appeals for a penalty turned down. Malcolm was out of the dugout bellowing at the officials. 'That's a penalty! A penalty! You're a fucking cheat!'

The linesman came over to the figure in the trademark long overcoat rampaging along the touchline. 'Get back inside the dugout, please.'

'Fuck off,' said Malcolm and continued to berate the referee.

The linesman waved his flag vigorously. The referee stopped play and came running over to the touchline.

'What's going on?' asked the referee.

'I told him to get back in the dugout and he refused.'

'That was a clear foul on Francis Lee. Why didn't you give the fucking penalty?' Malcolm demanded.

'I'm the only judge of what is and what is not a penalty.'

'You're a fucking ignorant cheat!'

'Right, I'm sending you off and reporting your comments to the Football Association.'

'Do, and I'll tell *them* you're a fucking cheat as well.'

Not even a late, if deserved, equaliser by Tony Coleman could lift the spirits at the club.

Walter Griffiths took a sadistic pleasure in informing Malcolm that he had been summoned to a hearing in front of the FA Disciplinary Committee in Leicester. Malcolm seemed unmoved and certainly unsurprised.

'Hire me a car to get down there, will you, Walter? Oh, and make sure it's a Roller. I wouldn't want to let down the image of this great club.'

Joe, meanwhile, was under pressure from the directors to curb the antics of his assistant manager.

'I understand how you feel, Chairman, but Malcolm's a passionate man. Take the passion out of him and he wouldn't be half the man he is.'

'Winston Churchill was a passionate man but he won the war.'

Joe was temporarily mystified. Was Malcolm being criticised for not having won the war instead of Churchill?

'The fact is, Joe, that Malcolm's behaviour is bringing this club a great deal of embarrassment. It's your job to control him.'

'The only way I can control him is if he sits in the stands with us.'

'Then we must make arrangements for him to do that.'

'He needs to be with the players.'

'The FA will ban him. If we ban him first, the FA might reduce the length of the official ban.'

'How can he communicate with the players sat in the stand?'

'Let Johnny Hart do it. He's the trainer.'

'How can Mal get hold of Johnny in the middle of a game?'

'Well . . . think of something because he's in for a long ban, I can tell you.'

Albert Alexander was right. It could scarcely have been longer. In addition to the £100 fine, which the club paid on his behalf with the money deducted in instalments from future wages, Malcolm Allison received a lifetime ban from touchline coaching. He was shocked. So was Joe. Malcolm felt the whole world was against him. And now he was going to have to sit in the stand for the rest of his life in football. Joe tried hard to raise his spirits. 'You'll enjoy sitting in the directors' box on Saturday.'

'How d'you know?'

'Jane Russell's going to be there.'

'Christ, I saw her films when I was about 15. She must be knocking on.'

'Long as you're not knocking her off.'

Malcolm tried to smile but it was hard. He felt wretchedly low.

'Come on, Mal, we've had bad times before. We'll get through them.'

'How?'

'We'll win the FA Cup. Why not?'

Malcolm finally managed to smile. 'That'll work. We only have to win six games.'

'And Booky'll be back by then.'

It was when they came back from a tough cup tie at St James' Park with a scoreless draw in the fourth round that they started to believe that the FA Cup was an attainable target. The 2–0 win in the replay was almost a foregone conclusion, as was the 4–1 victory away at Blackburn. They were in the last eight with a home tie against traditional victims Tottenham Hotspur when the phone rang, and Malcolm's old West Ham friend Noel Cantwell, now manager at Coventry, asked him to dinner to discuss something of mutual interest.

'It'd be more money.'

'How much more?'

'What are you on at City?'

Malcolm told him.

'A lot more.'

'Who picks the team?'

'We both do. We'd be joint managers in every sense.'

'Joe said I could have the City team for myself.'

'When did he say that?'

'When we started.'

'That was 1965. This is 1969.'

The money wasn't really the issue for Malcolm. He could get through £85 a week as fast as he got through £65.

'What's the board like?'

'The chairman is fantastic. He lets me manage. Come on, Mal, it'll be like the old days, you and me, discussing tactics in that greasy spoon and going back to Upton Park to see if it worked and upset the groundsman.'

The press soon learned the outline of the conversation, and the prospect of Malcolm leaving hit the dressing-room hard. Summerbee confronted him after training, when it had been the sole topic of discussion, and laid it on the line. 'Mal, if you go, you'll destroy the team.'

'We fight a lot. Maybe someone'll come in who gets more out of you.'

'Nobody could get more out of me than you. You made me an international player.'

'What about the others?'

'It's not just me, we all think like that. Belly, Bookie, Francis; none of us'll stay if you go.'

Malcolm nodded and went off to find Joe. 'Joe, I'm torn.'

'Nobody wants you to go, Mal.'

'Except the Secretary.'

'If you go, the team'll collapse without you. I can't do it on my own. I always said that.'

'I need to manage.'

'What's Cantwell offering you that I can't?'

'More money and the chance to manage.'

'Well, if it's just money,' said Joe quickly, ignoring the challenge of the second statement, 'go to the Chairman. Show him an offer in writing from Coventry. I'll bet he'll match it. I'll bloody well tell him to.'

Later, Malcolm sat drinking in the Fletcher's Arms, still undecided.

'How can you leave us now, Malcolm?' asked Ian Niven.

'I've got to stand on my own two feet. Joe won't let me manage and I think I can be a great manager.'

'I know you can,' Niven stated firmly. 'But for God's sake, be our manager. Don't waste yourself on Coventry City.'

'I've asked Joe when he's going to hand over the reins, but all he'll say is "soon". He's just stringing me along. He'll never do it.'

'It'll be just the same at Coventry, but you'll have worse players. How can you leave players like Colin Bell and Alan Oakes and Mike and Franny?'

In the end, that was what decided him. He had started that team. As Malcolm parked the car outside his house and turned off the engine he knew that his job at Maine Road was not yet completed. He would have to stay and finish it. They were going to win the Cup this year. He was quite sure of it. The attractions of life in the West Midlands paled, and he signed a new four-year contract with Manchester City at a higher salary, but one that still comfortably failed to meet his debts.

Quite how pressing were his debts was apparent the next morning during breakfast, when Beth opened the door to a man in a shabby fawn raincoat. 'Mrs Allison?' He raised his trilby hat in the conventional gesture of politeness. Beth was not fooled for an instant. There was only one reason why men dressed like this knocked on the door at this time of the morning, and she had at least ensured that the club house they were living in meant that there would be no more untimely visits from the rent man.

'TV or car?'

'Excuse me?'

'Have you come to repossess the television set or the car?'

The man smiled. It was quite refreshing dealing with people like this. Usually there was anger and even violence as desperate renters hurled their bodies on their cars and children cried bitter tears to see their television set carried out of the house. 'I'm really sorry. I'm a City supporter myself, you see. Have been since the days of Peter Doherty, before the war.'

'TV or car?' repeated Beth.

'Car, I'm afraid,' said the repo man mildly. He consulted his clipboard. 'Mr Allison has missed three consecutive payments, and we have written to him twice to warn him that if he missed another payment . . .'

'Malcolm!' yelled Beth. 'C'mere.' Malcolm appeared holding a half-eaten piece of toast and that morning's copy of the *Daily Express*. 'Give this man the keys to the car. He's repossessing it. You prat.' She pushed her way past him back into the kitchen. It really wasn't worth getting annoyed with her husband. That's what Malcolm was like. She'd always known it.

'Good morning, Mr Allison.' The repo man raised his hat again. 'I do apologise. About taking the car back.' Malcolm went into the living room, picked up the car keys from the mantelpiece and dropped them into the man's open palm. 'Thank you. How do you think we're going to get on against Tottenham, then?'

'We're going to win, of course,' Malcolm replied. There was no point getting angry with the bloke. He was only doing his job.

'Can I give you a lift to Maine Road?'

'Nah. It's all right.' Malcolm shut the door and picked up the telephone to order a taxi to take him into training.

'Cash or account?' asked the deadpan female voice on the other end.

She must be joking. 'Account.'

'What's the name or number of the account?'

'Manchester City FC.'

'We don't have an account in that name,' came the response after a moment's pause.

'I'm opening one,' said Malcolm shortly.

'Are you authorised to do that?' asked the voice.

'I'm the fucking assistant manager!' The irritation of the day's events was starting to get to him for the first time.

'Ooh!' squealed the telephone receptionist. 'Is this Malcolm Allison?' Malcolm smiled. He recognised that tone of voice. Everything was going to be all right.

TWELVE

S itting in the back of the taxi as it drove from Sale towards Moss Side, Malcolm became ever more convinced that City were going to win the FA Cup. Joe saw the problems ahead of them; Malcolm saw only Tony Book lifting the trophy and said so to everyone who would listen. But Tottenham proved to be nothing like the soft touch they had been over those two thrilling games in the Championship season. They fought like tigers for every ball, and only Francis Lee's second-half goal separated the two sides. It was a greatly relieved home crowd who heard the referee's final whistle. Everton in the semi-final at Villa Park looked likely to provide even tougher opposition.

As soon as it was clear that Tony Coleman's ankle would not heal in time for him to play against Everton, Joe and Malcolm came up with exactly the same response. It was vital for them to stop Alan Ball from controlling the middle of the park, particularly because – even though they would both play – neither Bell nor Doyle was fully fit. David Connor, who had marked Ian Gibson out of the game for them in their first match in charge at Middlesbrough nearly four years ago, was charged with the task of doing the same to Alan Ball. His performance was one of such dogged tenacity that he was never more than a few feet away from Ball throughout the ninety minutes.

It was a typical semi-final war of attrition. The football was dull and uncreative, but the tension, which gripped everyone in the ground, was almost unbearable. Individual battles were being fought out all over the pitch. Nineteen-year-old Tommy Booth, who had taken over the centre-half position from George Heslop after the debacle in Istanbul, was coping manfully with the twenty-year-old Everton centre-forward, Joe Royle. Conversely, Brian Labone was struggling to keep Francis Lee in check. With more than 15 minutes to go until half-time, Royle clashed with Doyle, who went down in great pain. The referee eventually stopped play, and Doyle was carried off the pitch. Standing up from the bench, the substitute Bobby Owen started to warm up. In the stand, Malcolm stood up and bellowed at the supine figure on the stretcher, 'Run it off! Get back on your feet and run it off!'

Joe asked the director Sidney Rose to go into the dressing-room and check how serious the injury to Doyle was. 'Sidney, for God's sake, get him back on. If we bring Owen on now, we'll have to pull Colin Bell back to right-half and the whole pattern of our play will be disrupted.'

Rose found Mike Doyle lying on the treatment table screwing up his face in pain as Peter Blakey gingerly pressed with his fingers on the bruise.

'I've broken it, Mr Rose, I'm sure.'

Sidney Rose took over from the physiotherapist and expertly ran his fingers quickly up and down Doyle's leg.

'Shall I tell the Boss to get Owen on, Mr Rose?' asked Blakey.

'Not yet.'

'It's broken, Mr Rose,' moaned Doyle.

'Peter, would you be so good as to tell Joe that I think Mike can probably get back after half-time.'

Blakey left the room as Doyle started to doubt the doctor's sanity.

'I can't even feel the leg, Mr Rose. How can I go back on in the second half? I've got a broken leg.'

'You haven't got a broken leg, Mike; you've got a dead leg. You just need to get the blood circulating again. Get down from the table and put your weight on it slowly, and then start shaking it and stamping it on the ground.'

Doyle went back out with the rest of the team for the second half with few noticeably ill effects, but as hard as they all tried they created few clear chances, and those openings that they did manage to find were quickly closed down by some desperate defending from Everton. In the very last minute, Neil Young broke clear and bore down on the Everton goal with only the goalkeeper to beat. He had scored so many times in similar situations that there was a huge roar of relief from the Everton section when Gordon West flung up an arm and Young's shot deflected off his shoulder for a corner. The disappointed Young trotted over to take it, and the ball floated to the back post, where the rejuvenated Doyle won the header, Summerbee slipped the bouncing ball sideways and Tommy Booth thumped it into the back of the net. Half of Villa Park erupted in ecstasy; the other half sat contemplating the injustice of the world. Everton were going back to Merseyside, but City were on their way to Wembley.

Afterwards, Joe was in his element as he told the world that the final would be like the champagne that was being consumed in industrial quantities in their dressing-room. The Cup final was a party compared with the semi-final, in which the sickening fear of losing one match away from Wembley was always so inhibiting. As ever, they were all in the winning dressing-room: the directors in search of identification with their successful players, the pressmen in search of a quote, the hangers-on in search of a drink and a ticket for the final. Malcolm was delighted to offer hospitality to a forlorn Gordon West. 'Fucking hell, Mal, the gaffer's going ape-shit in there. No one's talking, everyone's getting a bollocking . . .'

Malcolm thrust a glass of champagne into his hand. 'Come and join the party, son; you'll have a much better time in here.'

Later Malcolm found the City director John Humphreys, who, with his brother, had started the sports kit-manufacturing firm Umbro. He had been only too pleased to manufacture a new Umbro kit based on the *rossoneri* of AC Milan. 'Malcolm, this is a wonderful day.'

'For you, too. I think we should play in this red-and-black strip in the final.'

'Wouldn't that be giving Leicester an advantage?'

'How?'

'By allowing them to play in their regular blue strip.'

'I don't think so. I think this AC Milan strip is fantastic. We've won every cup match we've played in it.'

'You don't think it makes them look too . . . well, foreign?'

'Italians make the sharpest clothes.' He ignored the rather hurt look Humphreys flashed him and carried on with engaging enthusiasm. 'Besides, it worked for us at Blackburn as well as here. They look sleek; they look powerful. I think we should keep it for the final.'

'I'll tell the factory on Monday morning. What does Joe think?'

'Leave the Boss to me.'

When City walked out at Wembley at the end of April it was with those red-and-black stripes on their backs, but they deliberately made Leicester wait for three long minutes in the tunnel so they could hear the noise of the expectant crowd and let nerves do their damage. In the City dressing-room, Joe made his predictable plea for the players to go out and enjoy the party. They had worked so hard to get there that they would regret it for the rest of their lives if they didn't go out and play as well as they all knew they could. At this point, a Wembley official barged into the dressing-room and demanded that the players make their appearance in the tunnel. The players instinctively got to their feet.

'Sit down, we're not done here yet,' barked Malcolm, ushering the official out and slamming the door in his face. He opened a bottle of brandy, urging his players to take a nip and let the Leicester players listen to the crowd's moving rendition of the perennial favourite hymn 'Abide With Me'. 'When you go out there, keep your heads up. I don't want any of you looking at your feet. It's your stadium. Go out and show me that you own it. You deserve to be here. If we lose because we've played attacking football, I'll tell the Boss it was my fault. Ready? Let's go.' Then Malcolm slipped away to take his anonymous seat in the stand, shaking the hand of Leicester's manager, Frank O'Farrell, another of his mates from the Upton Park academy of the 1950s, as he slipped past him, and took the walk out of the tunnel at the head of . . . nobody. One hundred thousand people did not rise to their feet as he made his way slowly around the perimeter to the seats near the Royal Box. Scarcely had he sat down when the explosion of noise told him that the two teams were coming out. Leading the Manchester City team was Joe Mercer. Well, why not? He was the manager. He was the public face – at least, the more than acceptable public face – of the club, the genial, wise, experienced, jovial character beloved by everybody in the game and by supporters of all clubs. Malcolm sat in the stand because the FA had refused to lift their ban even for the Cup final. They thought that if Malcolm couldn't control himself at a League game when there were no television cameras around, it was even less likely that he would do so in the full glare of a Wembley final.

So Malcolm sat at the front of the stand, ironically closer to the pitch than the two benches for the managers, trainers and substitutes, which were traditionally placed directly under the Royal Box. He watched as his team was introduced to Princess Anne, and he couldn't help but think that it should have been him out there. He understood how popular Joe was and appreciated the chance he had given him, as well as the support he knew Joe provided for him when the directors examined the hotel bills Walter Griffiths placed in front of them. He was grateful – he would always be grateful – but this was his team, and he felt a knot of the purest jealousy in his stomach as he watched Joe Mercer being asked for his comments on the game by a BBC reporter, which were fed into the live transmission of the match. He wanted those cameras on him. He would be so much more entertaining than Joe, so much more insightful in his analysis. Instead he sat and suffered because, although his journalist friend Paul Doherty was sitting next to him with an illicit microphone up his sleeve and asking the occasional question, Malcolm's comments would be transmitted on ITV, and who the hell watched ITV on Cup final day? It was Joe that people would remember, not him. When his time in the sun came, he wouldn't let people forget who he was. Ever.

Although Summerbee and Coleman constantly had the beating of their full-backs, Nish and Rodrigues, Leicester performed far better than Malcolm had anticipated, and their two main forwards, Lochhead and Clarke, put the defence under continuous pressure. Even after Neil Young's 23rd-minute goal Leicester always looked likely to snatch an equaliser, and Malcolm was puzzled as to why his team couldn't find the second goal to kill the game off. Both City and Leicester continued to make and miss chances, but the match finished in a 1–0 victory, and City had won the FA Cup the year after the Championship, just as he had always known they would. Why, then, did he still have this nagging feeling of dissatisfaction?

Joe was understandably delighted as he became the first man in the history of the game to have won the League Championship and the FA Cup both as a player and as a manager. The Chairman was as ebullient as Joe had ever seen him, and he told the same joke he told after every big match when congratulating the players, by telling them their efforts had brought the club such wealth they could now afford to buy some good players. Everyone laughed dutifully. It was part of the tradition, as was the celebration banquet that night at the Café Royal, from where David Coleman introduced highlights of the match and interviewed the ecstatic winning team and their management. Joe and Norah thought it was one of the happiest evenings of their long and rewarding marriage. Malcolm had invited Joe Lowery as his guest, but the old scoundrel had needed some persuading. He had just been released from prison and he didn't want his criminal record to taint the night for his former associate. Malcolm insisted, but what depressed him was Lowery's appearance. This was a man who had never shown the world anything but style or contempt, yet prison – even the open prison in the West Country where he had served out the final months of his sentence – seemed to have broken him.

THE WORST OF FRIENDS

The champagne flowed, but even when they were done with the Café Royal the night hadn't yet started for Malcolm, the players and their wives, who went on to the Sportsmen's Club on Tottenham Court Road. Tony Coleman had started Cup final week by getting caught up in a fight in a pub, and now Lee and Summerbee managed to end the perfect day by brawling in the street with four aggressive Leicester supporters. Summerbee had come down the stairs from the club to find a cab when the altercation began. His wife, Tina, flew back upstairs to look for her husband's best friend. 'Francis!' she implored. 'Mike's on the pavement scrapping with half a dozen drunks.'

'Right,' said Francis Lee, running towards the exit. 'Don't worry, love, I'll sort it out.' And he did. The City players, blood-spattered and bruised, emerged victorious for the second time that day. The Leicester fans, defeated in battle on the pitch and in the gutter, dragged themselves painfully away. Summerbee, proud holder of a coveted FA Cup-winner's medal, spent the night on the floor of his hotel room, banished from the bed occupied by the disapproving figure of his pregnant wife.

Fortunately he and Lee had recovered by the following afternoon, when they sat on an open-top bus as it drove through the streets of Manchester, which were thronged with City supporters who had never known so much success. The players took it in turns to show off the famous old trophy to the quarter of a million delighted fans, all of whom claimed they had been among the 8,015 who had been present at the notorious Swindon Town game in January 1965. Malcolm felt a great sense of accomplishment when he lifted the trophy in time-honoured fashion to show to the fans, who cheered him every time he did so, yet he couldn't help acknowledging that this triumph was laced somehow with a deeper unhappiness.

Something was eating away at Malcolm, and he couldn't even describe the feeling of discontent to anyone until he received a visit from an Italian journalist who was in town to watch Manchester United take on AC Milan in the European Cup semi-final. It was less than three weeks since Neil Young's goal had won the FA Cup, and already United were threatening to undermine City's triumph by winning the European Cup, as they had the previous year. Malcolm, who was used to the dress style of football reporters based in Manchester, whose wives bought their clothes for them at C&A in Market Street, was impressed by the Italian's appearance. Beneath his fashionably cut smart suit was a silk shirt that City's own bespoke shirt salesman, Mike Summerbee, would have approved of. Its cuffs were held in place by gold bracelets. This was a man who knew how to dress and a man who revelled in his money. Malcolm itched to take him into Walter Griffiths's office and show the Secretary what smart dressing really was.

The man's English, though accented, was as impeccable as his clothes. 'Signor Allison, I have been sent by Juventus to enquire whether you would like to be their new manager.'

Malcolm had always known that a conversation containing those words would happen one day. It just took him by surprise when it did. 'Do you work for them?'

'I am, shall we say, "empowered" to ask you this question. It would be difficult for Signor Agnelli to ask you himself. He doesn't like to hear the word "no".' The reporter smiled. Malcolm smiled back. They both understood the affectations of the powerful. He just couldn't envisage the possibility of Albert Alexander sending Peter Gardner on a similar mission to Milan to see Helenio Herrera, should he and Joe ever need to be replaced.

'I'm on a hundred quid a week, you know,' said Malcolm, inflating his salary for negotiating purposes.

'Money will not be a problem.'

'Plus bonuses.'

'Signor Agnelli owns the Fiat motor-car company as well as Juventus. He is a very wealthy man.'

'I could do with a car.'

'That can be arranged.'

'I'll need to sign new players.'

'How do you know? You have not seen Juve.'

'If they weren't a crap team Agnelli wouldn't have sent you over here to sound me out. Plus you're here to watch AC Milan in the European Cup – not Juventus.'

The journalist nodded his head in appreciation of the accuracy of Malcolm's statement. 'Money will not be a problem. For the team or for you.'

'In that case you can tell him that I'm interested.'

The next step came a few days later. An Italian voice, which was not that of the well-dressed journalist who had come to Maine Road, telephoned and left the most cryptic of messages: Malcolm was to drive his Fiat saloon (which had arrived at the ground with two months' free rental paid as a gift from the manufacturer) to a designated isolated spot on the Lancashire moors outside Preston and wait. Another car would draw up opposite him and flash its lights. At this point he was to get out of his car, then go over and sit in the passenger seat of the other car. On no account was he to mention this meeting to anyone. Malcolm laughed. He thought he was being wound up. It all seemed like a Hitchcock thriller or one of those Harry Palmer films with Michael Caine. He hoped there would be a girl in this one somewhere.

The scenario played out precisely as described. A minute after Malcolm had arrived at the rendezvous point, the other car drove up and turned off its engine. The lights flashed as arranged and Malcolm got out of his Fiat, turned up his collar against the drizzle that blew in gusts across the moors into his face and opened the passenger door of the expensive Alfa Romeo, hoping to find a young Sophia Loren. But there was no sultry dark-haired Italian beauty in an expensively cut dress from one of Milan's top designers sitting in the driver's seat – just Gigi Peronace, the Italian agent.

'Fuck me,' said Malcolm. 'I had a feeling it was going to be you.'

Peronace had become notorious in English football for his role as the go-between in the transfers of John Charles from Leeds United to Juventus in the 1950s and Denis Law from Manchester City to Torino in 1961. 'Ciao, Malcolm.'

'It's freezing out there, it's blowing a gale and we haven't seen the fucking sun since last summer. Are you sure you need them dark glasses?'

'Yes,' said Peronace, making no move to dispense with them.

'All right, where's the secret message? Don't tell me it's written in invisible ink.'

Peronace took an envelope from his inside pocket and handed it over. Inside Malcolm found 50,000 Italian lire and a plane ticket to Turin.

'What's this for?'

'The money is a gift from Juventus. The plane ticket is for you to fly to Torino and meet Signor Agnelli.'

'How much is 50,000 lire?'

'About £330.'

'And this is for . . .'

'You. On condition you say nothing to anyone about these negotiations. It is imperative that they remain top secret.' Peronace took off his dark glasses and smiled. 'I know how much you like publicity, Malcolm.'

'My lips are sealed. When do I leave?' He was happy to obey the demand for secrecy from the Italians. He didn't yet know how he might feel if he left Manchester, and he didn't want to deal with the phone calls from people he knew and the abuse from fans he didn't know. He needed time to sort out his own feelings because the reality of managing a top Italian club was overwhelming. All right, Juve weren't the force they'd been ten years before in the great days of Sívori, Boniperti and John Charles, but they were still one of the great names in world football, and to manage them would immediately make Malcolm one of the great names in world football as well. He thought a few days in Turin in relative anonymity while he contemplated the situation was an attractive proposition.

For the trip to Milan he dressed in the most fashionable clothes he could find in Carnaby Street: a sharp light-blue suit with white shoes. Having seen the threads worn by the emissary, he knew it was important to create an immediate impression of style, even if it was only for the delectation of the Agnelli family. The secrecy surrounding his trip lasted until the door of the plane opened and he appeared at the top of the stairs. Clustered around the foot of the staircase was the entire Italian football press corps and the camera shutters clicked as soon as they spotted the imposing figure of the new English manager.

Juventus officials rushed Malcolm through the bureaucratic preliminaries and into a very acceptable red Ferrari, which soon became part of a gigantic cavalcade that swept him from the airport to the club offices in the centre of Turin. The cameramen that had greeted his arrival now mounted their Vespas and pursued him, at some danger to their own lives, still shooting film of him in the Ferrari as if they were all engaged in a Fellini film. He smiled as he remembered his arrival in Manchester four summers ago. Nobody knew who he was when he went to Maine Road to meet Joe Mercer. Now look at him. This was the big time. He was born for this. It was his Destiny.

It was ridiculous, but as the press conference started in Turin he began to think about Joe back in Manchester and his likely reaction even as the questions in broken English were being hurled at him.

'You sack all Juve players, Malcolm?'

'How much lire you have to spend?'

'You take Colin Bell to Juve?'

Gigi was with him, jabbering away, doing what Gigi did, protecting his English neophytes. This wasn't like dealing with the *Express* and the *Mail* in Manchester, and Malcolm was grateful. Then he heard the names

'Law' and 'Greaves', and though he couldn't understand the question he knew what they wanted to find out. Law and Greaves had both spent a most unhappy year in Italy and couldn't wait to get home – Law to Manchester United, Greaves to Spurs. They had found the cultural gap too wide to bridge.

'Tell them I'm a manager, Gigi, not a player. There have been good English managers here before.'

The chances of Malcolm keeping his visit to one of Italy's top clubs secret were always going to be remote as soon as he decided to take with him Alan Thompson of the *Daily Express*, Thompson's photographer Jimmy Milne and Paul Doherty, the son of Peter Doherty, who was a well-known freelance journalist. When Joe Mercer went down to breakfast the day after Malcolm's arrival in Italy, he immediately sensed that Norah was unhappy. There followed a domestic scenario familiar to the Mercer household.

'What's up, love?'

'Nothing.'

Good, thought Joe, she doesn't want to talk about it. 'Where's the paper, then?'

'It hasn't come.'

'I heard it coming through the letterbox.'

Norah said nothing.

'It's the close season. We've won the FA Cup. They can't be coming after me.'

'It's not you.'

'What then? If it's not me, what are you trying to protect me from?' It never occurred to Joe that Norah's behaviour could be explained by anything other than her strong instinct to protect him from anything that might cause him distress. She took the *Daily Express* out of the oven and handed it to him wordlessly, back page first. Joe read it carefully, laid it down and shook cereal out of its box and into a bowl, apparently unmoved.

'Aren't you bothered about it?' she wondered.

'About losing Malcolm? Nah. Plenty more where he came from.'

'But you've always said how vital he was to the team's success.'

Joe added milk and sugar and began to crunch. He hoped his studied nonchalance was convincing Norah. Inwardly he dreaded the prospect of Malcolm leaving City. 'I've got a team that's just won the League and the Cup in successive seasons. I've got international players who will be around for years. Do you really think I won't find good coaches queuing up to come and work for me? Coaches who wouldn't want to be the manager, either.'

Norah was pleased that Joe was feeling so resilient, so confident about the future, but she couldn't help sensing that he might be kidding himself. He had always been grateful that Malcolm had settled into the job so quickly and successfully. She knew well enough from personal experience what a difficult, insecure profession football was. It was wonderful that Joe had found such a perfect partner. She just wasn't sure how long it would last, and she didn't want Joe to be the one that was the big loser if, or more likely when, the split came.

In the meantime, Malcolm was having a ball in Italy. It was extremely flattering to be wanted. Of course, he'd been wanted before – by Bath City and Toronto, by Plymouth Argyle and by Noel Cantwell at Coventry – but nobody who had ever wanted him previously had had the resources of the Agnelli family. The medical facilities at Juventus overwhelmed him. He wondered what Sidney Rose or, more to the point, the old trainer Laurie Barnett would have thought of the gleaming new medical centre that put the NHS to shame. He wondered what Alan Oakes, who had made his debut for City ten years before, would think if he saw the well-appointed Juventus training ground and the five thousand spectators who gathered there every morning just to watch the players go through a regular training session.

He was almost relieved when Juventus lost a friendly match 1–2 at home and the crowd vented its anger in hissing and jeering. Malcolm turned to Paul Doherty. 'I recognise that sound,' he remarked ruefully.

Doherty couldn't help noticing the intensity of the derision being heaped on the heads of the hapless Juventus players. 'Reminds me of the time City lost 2–1 at home to Swindon before you and Joe came.' Malcolm knew all about that Swindon match; it had passed into City folklore.

'So what do you think, Mal?' asked Alan Thompson.

'Feels intense.'

'I thought that's what you were looking forward to.'

'I am. But it's not like the intensity of having to win at Newcastle or beating Leicester at Wembley.'

'City were winning. This lot are losing.'

'How much freedom would I have? Joe and me, we can do nearly anything we want at Maine Road.'

THE WORST OF FRIENDS

'Why don't you wait and see what the president says he's going to pay you? You can only tell how much they really want you when they have to put the cash on the table.' You could always rely on a journalist for a dose of common sense.

Malcolm was impressed with the offer when it came on the third day of his stay in Turin. A two-year contract at £20,000 a year and a further £10,000 guaranteed bonus each year would buy a lot of Dom Pérignon and a good few boxes of Montecristo cigars. He was tempted to accept there and then, just to be able to fly back to Manchester with a signed copy and thrust it in Walter Griffiths's face. He doubted that Juventus would be examining too closely the hotel bills that came their way for payment with his name on them. From having no money, he would suddenly be a rich man. But then he'd always acted as if he had been a rich man. He just never had the money that normally went with it. It amused him to hear that the presidents of Italian football clubs had been known to drop a thousand quid or so into the lap of a manager who had just won an important match. He couldn't see Albert Alexander ever behaving like that, but he liked the Italians' style – and the prospect of a little extra cash.

'When we all go back home and we're covering United versus Liverpool,' said Paul Doherty wisely, 'what will you do for company?'

'Agnelli said I could borrow his private plane any time I fancied flying anyone over – male or female.'

'So you're going to take it?'

'I want to see what I can achieve at a top club.'

'You're at a top club, Mal.'

'But I'm not the top man, am I?'

'You won't be here either. Don't kid yourself. They might call you the manager, but Agnelli calls the shots.'

'I want to see what happens here when I get players who want to attack. So many games end 1–0 in Italy. My team won't lose 1–0 if they go a goal down.'

'You're right there. It'll be three or four if you bring Ken Mulhearn and George Heslop with you,' observed Alan Thompson caustically. They all laughed.

'Christ, I'll be glad to be shot of you and Crowther at the *Mail*.'

'I think you might miss us when you have to deal with our Italian counterparts on the phone at 3 a.m. every morning for the week after you've lost a home match.' Malcolm was quiet. He had a feeling

Alan was talking from genuine knowledge of how the Italian press operated.

'How long have you got to tell him?' asked Paul.

'A few days.'

'Great. We can go to the French Riviera,' said Alan.

'I thought we were all going to Rome,' said Paul.

'We're going to both,' announced Malcolm decisively.

Joe sat with Albert Alexander and watched him devour the last of his smoked salmon sandwiches. The Chairman drained the cup of Earl Grey tea, wiped his mouth with the large white linen napkin and sank back contentedly into the overstuffed armchair in the lounge of the Midland Hotel.

'Joe, you're the manager. You're the one everyone associates with Manchester City. The fans love you, the players love you, even the board of directors loves you, and I have to say that's quite a rare thing to be said about any manager of Manchester City in my experience.'

'Albert, you know exactly how much Malcolm means to me, to the players, to this football club.'

'Yes I do. According to Walter Griffiths, his latest unauthorised use of the club's name cost us about £450.'

'You know what I mean. I can't go back to being a tracksuit manager again. I'm past it.'

'But Joe, the world must be full of players in their mid-30s who have just finished playing and who would give their right arms to come and work here under you.'

'Name me one.'

'Dave Mackay. Isn't he due to retire soon?'

'Dave's still playing, and he'll do it till he drops. Besides, whenever he finishes he'll be able to walk into a manager's job. He won't need to coach.'

'There are others. Bound to be.'

'Malcolm wanted Dave Mackay the day he came here. And he was right. Malcolm can spot players like no one I've ever known. Malcolm's the best coach I've come across in 35 years in professional football. He's irreplaceable.'

'He's not. I've been in football a long time. So have you. You know no one's irreplaceable. The game will continue without us. You'll find someone.'

'I hope I don't have to. I really hope Mal turns Juventus down. And if it's a question of money, if he uses Juventus to get his money up here . . .'

'I'll tell him Walter says we can't afford it.' He smiled. Joe did not.

'Chairman . . .' he warned. 'Don't. Please.'

Malcolm and his companions went to Rome to see the sights and they went to Menton on the French Riviera. Malcolm pointed out that there was something undeniably attractive about being able to shoot off to the beach for the day.

'You can do that in Manchester,' Paul said.

'No you can't,' replied Malcolm scornfully, thinking of the blue sky, the golden beaches, the constant sunshine and the very real possibility of coming across attractive young women sunbathing topless, as they drove along the coastal road.

'Course you can,' said Paul reasonably. 'Blackpool's only 50 miles away, and St Annes is closer.'

Malcolm just looked at him.

The nightlife in Turin produced one memorable encounter with a Hungarian stripper, who helped Malcolm to forget, at least temporarily, the problem of how to unpick a defence that played five men across the back with a sweeper behind to lock the bolt: the *catenaccio* so beloved of Herrera and the Italian coaches. It would take more than Summerbee and Coleman kicking their way to the byline to unlock that kind of bolt.

Women, it seemed, were never in short supply in Italy, but that also applied in London and in Manchester. There was no point coming to Turin just for the birds. He didn't need much Italian for sex. He thought when he arrived that he wouldn't need much Italian for football, either, but he started to worry that his tactics were complicated and couldn't be contained by Matt Busby's well-known weekly tactical talk, which Noel Cantwell had told him amounted to 'Go out there, express yourself and pass the ball to another player in a red shirt.' What horseshit that man spoke.

More worrying than the language, though, was the culture. Much as Malcolm wanted the money, much as he wanted the challenge of proving himself in another country, much as he wanted to show the world what he could do as a manager, he was at heart, he knew, still in love with English football. And he was in love with his players. He had made Lee, Bell and Summerbee into international footballers. Neil Young should be in Alf Ramsey's plans – would be already if he wasn't such a fucking coward when it came to a tackle. Malcolm also knew that Oakes and Pardoe were being seriously considered and that Tommy Booth was a certainty. Even big Joe Corrigan, the young giant of a goalkeeper, was an England prospect in Malcolm's eyes, although he had yet to make a first-team appearance. Was he really ready to give up all this just for money?

If Joe guaranteed that Malcolm would take over as manager at Manchester City within 12 months, he would turn his back on the biggest opportunity of his life. It might never come again, but if he got his way in Manchester that would be irrelevant. He didn't want to be Malcolm Allison, the manager of world-famous Juventus. What he wanted to be was the world-famous Malcolm Allison, the manager of Manchester City.

THE WORST OF FRIENDS

1968–69: MANAGER JOE MERCER

1	AUG	10	(A)	LIVERPOOL	L	1–2	YOUNG	51,236
2		14	(H)	WOLVES	W	3–2	SUMMERBEE 2, LEE	35,835
3		17	(H)	MANCHESTER U	D	0–0		63,052
4		21	(A)	LEICESTER C	L	0–3		30,076
5		24	(A)	QUEEN'S PARK R	D	1–1	DOYLE	19,716
6		27	(A)	ARSENAL	L	1–4	BELL	40,767
7		31	(H)	IPSWICH T	D	1–1	BELL	31,303
8	SEP	7	(A)	STOKE C	L	0–1		22,015
9		14	(H)	SOUTHAMPTON	D	1–1	COLEMAN	29,031
10		21	(A)	SUNDERLAND	W	4–0	LEE 2, BELL, SUMMERBEE	31,687
11		28	(H)	LEEDS U	W	3–1	BELL 2, YOUNG	46,431
12	OCT	5	(A)	EVERTON	L	0–2		55,649
13		9	(H)	ARSENAL	D	1–1	BELL	33,830
14		12	(H)	TOTTENHAM H	W	4–0	LEE 2, CONNOR, COLEMAN	38,019
15		19	(A)	COVENTRY C	D	1–1	OPP OWN-GOAL	30,670
16		26	(H)	NOTTINGHAM F	D	3–3	BELL, YOUNG, OPP OWN-GOAL	32,937
17	NOV	2	(A)	CHELSEA	L	0–2		40,700
18		9	(H)	SHEFFIELD W	L	0–1		23,861
19		16	(A)	NEWCASTLE U	L	0–1		36,400
20		23	(H)	WEST BROM A	W	5–1	YOUNG 2, BELL 2, DOYLE	24,667
21		30	(A)	WEST HAM U	L	1–2	LEE	33,082
22	DEC	7	(H)	BURNLEY	W	7–0	BELL 2, YOUNG 2, DOYLE, LEE, COLEMAN	31,009
23		14	(A)	TOTTENHAM H	D	1–1	LEE	28,462
24		21	(H)	COVENTRY C	W	4–2	YOUNG 2, BOOTH, OPP OWN-GOAL	27,760
25		26	(H)	EVERTON	L	1–3	BELL	53,549
26	JAN	11	(A)	CHELSEA	W	4–1	OWEN 2, LEE, YOUNG	35,606
27		18	(A)	SHEFFIELD W	D	1–1	YOUNG	33,074
28	MAR	4	(A)	BURNLEY	L	1–2	BELL	18,348
29		8	(A)	MANCHESTER U	W	1–0	SUMMERBEE	63,388
30		11	(A)	IPSWICH T	L	1–2	DOYLE	24,312
31		15	(H)	QUEEN'S PARK R	W	3–1	LEE, YOUNG, BOWYER	28,869
32		24	(A)	NOTTINGHAM F	L	0–1		24,613
33		29	(H)	STOKE C	W	3–1	BELL, OWEN, DOYLE	27,337
34	APR	4	(H)	LEICESTER C	W	2–0	SUMMERBEE 2	42,022
35		5	(A)	LEEDS U	L	0–1		43,176
36		8	(H)	WOLVES	L	1–3	LEE	28,533
37		12	(H)	SUNDERLAND	W	1–0	YOUNG	22,842
38		16	(A)	WEST BROM A	L	0–2		25,030
39		19	(A)	SOUTHAMPTON	L	0–3		26,254
40		30	(H)	WEST HAM U	D	1–1	PARDOE	31,846
41	MAY	5	(H)	NEWCASTLE U	W	1–0	YOUNG	20,108
42		12	(H)	LIVERPOOL	W	1–0	LEE	28,309

FINAL LEAGUE POSITION: 13TH IN DIVISION ONE

FA CUP

3	JAN	4	(H)	LUTON T	W	1–0
4		25	(A)	NEWCASTLE U	D	0–0
R		29	(H)	NEWCASTLE U	W	2–0
5	FEB	24	(A)	BLACKBURN R	W	4–1
6	MAR	1	(H)	TOTTENHAM H	W	1–0
SF		22	(N)	EVERTON	W	1–0
F		26	(N)	LEICESTER C	W	1–0

LEAGUE CUP

2	SEP	3	(A)	HUDDERSFIELD T	D	0–0
R		11	(H)	HUDDERSFIELD T	W	4–0
3		25	(A)	BLACKPOOL	L	0–1

THIRTEEN

· ·

It was in the early hours of the morning when the telephone rang in Walter Griffiths's house. Fortunately he had recently installed a second phone in the bedroom, which at least meant he didn't have to go downstairs in his pyjamas to stop the shrill ringing tone and then stand around in the freezing-cold hall.

'Walter,' said Mrs Griffiths as she stared at the little travel alarm clock that stood on her bedside table, 'it's two o'clock in the morning. Who do you know who rings people at two o'clock in the morning?'

'I'll find out,' he said, picking up the receiver. 'Hello?' There was no need to ask, though – he knew who it was going to be before the voice spoke. There was only one person who could cause him to be woken at this time.

'Is that Mr Walter Griffiths?'

'It is.'

'This is Sergeant Leonard Nuttall of the Lancashire Constabulary.'

'Hello, Sergeant.'

'I'm sorry to disturb you at this time of night, Mr Griffiths, but are you acquainted with a Mr Malcolm Allison?' Walter Griffiths groaned audibly.

Mrs Griffiths, thoroughly alarmed, poked her husband in the ribs. 'Walter! What is it? Is it one of the children?'

'No! What's he done this time, Sergeant?'

'He just walked away, Joe,' complained the Secretary to the manager the following morning.

'He's a rotten driver.'

'It's not just the fact that he wrapped his car round a lamp post in Bolton that bothers me.'

'It's on the HP. He probably couldn't afford to keep up the repayments.' Joe smiled at Walter, but the Secretary was in no mood for levity this morning.

'I know that. I've had his bank manager on the phone. He's threatening to take away his cheque book.'

'Again? Well, look: he got drunk. It's not a crime.'

'Driving under the influence of alcohol is a crime. Leaving the scene of an accident is a crime.'

'I'll have a word with him. Make sure it doesn't happen again.'

'You've been having a word with him for four years. It happens over and over again.'

'We don't want this in the papers, Walter. It's not good publicity for the club.'

'Well, there I agree with you. But one of these days that man will do something that'll get him sent to prison. In my opinion it would be the best place for him. In my long career in football I have never met any member of my staff who was so irresponsible.'

'Malcolm's late nights and what you call "irresponsibility" has a positive aspect to it, you know.'

'No, I don't know.'

'He's very close to the players partly because he does the daft things that they do.'

'I hope he knows his life would disintegrate if you weren't around to protect him, Joe.'

'We've got this problem with Stan Bowles and Tony Coleman. I can talk to them both till I'm blue in the face, but Malcolm's with them on their evenings out and he knows exactly what's going on.'

'I'm sure he does. I'm sure he's as out of control as they are.'

Joe Mercer shook his head and smiled his wise-owl smile as he stood up and turned to go. As his hand came to rest on the door handle he turned and said softly, 'Walter, trust me, there's more good than bad in Malcolm. You mustn't underestimate him.'

Despite Malcolm's late nights bonding with Tony Coleman and Stan Bowles, he knew that it was bad news for the club to have to deal with their constant lack of respect for authority. In the end it came down to a choice between the two talented left-footed forwards. Joe wouldn't keep both of them, and Malcolm knew in his heart that the Boss was right. TC was a scally, but on his own they could just about cope with his lack of discipline. Just before the Cup final he'd confessed that the presence of so many tattoos on his hands was making him very nervous at the prospect of shaking hands with Princess Anne on the big day. Malcolm arranged for a local dermatologist at the Christie Hospital to remove them in exchange for two tickets for the Wembley final. Coleman was grateful, but he wasn't going to change his character.

Stan Bowles was one of the most talented of the many youngsters Malcolm and Joe were shepherding towards first-team stardom. Since the arrival of the two men and the astonishing success they had achieved, the balance of power in the city had swung from Old Trafford to Maine Road. United had always prided themselves on being the team that developed its own stars. It was one of Busby's key beliefs, and the remarkable production line ensured that United won the FA Youth Cup for the first five years of its existence in the 1950s. Those players formed the core of the Busby Babes.

The quality of players in the City reserves was now better than that possessed by United, which boded well for the future. One of the best prospects was Stan Bowles, an old-fashioned dribbler of the ball with an eye for goal. Unfortunately, he also had an eye for a betting shop, a pretty girl and a glass of alcohol. His talent and his irresponsible social behaviour made for a combustible mixture. For Tony Coleman it was irresistible, for Stan reminded him of himself when he was 18, but instead of imparting the wisdom of his own experience and guiding the young lad onto the straight and narrow he encouraged all the worst elements of his behaviour.

Just like his mentor, Stan didn't give a toss if he was carpeted by Joe or Malcolm. They could scream at him all they wanted; he wasn't going to change. TC loved that streak in his young protégé and thought that it was a big joke when Stan missed the flight to Amsterdam for a friendly against Ajax at the start of the 1969–70 season. Nobody else was thinking along similar lines. It was unprofessional and disrespectful. Stan was on a final warning a few weeks later when he was discovered in the Cabaret Club by Malcolm. 'What the fuck are you doing here?'

'What the fuck are you?' replied Stan, clearly unfazed by being discovered breaking his curfew. Malcolm's attention was momentarily diverted by the sight of another figure he recognised coming out of the Gents and making for a girl with long blonde hair in a skirt whose hemline gave an unobstructed view of her underwear. Malcolm strode over and put his hand on Tony Coleman's shoulder, like the long arm of the law apprehending a villain.

'Hello, Mal,' smiled his outside-left. 'This is Rita. You wanna dance or a fuck? She's great at both.'

'Tony!' complained the object of his praise, flouncing away.

'I don't care what you do to yourself after the way you played against Liverpool, but I fucking warned you about Stan.'

'He's 18, Mal. He's legal. He can do what the fuck he likes. Now get your fucking hand off me.' He tried to take Malcolm's hand off his shoulder but did so more aggressively than he meant to, throwing Malcolm off balance.

'Don't you fucking push me around me, sunshine,' warned Malcolm, and then the situation quickly reached boiling point, fuelled by alcohol and passion. Stan Bowles took a look at the fight between Malcolm and Coleman, and instead of leaving swiftly, as most 18 year olds would have done in similar circumstances, he ordered another drink and pushed his way to the front of the crowd that had gathered around them. The scrap was over before it started, but Coleman had broken an unwritten law. Whatever the justification, you couldn't raise your hand to the manager or his assistant. The respectful Ogley had been moved out of the club after one half-time rant. Coleman didn't stand a chance once Malcolm turned against him.

In the morning, Malcolm found Joe in complete agreement when he suggested selling the winger. 'I think Ian Bowyer's good enough to play there regular, and there's that youngster called Ian Mellor who'll be ready in a year or two.' Malcolm was never sure whether Joe knew who he was talking about when he mentioned the youngsters. Joe didn't really concern himself with the kids the way he did. 'I had an enquiry from Danny Williams at Sheffield Wednesday in the close season. I thought you wouldn't be interested in getting rid of TC, so I turned it down.'

It was typical of Joe, thought Malcolm. He did something because he trusted his assistant manager but wouldn't give him control of the club in the way he wanted. If Joe was merely rubber-stamping Malcolm's decisions, what was the point of him being the manager? Still, it was better that Joe should be the one to give TC the push. The players would always take bad news better from the Boss. They trusted him, oddly enough, in a way somehow different from the way in which they trusted their coach.

Joe and Malcolm brought Stan into the office and told him that he was on a final warning.

'I thought I already was on a final warning.'

'Do you want me to sack you?' asked Joe impatiently.

'Stan, you can be a great player but you won't if you piss it all away,' said Malcolm.

'Like you, you mean?'

'No, you little fucker, we mean like TC.'

In fact it was Stan who took the number 11 shirt on the Saturday in the match against Sunderland at Roker Park. It brought a crushing 4–0 win, which was comforting after three defeats in the first five games of the season, although the young star of the game was Ian Bowyer, not Stan Bowles. Bowles continued to frustrate his managers in the two dull draws that followed against Burnley and Chelsea. He looked lethargic and uninterested in both matches, and was dropped back into the reserves. Within a year he was released.

On 1 October Tony Coleman signed for Sheffield Wednesday, the first of the great Championship- and Cup-winning side to leave the club. The other players recognised the fact that TC was living on borrowed time as his relationship with Joe and Malcolm hit the buffers. Players couldn't win in that situation, but Malcolm in particular had always fought Coleman's corner so strongly that the situation only became impossible because TC lacked the will even to make a formal nod in the direction of the management. He was never going to change, and if that meant leaving Manchester City, so be it. Like Jimmy Cagney on his way to the electric chair or certain capture, all TC could do was to break the rules and yell 'Come and get me, copper!' TC had added something to the dressing-room spirit, but he was a headcase and his demise had been inevitable.

Meanwhile, another infuriatingly inconsistent season in the League was matched by a smoothly impressive one in the cups. This time round, Joe and Malcolm made quite sure they travelled to watch their European opponents in action long before the City team was due to play them. A spirited 3–3 draw in Bilbao was followed by a comfortable 3–0 home win. The Belgian side Lierse offered even less resistance, and City eased past them 8–0 on aggregate to move effortlessly into the quarter-finals of the European Cup, which were not due to be played until March the following year.

In the domestic knockout competitions, they were fortunate in that tough League Cup games were eased by their being drawn at home to play Liverpool, Everton and Queens Park Rangers. Their progress in the semi-final was barred by Manchester United, whom they had already beaten in the League by a crushing 4–0. It was a sign of the times that when Malcolm went into the Fletcher's Arms nobody doubted him when he predicted another win. How different it had been less than two years before, when the Reds ruled the town and the 3–1 victory at Old Trafford had been the triumph of the underdog. Who now could see a United side that was visibly ageing before its manager's eyes overturning the rampant Blues?

Everywhere Joe and Malcolm looked they saw evidence of City's rise to dominance. It was no surprise to Malcolm, who had wanted it with a passion since that infamous night when he had been ordered to the centre of town to celebrate Manchester United's 1965 League Championship victory and had to suffer the slings and arrows of outrageous United supporters. Now there was as much City merchandise on general display as there was United; City were talked about as much in the press as United; and in Lee, Summerbee and Bell they had three current England internationals. Most important of all to Malcolm was the startling growth of the Junior Blues. It meant that not only would the best young players find their way to Maine Road before turning to Old Trafford but also that the bedrock of support for City in Manchester and surrounding parts of Lancashire was being assured for years to come.

'The only player we have to worry about is Bestie,' said Malcolm to Joe as they sat down to talk about the first leg of the League Cup semi-final.

'I don't know, Mal, they won't be as bad as they were here two weeks ago.'

'Look at the two teams, Boss; we're better all over the park except for Bestie.'

'I wouldn't give the players too much of that. I was talking to Matt. He feels this shift in the way things are in Manchester really deeply.'

'Good. Nobody's had the guts to challenge the old man since he came here 25 years ago. Well, he's in a fight now, and he's going to lose.'

'Matt's all right. You don't understand him.'

'I understand he's had things all his own way in this town. Well, that's over. They'll never win the European Cup again in his time as manager. Even Bestie can't do that by himself. Denis's reflexes aren't as sharp as they were two seasons ago, and Bobby's legs have gone.'

'How can you say that?'

'Just watch what we do to them on Wednesday.'

'Mal, you don't need to tell them we can beat United any more. They know that.'

'That's why we'll beat them again. They're on the run.'

Joe sighed. When Malcolm was in one of these moods it was impossible to reason with him.

'Joe, when are you going to retire?'

'Retire, Mal?' Joe's eyes flashed with alarm. Retirement was the last thing on his mind.

'It's been more than two years since we sat on that coach to Middlesbrough. You said I could have the club in two years.'

'I know, Mal, but did you ever think it'd be like this?'

Malcolm was thoughtful. In fact he had thought it would be absolutely like this, but even he knew it would sound odd if he confessed as much.

Joe could see the seed of ambition eating away at his assistant. The last thing he wanted now was to drive a wedge between them. 'Mal, look, if we win the League Cup and we win in Europe, I'll take a back seat.'

'A back seat?' Malcolm wasn't quite sure what he was being offered.

'You'll be the manager. I'll be around, and we'll talk just like we're talking now.'

'I'll be the manager, then?' Malcolm wanted Joe to say it out loud so there was no mistake.

'You'll be the manager if we win both the trophies.' They both knew no English club had ever won a domestic and a European trophy in the same year, but whereas Joe took satisfaction in knowing it was virtually impossible Malcolm just accepted it as another challenge.

'Right, we'll start by stuffing United.'

'Mal, please, let's not underestimate them. Matt's hurting. They'll really go for us. We need to tell the players that United will come back at us.'

'Whatever they've got it's not enough.'

The match proved both of them to have been right. United were vastly improved from the spineless collection of individuals that had submitted so tamely in the middle of November. It was only three weeks later, but United seemed to be a different team after Bell put City ahead with only twelve minutes gone. In the mudbath of a filthy winter's night in Moss Side, United, with Charlton and Best causing constant problems for the City defence, gradually won the battle of the midfield and midway through the second half gained a deserved equaliser. Tony Book failed to clear a centre from Kidd properly and accidentally rolled the ball invitingly into the path of Bobby Charlton, the outstanding player on the field, who hammered it past Corrigan.

'Now we'll see what they're made of,' said Joe to Malcolm.

'I know what they're made of,' Malcolm replied. 'I'd like to see a bit more of it.'

It was Francis Lee who came to City's rescue two minutes from the end. He took a chipped pass from Oakes in his stride and turned to shoot as Ian Ure slid in with a tackle. Lee went down and the referee, Jack Taylor, walking slowly into the penalty area, having been many yards away from the place where the incident had occurred, pointed to the spot as the unfortunate Ure openly demonstrated his frustration.

Joe looked at Malcolm and smiled. Football was like this. How many times had they each known a similar situation in which fortune had frowned rather than smiled? Was Taylor unduly influenced by the screams for a penalty from the home supporters? Probably not. Would the penalty have been given at Old Trafford? Probably not. That was football. You shrugged your shoulders and got on with it. Lee placed the ball on the spot and turned away. There was no Tony Coleman to worry about now. His shot was low to Stepney's right. The goalkeeper didn't dive so much as scramble across the line, but the ball found the back of the net and City had a vital advantage to take to Old Trafford in the second leg.

George Best remained incensed when the final whistle blew a couple of minutes later. Ian Ure was still vehemently protesting his innocence and Wilf McGuinness, the United coach, was marching towards Taylor demanding an explanation for the contentious penalty. George walked across to the referee and, rather in the manner of an irritating seven-year-old child, knocked the ball from Taylor's hands. In due course he would be heavily fined and banned from the game for this act of outrageous effrontery.

The return leg at Old Trafford two weeks later attracted a full house of sixty-four thousand people. Colin Bell wasn't fit, so Joe and Malcolm had no hesitation in selecting David Connor and asking him to do his usual job on Bobby Charlton, United's perceived danger man, that he had done so successfully in the past on Alan Ball, Ian Gibson and others. The City players knew they had been slightly fortunate to have won at Maine Road and were well aware that the crowd would make Old Trafford a ground of unremitting hostility. They were just 90 minutes from Wembley, but the tension of the semi-final had finally got to the players for the first time since Fenerbahçe over a year before. Malcolm took one look at the drawn faces of his players and told them they were going outside.

'There's half an hour till kick-off, Mal.'

'Outside, everyone, now.'

'What's up, Mal?'

'You'll find out.'

It was as much a surprise to the crowd as it was to the players when they emerged from the tunnel and walked across the pitch towards their own fans, who were mostly standing up on the open terrace to their right. They were received ecstatically there while the boos from the Stretford End resounded in their ears.

'Right,' said Malcolm, who was holding a large Montecristo cigar in one hand with which he gestured towards the Stretford End. 'Now we're going there.'

'Mal, that's the Stretford End,' warned Alan Oakes, who had been playing in local derby matches for ten years.

'That's why we're going there.' And with that he strode off towards the ranks of the enemy with his players following behind. By the time they got there the booing had started to fade. There was only so much booing you could do at a dozen men in blazers, ties and smartly tailored slacks walking slowly across a patch of grass. The City players began to see the Stretford End not so much as a nest of dangerous vipers but as a football terrace, no worse than any other. After all, this was where they had started in their final run-in to the Championship nearly two years ago. Malcolm stood in front of the Stretford End and waved at them. The Stretford End booed back heartily, but it was entirely different in tone from the earlier hostility: this was more of a pantomime catcall. The players' heartbeats began to slow down. Then Malcolm slowly raised the palm of his left hand and held it up in front of the crowd, the five fingers clearly indicating they would score five goals. He clamped his cigar in his mouth and touched his right thumb with the tip of his right forefinger to create a circle. The crowd's booing intensified, but the players could hear shouts of laughter and the derision that the gesture produced was mostly good-natured.

'Fuck me, Mal,' said Summerbee as they walked back towards the dressing-room. 'Five? Five–nil? Can't you make it four next time? Five puts a lot of pressure on us.'

THE WORST OF FRIENDS

City came out and demonstrated few of the nerves that had looked likely to paralyse them earlier. After seventeen minutes Bowyer put them a goal up, stretching the aggregate lead to 3–1, but just as in the first leg City's opening goal seemed to elicit an immediate response from United, who equalised only seven minutes later. It was the very best of English cup ties, with total commitment from all 22 players and a passionate partisan crowd to urge them onwards. Despite Connor's magnificent effort to stifle Charlton there was still plenty of room on the pitch for George Best to do some damage, which he had failed to do in derby matches for some time.

It was Best's powerful shot in the middle of the second half that Corrigan couldn't hold. The ball squirmed out of his grasp for only a second, but that was long enough for the predatory Law, who had looked a shadow of the dangerous player he had been for over ten years, to seize on the mistake and put United ahead on the night. Now City were under the most intense pressure. For the first time in the tie, United felt that the momentum of the match was with them and that if anyone was going to score before the game went into extra time, it would be the home side.

Eight minutes from time, Morgan obstructed Bowyer, giving City a clear indirect free kick in the centre of the goal just outside the penalty area.

'What's Francis going to do?' asked Joe of Malcolm, aware that his assistant spent a considerable amount of time on the training ground practising with Lee for just such an eventuality.

'I don't know,' acknowledged Malcolm honestly. 'He'll probably hit it straight at Stepney.'

'It's indirect, Mal.'

Before Malcolm could explain that he was probably looking for a deflection off the wall, Lee ran up and, to everyone's surprise, fired the ball through the wall, forcing Stepney to make a hurried save. The ball struck the United goalkeeper on the wrist and rebounded to the other side of his goal, where Mike Summerbee, who was the only player following the ball, had nobody within six feet of him as he calmly stroked the loose ball into the roof of the net. It was over. City had dealt United another crushing blow. There was no doubt now as to which was the top team in Manchester. Malcolm gave a disconsolate Paddy Crerand an extra-large smile as he came off looking devastated.

As an ecstatic Malcolm ripped off his clothes and leapt into the bath with his players, who were on the way to Wembley for a second Cup final in successive seasons, Joe was upstairs in the directors' lounge with Matt.

'Well done, Joe, the better team won.'

'It was a hell of a battle, Matt.'

'I hope you win at Wembley. It's good for Manchester to keep winning things.'

'You'll be back. You've had tough periods before. Like after Munich.'

'Munich was different and, besides, I was younger. I haven't got the fire in the belly like I used to. And I have to give young Wilf his head.'

'How's that working out?'

'You saw what happened tonight. And you know where we are in the League. I wish I had Malcolm.'

'Somehow I don't think you would. He'd want complete control.'

'Well, are you going to give it to him?'

'Things are just great as they are, Matt. You can see the spirit in the side. Malcolm's building a great reputation for himself, but he needs me by his side. He upsets referees, he upsets the FA, he upsets the directors. The directors know how important I am in controlling Malcolm. If I wasn't around, God knows where he'd take the club.'

'You think he'll be happy being your number two for the rest of his life?'

'It won't be the rest of his life. I'll give it up. I've told him he can have the club when I go.'

'When are you going to go?'

'Blimey, Matt, you sound like Malcolm. I'm not going till we've won this one, and I think we have a real shot at Europe this year, but what I really want to do is to win the League again.'

'That's going to take a few years.'

'Maybe, but you're five years older than me, so if I go at your age having done all that, I'll be happy.'

'But will Malcolm?'

'As long as we're winning he'll be as happy as a sandboy. It's different when you start losing.'

'That's for sure,' said Matt Busby with a sigh, and reached for the bottle to top up both their drinks.

Joe was right that Malcolm wasn't going to upset the apple-cart as long as the team was winning, but it bothered the manager that their League form had fallen off so dramatically since the title win at Newcastle. The FA Cup had saved last season just as this season was being saved by the League Cup and the European Cup-Winners' Cup. It wasn't the side he wanted to build. He thought that with the blend of youth and experience at his disposal they should be challenging for honours every year, like Leeds.

He hated Leeds, hated their negative outlook, hated the way they turned every contest into a battle when they had the skill to win without any of the rough stuff Don Revie seemed to think was mandatory. Still, he had to admire the way Leeds performed, and he knew from speaking to other managers that nobody ever looked forward to a match against Leeds United. As far as City, United, Liverpool and Everton were concerned, each of those teams could beat anybody on their day, but if you caught them in one of their less interested moments they wouldn't give you much trouble. Leeds were never like that, and Malcolm wondered why he couldn't establish that kind of consistency with his team.

They were subject to losing streaks, when every player just seemed to switch off. One of the defeats was a particularly unfortunate 5–1 reverse at home to West Ham in front of the *Match of the Day* cameras. Malcolm had really let the players know the full extent of his displeasure at that one. One goal in particular infuriated him. Young Joe Corrigan aimlessly booted the ball out at the edge of his area, turned his back on play and trotted back to the goalmouth, only to find that Ronnie Boyce had volleyed it back from the centre circle over his shoulder and into the net. The young goalkeeper looked like a fool, which was the way Malcolm felt when he realised it would be Saturday night's talking point up and down the country. At the end of the game he grabbed the luckless Corrigan and forced him against the wall of the dressing-room. 'What the fuck were you thinking about?'

'I wasn't thinking about anything.'

'Christ, you can say that again. Don't ever, *ever* turn your back on play like that again! Understand?'

All Corrigan could do was nod as Malcolm gradually released his grip on the goalkeeper's green jersey.

'It's not his fault, Mal,' said Francis Lee with his usual bluntness. 'We were all shit out there.'

On the Monday after training, Walter Griffiths's secretary Dorothy knocked on Joe Mercer's office door clutching a sheaf of letters.

'Hello, love, what have you got there? Is that all my fan mail?' Dorothy blushed, and Joe knew it wasn't fan mail.

'Mr Griffiths said you ought to see these.' Joe picked up the first letter. *Dear Joe Mercer,* it began. *I've been watching City for over 50 years and never have I seen a worse team that the one I watched on Saturday . . .* Joe put it down and picked up the next one. *You're fucking useless, you and that fucking loudmouth you call a coach . . .* The rest of the letters were in a similar vein. He filed them neatly in the wastepaper basket. He'd been through all this at Sheffield United and Aston Villa. Apart from knowing for sure that these people were idiots and not worth responding to, he remembered quite clearly how his health had suffered when he had taken such comments to heart. Never again.

What made the letters even more ridiculous was that even in the middle of this latest poor run of League results the team had come together for some of its best performances. The cups seemed to inspire the players in a way that the bread-and-butter League games never could. For Joe and Malcolm it was irritating that City no longer offered a challenge in the League, but there was no gainsaying the fact that they all thrilled to the danger of a knockout competition. The quarter-final tie against Academica Coimbra proved the point.

Theoretically Coimbra were a university side, but the cynical players who kicked and spat their way through two legs and extra time bore little resemblance to the enthusiastic and polite young men Malcolm had coached at Cambridge University. A scoreless draw in Portugal was regarded as a good result, but City were unable to break down the stubborn Portuguese rearguard at Maine Road and their cause was not helped by a referee who seemed to regard kicking, shirt-pulling and spitting as acceptable tactics. In the last minute of extra time, with the unenviable prospect of the semi-final place being decided by the toss of a coin, Tony Towers, the 17-year-old substitute, scored with a Roy-of-the-Rovers shot from outside the penalty area. The entire ground, including the directors' box, rose to acclaim a thoroughly merited victory.

Joe and Malcolm embraced. They were not in the habit of losing semi-finals, and they could almost taste the European victory that awaited them at the end of April. Whatever the tensions that continued to exist between the two men, they both knew that success has many fathers but failure has none. So for the moment they revelled in their triumphs – for between the two legs of the Coimbra tie, they had won the League Cup at Wembley.

THE WORST OF FRIENDS

For all the meticulous planning that Joe and Malcolm had believed in since their traumatic experience in Istanbul, they had been unable to control either the weather or the state of the pitch at Wembley. They were supposed to spend the Wednesday night after the away leg against Coimbra in the comfort of a monastic retreat high in the hills that had once been a palace of the kings of Portugal, 16 miles from the Municipal Stadium, before flying back to London the next morning in time to prepare for the League Cup final against West Bromwich on the Saturday afternoon. In the event, bad weather in London caused the flight to be delayed and then fog closed in around Heathrow. The flight was diverted to Birmingham, where a coach had to be hastily hired to take the team to London. When they finally got into bed at 3 a.m. on Friday morning, it was just 36 hours till kick-off in one of the showpiece events of the English season.

Joe was even more frustrated when he saw the state of the Wembley pitch. He demanded to talk to the groundsman. 'It's a fucking cabbage patch out there!'

'It's not my fault,' protested the distressed groundsman.

'How did you let it get like that?'

'It's the BBC!'

'Eh?'

'The BBC arranged to televise the *Horse of the Year Show* here.'

'You let horses on this pitch the week before a cup final?'

'I'm just the groundsman, Mr Mercer.'

'It's a bloody disgrace. How can you expect good footballers to pass the ball to each other over a ground like that?'

'I agree with you, but you'll have to talk to the BBC.'

'No point. The game's on ITV.'

It was Joe's second awkward conversation of the day. Neil Young had just complained that Malcolm had told him he was dropped for the final. 'I won the Cup for you here, last year, Boss.'

'I know, but your form's suffered and we can't take the chance.'

'I did OK on Wednesday, didn't I?' Joe didn't respond, and Young knew perfectly well he hadn't been playing well for some time. 'I can't even watch it on telly. I'm hopeless at watching.'

'When's your wife due to give birth?'

'Any day.'

'Any day, and you're sitting here moping? Go back to Manchester and watch your baby being born.'

'They don't let you in the room.' Young walked miserably away from the scene of his greatest triumph as Malcolm joined Joe.

'Look at it, Mal. It's a cabbage patch!'

'We can play on it, Boss, don't worry. We've had a five-a-side. I think that's all they need. I fancy taking them to the pictures tonight.'

'What's on?'

'D'you like Paul Newman?'

'*Cool Hand Luke*? Course.'

'*Butch Cassidy and the The Sundance Kid*'s on at the Odeon.'

'I've seen it,' said Joe, rather disappointed. 'Me and Norah went to it in Manchester last week.'

'I'm thinking about the players, Joe,' said Malcolm heavily, trying not to let his impatience show.

'Sure. That's fine. They'll enjoy it. Have you talked to George and Tommy about how to deal with Astle in the air?'

'Till I'm blue in the face.'

'Good job we're wearing red-and-black stripes then, isn't it?'

On match day, within five minutes of kick-off Ray Wilson had sent over a cross, which Jeff Astle reached first with his head despite the attentions of George Heslop and Joe Corrigan, and City were a goal down.

'Bloody good plan this two centre-halves thing is!' Joe said bitterly to the rest of the bench.

'It was on the bloody six-yard line! He should have swallowed that,' muttered Malcolm to himself, his mind racing ahead to the half-time team talk. He could see Heslop, Booth and Pardoe gesticulating furiously at the goalkeeper. Corrigan probably wouldn't need reminding of his error. At least West Brom had scored early – there was plenty of time for City to come back.

It was the day that Francis Lee showed how great a player he had become in the two and a half years since he had signed from Bolton. At the end of the 90 minutes City had drawn level but had been unable to find the winner their overall play had deserved. Malcolm and Joe faced the players, who weren't anticipating another strength-sapping 30 minutes on the Wembley mud heap with much pleasure. Summerbee, who had helped to set up Doyle's equalising goal, had already gone off with what turned out to be a hairline fracture of the leg. Joe started as he always did. 'You have to forget about Wednesday, forget about the last 90 minutes. You've got 30 minutes to get another winner's medal at Wembley. How many times will you get that chance in your careers?'

Malcolm waited till Joe's ringing words had made an impact, then said quietly but urgently, 'Francis, drop back behind the front man. I just want to leave Ian Bowyer up front so the midfield can come and support him.'

Lee was in no mood to listen to what he thought was defeatist talk. 'Never mind all that shit,' he shouted at the rest of his teammates. 'Just give me the fucking ball. I'll win this match for you. Give it to me.'

Malcolm looked at Joe and nodded. 'You do that, Francis.'

Francis Lee was as good as his word. Time and again, he gathered the ball and set off towards the West Bromwich goal. The defenders, particularly Doug Fraser, made frantic efforts to stop him by any means, but that day he was irresistible. In extra time it was his chip that was headed on by Bell at the near post for Pardoe to turn in for the winning goal. Once again Tony Book climbed the long flight of steps to the Royal Box and lifted the trophy, showing it to the adoring fans who, five years before, had been warned their club might have to merge with Manchester United. It wasn't exactly a chore, picking up silverware like this, but Joe knew only too well that the gravy train would have to stop somewhere, sometime, and they would all have to get off. Meanwhile, the new trophy demanded its own civic reception at the Town Hall in front of the adoring, if freezing, City fans. For all Joe's realism, it seemed to the ecstatic fans that the triumphal procession would never come to an end. Malcolm was of their opinion and told the press that Wembley now felt like their home ground.

Certainly, FC Schalke's attempts to halt them in the semi-final of the European Cup-Winners' Cup were convincingly repulsed. A 1–0 defeat in Germany was soon wiped out by a goal from Neil Young, who had finally recovered the form that had been so elusive all season. Then the floodgates opened, and a consolation goal for the Germans in the last minute did little to lessen the indignity of a 5–1 thrashing. City were going to another final. This time it was to be in Vienna, and for Malcolm Allison it was to be the fitting culmination to a football career that had started 20 years before, when he had been stationed there as part of his national service.

Malcolm opened up to Joe one day after training, as the League programme drew to an irrelevant close. They had beaten Leeds 3–1 at home, always a satisfying experience, although Revie's side also had their eye on a final – in their case against Chelsea at Wembley. Joe and Malcolm both faced the prospect of the Cup-Winners' Cup final in

Vienna with a fair degree of relaxation. After the disaster at Fenerbahçe in 1968 they had succeeded in proving to the rest of the football world that they were capable of competing successfully in Europe. With one trophy already secured it was hardly going to be a bad season even if they lost, and they had no intention of doing that.

Malcolm lit a cigar and put his feet on Joe's desk. 'I played for the Army at the Prater Stadium, you know. Then I saw Austria play Italy there. Ocwirk was playing for them.'

Joe's head jerked up. He knew all about the great ball-playing Austrian centre-half. 'When?'

'Nineteen-fifty. I was stationed in Klagenfurt and then in Vienna. There was a girl called Heidi . . .'

'Like the girl in the story?'

'What story?'

'Children's story.'

'Yeah – she was 17, blonde, beautiful.'

Joe shook his head. 'Sounds like a different story to me.'

'She took me home. You're probably right. What happened was no children's story, I can tell you!'

'I hope her Dad was very welcoming.'

'He was a 17-st. butcher. I had to creep past his bedroom door in the morning. Thank God he snored.'

'The football, Mal, tell me about the football.'

'Whenever I could, I used to go along and watch them training at the Prater. Ocwirk was one of them – what a magnificent player. So much time.'

'That's it,' agreed Joe. 'You can always tell the great players because they seem to have the time to do things – that's why they look so much quicker than anyone else.'

'They trained with the ball. Soon as I came back to Charlton, I never saw the ball.'

'It wasn't just Charlton.'

'Why are we so far behind the rest of the world in this country?'

'It's the sea.'

Now it was Malcolm's turn to look surprised.

'Getting across the English Channel is like flying to America. It's miles away. It's not part of us. That's why all this talk about the Common Market is so stupid. The British don't want to be part of Europe. Never have,' said Joe.

'Puskás and Hidegkuti were part of Europe. Beckenbauer and Cruyff are part of Europe.'

'Who?'

'Cruyff. Johann Cruyff. Plays for Ajax in Amsterdam. Going to be a big star.'

'Not if he's from Holland. Holland have never been much of a football country.'

'That might change, Joe.'

'Well, we're playing the Poles, so perhaps we should talk about them instead.'

'If Summerbee's not fit we should play Towers in midfield and bolster the defence with Heslop and Booth, like we did at Wembley.'

And they were off. These were the good times. This was like when they had first started out together nearly five years before. Joe couldn't help recalling that dreadful friendly against Dundee, the sinking feeling that he had made a terrible mistake coming to this graveyard of a ground in Manchester, where he doubted anyone would even turn up to watch his team of no talent. Now look at him. Look at *them*. He turned to his assistant and said slowly but sincerely, 'These have been the best five years of my life, Mal. I wouldn't have traded them for anything.'

Malcolm just nodded. He knew that dreams of European glory had been a long way from their minds back in 1965, but they had set out on the journey with a common purpose. Now, with the imminent arrival of their first European final, they seemed to be starting a new journey. There were moments throughout the season when they had disagreed over something or other, but in the end they were both football men and Joe knew that what was good for City was good for both of them. The problem was that Malcolm was no longer quite so sure that was still true.

1969-70: MANAGER JOE MERCER

1	AUG	9	(H)	SHEFFIELD W	W	4–1	YOUNG 2, BELL, LEE	32,583
2		12	(A)	LIVERPOOL	L	2–3	BOWYER, OPP OWN-GOAL	51,959
3		16	(A)	NEWCASTLE U	L	0–1		46,850
4		20	(H)	LIVERPOOL	L	0–2		47,888
5		23	(H)	EVERTON	D	1–1	BOWYER	43,676
6		27	(A)	SUNDERLAND	W	4–0	BOWYER 2, OAKES, BELL	21,515
7		30	(A)	BURNLEY	D	1–1	BOWYER	26,341
8	SEP	6	(H)	CHELSEA	D	0–0		35,995
9		13	(A)	TOTTENHAM H	W	3–0	OAKES, BELL, BOWYER	41,644
10		20	(H)	COVENTRY C	W	3–1	BELL 2, LEE	34,320
11		27	(A)	STOKE C	L	0–2		29,739
12	OCT	4	(H)	WEST BROM A	W	2–1	BELL, YOUNG	34,329
13		8	(H)	NEWCASTLE U	W	2–1	YOUNG, LEE	32,172
14		11	(A)	NOTTINGHAM F	D	2–2	LEE 2	30,037
15		18	(A)	DERBY C	W	1–0	LEE	40,788
16		25	(H)	WOLVES	W	1–0	DOYLE	34,425
17	NOV	1	(A)	IPSWICH T	D	1–1	LEE	24,124
18		8	(H)	SOUTHAMPTON	W	1–0	BELL	27,069
19		15	(H)	MANCHESTER U	W	4–0	BELL 2, YOUNG, OPP OWN-GOAL	63,013
20		22	(A)	ARSENAL	D	1–1	BOWYER	42,939
21		29	(H)	LEEDS U	L	1–2	LEE	44,590
22	DEC	6	(A)	WEST HAM U	W	4–0	BOWYER 2, LEE, DOYLE	27,440
23		13	(H)	TOTTENHAM H	D	1–1	OAKES	29,216
24		20	(A)	CHELSEA	L	1–3	SUMMERBEE	34,791
25		23	(A)	EVERTON	L	0–1		51,864
26	JAN	6	(H)	BURNLEY	D	1–1	LEE	22,074
27		10	(A)	COVENTRY C	L	0–3		29,386
28		17	(H)	STOKE C	L	0–1		31,565
29		31	(A)	WEST BROM A	L	0–3		30,722
30	FEB	7	(H)	NOTTINGHAM F	D	1–1	DOYLE	27,077
31		18	(A)	ARSENAL	D	1–1	BOWYER	25,504
32		21	(A)	WOLVES	W	3–1	SUMMERBEE 2, BELL	30,373
33		28	(H)	IPSWICH T	W	1–0	LEE	29,376
34	MAR	11	(H)	CRYSTAL P	L	0–1		25,381
35		21	(H)	WEST HAM U	L	1–5	LEE	28,353
36		27	(H)	DERBY C	L	0–1		42,316
37		28	(A)	MANCHESTER U	W	2–1	LEE, DOYLE	60,286
38	APR	4	(H)	SUNDERLAND	L	0–1		22,006
39		6	(A)	CRYSTAL P	L	0–1		27,704
40		8	(A)	SOUTHAMPTON	D	0–0		24,384
41		18	(A)	LEEDS U	W	3–1	TOWERS, BELL, YOUNG	22,932
42		22	(A)	SHEFFIELD W	W	2–1	BOWYER 2	45,258

FINAL LEAGUE POSITION: 10TH IN DIVISION ONE

FA CUP

3	JAN	3	(A)	HULL C	W	1–0
4		24	(A)	MANCHESTER U	L	0–3

LEAGUE CUP

2	SEP	3	(A)	SOUTHPORT	W	3–0
3		24	(H)	LIVERPOOL	W	3–2
4	OCT	15	(H)	EVERTON	W	2–0
5		29	(H)	QUEEN'S PARK R	W	3–0
SF	DEC	3	(H)	MANCHESTER U	W	2–1
		17	(A)	MANCHESTER U	D	2–2
F	MAR	7	(N)	WEST BROM A	W	2–1

FOURTEEN

Vienna had been home to some remarkable sights down the centuries. The capital of the Habsburg Empire, the city became the cultural centre of *Mitteleuropa* after the Congress of Vienna settled the Napoleonic Wars. In most people's minds Vienna is the home of the waltzes and polkas composed by the Strauss family, and the place where Mozart, Beethoven and Schubert composed their greatest music. To others it might conjure up Harry Lime's journey through the sewers of a city struggling to recover from the ravages of war, operated by four occupying powers and a thriving black market. Until 29 April 1970, however, Vienna had never witnessed Francis Lee dancing on a piano in his underpants.

Bolton's answer to the elegance of *fin-de-siècle* orchestral music was occasioned by Manchester City's 2–1 victory over Gornik Zabrze in the final of the European Cup-Winners' Cup competition. The only disappointed member of the squad was Mike Summerbee, who had come off injured during the last League match at Hillsborough. He was given a fitness test under the supervision of Sidney Rose, Joe and Malcolm. The managers turned to the doctor for his final verdict, which they knew in their hearts was going to be negative.

'I'm sorry, Mike,' said the doctor in his best bedside manner. 'You're not fit to play.'

'I can do it, Mr Rose,' protested Summerbee. 'I can run it off.'

'Mike, we can all see you're carrying an injury,' said Joe. 'We all know how much you want to play, but Sidney's right.'

'If we can see it, Gornik can see it,' said Malcolm briefly. His mind was already dealing with the practical necessities occasioned by the last-minute change to the line-up. Summerbee was out, Heslop was slotted in alongside Booth, Young and Lee up front; Towers would have to provide the width Summerbee's absence would cause.

THE WORST OF FRIENDS

Late in the afternoon on the day before the final, the squad lined up for a final run through the Vienna Woods.

'Remember this, do you Mal?' asked Francis Lee, who had heard all the grossly exaggerated stories of Malcolm's national service in Austria.

'Yeah, I screwed a blonde bird just through there.'

'Bert Trautmann's missus, was it?' someone chortled.

'Bert's German; this is Austria,' said Malcolm dismissively. Honestly, players today: they knew fuck all. Malcolm lagged, as he always did, towards the back. The group of runners in front of him put on a bit of a spurt and opened up a 20-yard gap between themselves and their trailing coach.

Lee nudged Doyle as they neared a thick clump of trees. 'Right, that's where we go.'

Malcolm's mind was on the match rather than the memory of the beautiful Heidi, and when he looked up he was entirely alone in the *Wienerwald*. 'Oi!' he yelled, and stopped to listen, but there was no answering call and no telltale sound of running feet on soft earth. He looked around. He had absolutely no idea where he was. Bastards, he thought and sprinted for 300 yards through the dense thicket of trees until he emerged in a clearing. 'Oi!' he yelled again, but all he heard was the sound of birdsong and the distant hum of traffic in the suburbs of Vienna. 'Shit!' he swore ferociously. If I find out this was planned, I'll have them all on a charge, he thought, and then his mind wandered back to the time in 1950 when he was supposed to have been guarding a Liverpudlian soldier called McCarthy, who had wandered into the Russian sector under the influence of alcohol and killed one of their soldiers. The task was boring and their stomachs were empty, so Malcolm and his prisoner went out for a walk, stole a chicken, saw off two Yugoslav border guards and got the chicken safely back to the cookhouse. It was still roasting on a makeshift spit when a colonel in the Yugoslav army arrived with a full military escort to reclaim the chicken at gunpoint.

His reverie was broken by the sound of evening thunder and the feel of rain on his face. He swore again briefly. He tried to lengthen his stride, but at forty-two and with only one lung distance running was no longer his strong point. Plus he had no sense of direction and no idea where the hotel was. He ran nine miles instead of the two or three the players covered, and it took him nearly three hours to get back to the hotel. For the players who were in the lobby when they saw their bedraggled coach staggering in, it was, after the memory of Tony Book holding up the League Cup and Mike Summerbee's goal in the semi-final, the sight of the season. Malcolm pointed at the smirking faces of his players, who could barely conceal their joy. 'I'll have you – and you and you.' Then he burst into laughter himself. He knew what an absurd figure he must cut, but at least it was helping the players to conquer whatever nerves might have been afflicting them on the night before their first European final.

On match day, Joe looked out of the window as the coach drove them from their hotel to the Prater Stadium, which was underneath the great wheel where Harry Lime had met Holly Martins. 'Christ, Mal, look at it. It's coming down like stair rods.'

'Any idea how many of our fans have travelled?'

'Walter thinks about 4,000.'

'Four thousand? Gornik won't send many, and the place holds 80,000.'

'The locals'll come.'

'Not tonight. Not in this. Besides, it's on the telly here. The place is going to be empty.'

'Well, since we're not on telly at home, if we lose nobody'll know about it.' It was a sore point with the City fans and management that the 2–2 draw between Leeds and Chelsea at Wembley the previous Saturday had caused a replay of the FA Cup final at Old Trafford on the same night that City were attempting to become the first English club ever to win a European and a domestic trophy in the same season. The BBC had decided to cover the Leeds v. Chelsea rematch live and feed score flashes from City's game through to the domestic audience.

'There's only about 10,000 out there,' said Joe in the dressing-room. 'I know we're a team that's used to the big stage and full grounds, but this is your next Wembley even if there's only half a dozen blokes with umbrellas out there. It's not a training session; it's not a friendly. Ignore the rain; ignore the lack of atmosphere. Play like you know you can play.'

'This lot shouldn't even be here,' said Malcolm bluntly. 'They only got past Roma on the toss of a coin – you beat Schalke 5–1. They're frightened of you. They're frightened because they know you'll attack them and they won't be able to cope. So go out there and attack them. Take the play to them. Take them on when you've got the ball, harass them, challenge them, pressurise them when they've got it. And forget about the fucking rain. Me and the Boss are sitting in the rain too.'

THE WORST OF FRIENDS

The rain continued to fall in torrents. Malcolm and Joe draped towels over their heads in a vain attempt to stem the tide. They felt their coats absorb the rain for the first ten minutes before it started to run in rivulets down the backs of their necks and into the waistbands of their underwear. By this time Neil Young had gathered the rebound from a Francis Lee shot that had hit the post and fired City ahead. At just about the time their shoes began to fill with water, the Gornik goalkeeper Kostka body-checked Young as he was going round him, and Lee scored from the penalty as the soaking-wet ball slipped between the despairing goalkeeper's legs. A consolation second-half goal for the Poles couldn't halt the march of Joe and Malcolm's team towards their European destiny.

Yet it irritated them that nobody back home had seen it happen and they couldn't help contrasting it with the night two years before, when the country had come to a halt to salute Manchester United's win over Benfica in the European Cup. Nevertheless, City had conquered Europe at their second attempt, and when the Mercers eventually returned to their bedroom, Joe carefully placed the European Cup-Winners' Cup on the dresser next to Norah's cosmetics, so it would be the first thing he would see when he woke up. He got into bed and stared at the trophy for the longest time. Norah was already asleep as Joe turned to her. 'Norah,' he said softly. 'Norah.' With a mighty effort his wife opened one eye. 'Are you glad I gave up football and went back to the grocery business?'

Norah smiled. 'I'm glad you're well and happy, Joe.'

'Malcolm's right, love. There's no limit to what we can achieve together.'

'If you stay together,' yawned Norah and turned over.

'Course we'll stay together,' scoffed Joe. 'What kind of success could Malcolm find on his own? Don Revie's not going to walk away from Leeds, and Shankly's not leaving Liverpool. The only big club that might want him is United, and somehow I don't think Malcolm's going there. He's upset too many people at Old Trafford. Besides, who can get between us?' But Norah was fast asleep.

In the early morning, Malcolm looked from his hotel balcony with great satisfaction at the sight of the city below. In the bedroom Beth was packing as Jim Lawton of the *Express* came in to talk to Malcolm for his weekly column. 'How do you feel, Malcolm?' he asked.

'I feel like Napoleon.'

'Is that all?'

'Maybe bigger than Napoleon. I mean, he lost at Waterloo, and he never won the European Cup-Winners' Cup, either.'

'Is this the pinnacle of success for you?'

'The pinnacle? No way. Not for this team and not for me. I'm going to win the lot before I'm through. On my own.'

Joe had supposed that the only people who could get between Malcolm and himself were the directors of another club that might come looking to poach his assistant, and he was confident he could see off any such approach. What he was not prepared for was for Malcolm to become a star of the 1970 World Cup, as Joe had been in 1966. After the commercial television franchises had been reallocated by the government in 1968, ITV had entirely reconstituted its sport department, and ITV Sport was now a serious competitor for the BBC's audiences for the World Cup, which started a few weeks after the triumph in Vienna.

ITV Sport was under the inspired leadership of its executive producer, a former *Daily Mirror* journalist with an instinctive popular touch called John Bromley, whose great innovation was the World Cup panel. Having signed football men with diverse views, such as Paddy Crerand, Derek Dougan and Bob McNab – the last the Arsenal left-back who had returned to England when Ramsey had cut his original squad of 28 down to the permitted 22 – Bromley picked up the phone to call a fellow client of the Bagenal Harvey Agency, to which all the movers and shakers in the world of sport belonged. Malcolm had never been shy of publicity, and whatever plans he had made for the summer were quickly shelved. Watching the World Cup, particularly the progress of Colin Bell and Francis Lee – the two stars he had 'made' – while becoming a national television star suited him perfectly.

He knew that bold opinions forcefully expressed weren't all that was required – the panel wanted outrageous opinions and an attack on Alf Ramsey, whom he had never really respected. Alf was of the old school: safety first, wingless wonders – the Stanley Baldwin of English football. It wasn't hard for Malcolm to work himself up into a fine fury, particularly after a good lunch at the Hendon Hall Hotel – ironically where Alf and the England team had stayed during the 1966 campaign.

'How shall we play this, Mal?' asked Dougan over lunch before the Mexico v. USSR match that would open the tournament.

Malcolm was busy summoning the waiter. 'We'll have another bottle of Dom Pérignon and the wild strawberries.'

The waiter acknowledged the order as the Doog looked at the price of the champagne and blanched. 'Mal, we're only being paid £500. I have to take some of it back to Jutta Maria and the kids.'

'You're not paying for it, Doog.'

'Well, that's very generous of you, Mal . . .'

'And I'm not paying for it either, so just relax, will you?'

'They're not going to be pleased at ITV.'

'Trust me, they're going to be thrilled at ITV. Fancy a cigar?'

'Well, sure, but shouldn't we save some of this champagne for when we get back tonight?'

'What's the matter, Doog? Worried you'll start slurring your words?'

'I can drink you under the fooking table, Malcolm Allison.'

Malcolm grinned. It was exactly the sort of challenge he enjoyed. 'Waiter!'

The opening match, a disappointing sterile nil–nil draw between the Soviet Union and the Mexican hosts, was just a prelude to the discussion the rest of the country had been deeply engaged in for weeks. Would England retain the trophy won so famously in 1966?

'Not with this team playing the way they do,' said Malcolm decisively.

'Not even with Francis Lee in the side?' asked Crerand mischievously.

'Francis Lee is a great player,' snapped back Malcolm instantly, 'but if he's going to play without service from the wings he's going to spend his time running up blind alleys. What Alf needs is a complete rethink of his tactics.' It was a stance Malcolm would reiterate throughout the whole of the World Cup. He was thrilled to see Lee and Bell as major players on a world stage. He had been right about them from the start. He always knew he was right. He should be manager of the England team. He knew how to harness their talent in an attacking manner. He'd love to have those players under his control: Moore, Hurst and Peters, Lee and Bell, Banksy and Bally . . . And then there were all those youngsters he'd been keeping an eye on who were coming through: Alan Hudson and Rodney Marsh, probably even Stan Bowles one day, for he'd never doubted the boy's original talent . . . It was an engrossing fantasy.

Back in Manchester, Joe and Norah sat in the living room of their semi-detached house in St Werbergh's Road and watched Malcolm's television debut with admiration, if not, on Joe's part, a little envy. At the conclusion of the programme Joe turned off the television and followed Norah into the kitchen, where they began the familiar ritual of the washing-up.

'He wears nice ties,' observed Norah.

'I'm glad Alf's in Mexico and couldn't hear what he said.' Joe had his own reservations about Alf, but he understood the pressures the England manager was under and was inclined to be much more sympathetic to him than Malcolm ever had been.

'Does Alf like Malcolm?'

'They're polite to each other. Mal wants Colin, Mike and Francis to play for England. He's not going to ruin their chances.'

'Does Alf see Malcolm as a rival?' asked Norah naively as she took the clean soapy dishes out of the dull-yellow plastic washing-up bowl and stacked them carefully in the plastic tray to drain. Joe laughed at what seemed at first the absurdity of the question as he collected the tea towel from the rail and slowly began to dry the dinner plates. Then he thought a little longer before answering.

'The FA find Alf hard work, never mind Malcolm.'

'Why is he being so horrible to Alf?'

'He's always said this sort of stuff to me. But it's one thing to say things in the privacy of the office. It's another to go on television and say it. Maybe you're right. Maybe he does want Alf's job, but I still don't think the FA will ever go for someone like him or Cloughie. Alf has his faults, but he knows when to keep his mouth shut.'

'I think Malcolm's very ambitious, Joe. Maybe it would be better for you if he went to England. He'd be off your back then.'

'I'd never find anyone else like Malcolm, love. We've won all those trophies together. As long as I'm the manager and I have the final say, I don't really mind what he does. I'll always be around to smooth things out. Did I tell you what happened when the police stopped me on Princess Parkway?'

'Joe. The police!'

'Don't worry, love. I was doing 50 in a 40 zone. Soon as they saw it was me, we had a chat about the World Cup and that was it.'

'So the police were after you, not Malcolm.'

'Well, that was the funny thing. Soon as I saw the light going in the rear-view mirror and the police were pulling me over, the first thing I thought was "Oh blimey, what's Mal done now?"'

'Joe, love, you remember how things changed for you when you were on telly for the last World Cup?'

'Yes.'

'Malcolm's going to be worse when he comes back.'

'It's all right. I know exactly how to handle him. I always have, haven't I?'

Norah tipped the dirty water out of the plastic bowl in the sink and dried her hands thoughtfully. She hoped her husband was right, but somehow something inside her made her doubt it.

In the *World of Sport* offices, Stuart McConachie showed John Bromley the sacks of fan mail that had been arriving for the panel. 'Look at this, Brommers. I've never seen anything like it.'

Bromley's heart swelled. He knew he had just given birth to a winning television series. It was the summit of any television producer's ambition. 'It's pub and club talk isn't it?' he said delightedly, ripping open an envelope at random. He scanned the contents briefly and laughed. 'Listen to this: *If you don't get rid of that loudmouth Allison I'll never watch your programme again*. Fantastic!'

'You think he means it?'

'Nah. He'll be turning on every night to see if we've got rid of him or not.'

'I had the manager of the Hendon Hall Hotel on the phone today . . .' started McConachie uncertainly.

'Yes?'

'It's about Mal's bill. It's getting rather high.'

'How much?'

'It's nearly 700 quid and we're only at the end of the first week.'

Bromley looked at the piles of unopened mail. 'Tell him to send the bill here.'

For Joe it had meant taking half an hour to walk up Bridge Street to Kendals. For Malcolm television fame meant, amongst other things, sex. Not just sex with the attractive young women who had been his staple diet for a few years, but sex with one of the few women who had really impressed him. He was in the green room, where all of the panel went for hospitality after transmission, when the phone rang. One of the researchers picked it up. Malcolm was continuing his tirade against Alf Ramsey, which had been in full flow on the air 20 minutes previously, when the researcher called out. 'Malcolm! For you!'

'Who is it?'

'Christine Keeler,' came the matter-of-fact reply.

Malcolm laughed and the other panellists jeered. He picked up the receiver. 'Hello?'

'Is that Malcolm Allison?'

'Yes.'

'It's Christine Keeler.'

'Fuck off.' The chatter in the room went quiet as all eyes turned to Malcolm who, unaccountably, had gone rather quiet himself. Maybe this wasn't another hoax call after all. 'Where are you?'

'I'm in the Star pub in Belgravia. I've just seen you on telly. I like your tie.'

'That all?' asked Malcolm, his voice recovering its normally powerful tone.

'You want to have dinner with me one night?'

'Sure. Do you know the Guinea Grill? It's a steak restaurant in Bruton Place, just off Berkeley Square.'

'Of course.'

'I'll see you there at eight tomorrow,' he said and put the phone down. He turned round to find 20 people staring at him.

'Shit, Mal, was that really her?'

It was obvious from his uncontrollable smirk that it was.

On the way back to the hotel that night, he thought about Christine Keeler. It had only been a few years before that her legendary sex appeal had effectively brought down the Conservative government. He wondered what it must be like to make love to a woman who exercised such fascination over men. He thought he would find out in 24 hours' time. A woman like Christine Keeler didn't ring men like him and ask them to go out with her if she didn't have something more in mind than a discussion about the merits of Ramsey's overlapping full-backs.

He was right, but what intrigued him about the courtship that preceded the dance itself was how sure of herself Christine Keeler was. He thought he would recognise her from the infamous photograph of her naked astride a chair, which had been imprinted on his mind in 1963 as it had been on the minds of so many men, taken when the Profumo scandal had broken. However, her dark hair had been dyed blonde, and though she was still magnetically attractive her face now betrayed a little of the hard life she had experienced. Malcolm was used to being the centre of attention when he walked into a restaurant with an attractive woman, so when they walked from the front door to their table at the Guinea it was a surprise to find that all eyes were fixed on his companion rather than on him. Despite the dyed-blonde hair, she remained instantly recognisable to everyone. Every man in the restaurant wanted to be in his shoes – and probably out of them as well. He might now think of himself as a television star, but Christine Keeler was a piece of imperishable British sexual history.

He found much to empathise with. She was a girl from a poor background who had existed on the fringe of criminal activities but had used what talents God had given her to better herself. He had known models and call girls, but none were like her. In all those relationships, he had always called the shots. This was the first time in his life that he had been involved with a woman and felt that she was in control of the relationship. They would make love on her terms when she chose. It was odd, but it was seductive for a few nights. Then she had enough of him and dropped him, just like he had dropped Ken Mulhearn after the defeat at Fenerbahçe. This was the life of stardom. They had sniffed around each other like a pair of dogs, taken as much as they wanted from each other and parted without a backward glance – at least on her part. He had heard something from America about the start of a women's liberation movement and how women were campaigning against traditional male hegemony to take control of their lives. It was Malcolm's first experience of a woman being in control, and he didn't much care for it, frankly. Her rejection of him continued to rankle.

He was in Tramps after a late-night highlights transmission and a belligerent exchange of views with Bob McNab about Alan Mullery, the Spurs midfielder whom Malcolm thought not good enough to play for England. McNab and Crerand were complaining about the lack of activity in the nightclub when Malcolm made an announcement. 'I'm fed up of this. Do you want to come and meet Christine?'

The two fellow-panellists gave Malcolm just the reaction he was looking for, and they quickly pulled him outside and hailed a cab.

'What's she like, Mal?' asked McNab.

'The best I ever had.'

'What does she do? Come on, you've got to tell us.'

It was greatly amusing. The two men were almost slavering. 'I'm not taking you over there so you two can fuck her, you know.'

'Course not,' agreed McNab indignantly. 'We just want to know . . .'

'Yeah, what's so fucking special? It's got to be something.' Crerand was not to be pacified with generalities.

Malcolm said nothing, partly because he was quite drunk, but he also knew that the less he said the more he implied and the crazier the two men would become.

The taxi eventually drew up in a mews very much like Wimpole Mews, the famous alleyway in Marylebone where Keeler had allegedly slept with both John Profumo, who was at the time the Secretary of State for War in Macmillan's cabinet, and Eugene Ivanov, a Soviet naval attaché. The copious volumes of alcohol Malcolm had consumed at ITV Sport's expense combined with the cold air blowing into his face from the open window of the taxi had rather served to scramble his brains more than usual.

He hammered on the door of Christine Keeler's apartment. 'Christine! Christine! Open the door, sweetheart. I've brought some friends to fuck you!'

'Malcolm,' said Paddy Crerand nervously, 'we haven't come for that.'

'S'all right, Christine. They haven't come to fuck you.'

McNab was paying off the taxi when he realised this might be a very short visit. 'Hang on for a minute will you, mate? You can restart the meter if you want.'

'I'm not going anywhere,' said the cabbie, restarting the meter. Frankly he'd have hung around for nothing for this entertainment. This would get the other cabbies talking at the Warwick Avenue shed.

'Christine, you bitch, open the fucking door.' Malcolm kept up his relentless tattoo on the door and eventually a window opened on the first floor. 'Christine!' He turned to the others with a beatific smile on his face. 'See, I told you she lived here.'

'It's three o'clock in the morning. Fuck off, Malcolm, and don't come back,' said the world's leading sex siren. The window shut with a decisive bang.

'Come on, Mal, let's go.' Paddy Crerand was already tugging at Malcolm's sleeve.

He shook his arm free. 'Christine! Christine!' He started to beat on the door again as lights went on all along the mews and the sound of complaints started to pour from other windows. Eventually McNab and Crerand managed to bundle Malcolm back into the cab, which roared away towards the safe haven of the Hendon Hall Hotel before the police arrived.

Malcolm felt somehow vindicated when England went out of the World Cup to West Germany at the quarter-final stage, though he spent a lot of time defending Colin Bell, whom Ramsey had brought on to replace Bobby Charlton midway through the second half with England still in the lead. In the end the World Cup tournament of 1970 had proved a triumph for Malcolm, if not for the England football team. Yet his caustic and constant criticism of Alan Mullery as a player unworthy of an England cap had left a bitter taste amongst the other panellists, who didn't like to see a decent player remorselessly pilloried on television. When he realised he might have gone too far, he came into the studio and announced to everyone in earshot that he was lunching with Christine Keeler the following day and that they were all welcome to attend, provided they paid their own way. A table for ten was booked at one of London's most exclusive restaurants. At lunchtime, nine men dressed in their finest and trendiest suits made their way to the table at the far end of the dining room for the one o'clock appointment. By quarter past two they all accepted that they were never going to fulfil the ambition of a lifetime and meet Christine Keeler, so they opened ten bottles of wine and talked about football.

Norah was right about Malcolm. He returned to Manchester significantly different from the brash man who had gone down to London at the end of May. Maybe it had something to do with the mood in the country. Four days after England lost 3–2 in extra time to West Germany in Mexico, the country took its revenge – not on Alf Ramsey but on Harold Wilson. In one of the most surprising results of recent general elections, the Labour government that had been in power for six years was turned out of office and Ted Heath, who had started the campaign in what was generally perceived as a hopeless position, took his grand piano and his sailing medals into 10 Downing Street.

The shock result seemed to revitalise the country. With a new decade and a new government it was hoped that the end of a long period of industrial unrest and economic turbulence was in sight. Malcolm recognised the national mood as something akin to what happened to every football club when it replaced a manager. There was always an extra energy about the ground. You could sense it among the players and the staff, as well as the newspaper reporters and the fans. Driving back to Manchester at the start of July he was overwhelmed by the strength of the feeling that his destiny was not going to come next season or the season after. It was here, right now, this minute. City had won two trophies last season, five in the five years he had been there, and he was going to demand some kind of recognition for what he had achieved. Not Joe. Him. Malcolm.

When the staff and players returned to pre-season training in July 1970, there was something slightly odd about the atmosphere. Superficially everything was the same as it had been at the close of the previous triumphant season. There were still the same jokes in the dressing-room; the same confidence that the team could win more and more trophies; the production line of excellent young players: Towers, Jeffries, Carrodus and Mellor showed no sign of slowing down, which added competition for the first-team places. Joe was still smiling; Malcolm was still bellowing. But something had gone. Something intangible at the heart of the Mercer–Allison relationship.

It was after training in Altrincham at the Silver Gates ground one morning that Malcolm decided to confront Joe. It was odd. He scarcely knew the meaning of fear. He certainly never backed away from a verbal confrontation of any kind. Even when ITV Sport had asked him to go head-to-head with Alan Mullery after the player's return from Mexico, he hadn't shirked the opprobrium that he knew was bound to come his way. He had said what he thought, and as far as he was concerned that was the end of the matter.

His relationship with Joe was different and extremely difficult. He couldn't quite grasp it. He didn't know where he stood. He thought it had been two or three times now that Joe had told him that he would supervise a seamless transition: Malcolm would become the manager, and Joe would move upstairs in some advisory capacity. It would be friendly and it would make sense. Malcolm had done the hard yards, the foot-slogging of a long apprenticeship, and nobody in the world of football could deny that he hadn't graduated with honours: five of them, to be precise, in five years. He opened the door to the manager's office, the office that should rightfully be his already, and walked in. 'Joe, we need to talk about the manager's job.'

'You're not off somewhere glamorous again, are you, Mal?'

'Here, Joe. What we talked about last year at the League Cup tie against United, and after Vienna, and before that very first game at Middlesbrough.'

Joe's eyes flashed with alarm. He knew exactly what Malcolm was talking about and he didn't want another conversation about it. He wanted things to continue as they were, to win the League again and have another crack at the European Cup, like Matt had done. Why wouldn't Malcolm leave well enough alone? 'Is it money, Mal? Because I can . . .'

'No, Joe. It's not money. I've never been interested in money, you know that.'

'Not if you can use someone else's.'

Malcolm was on the verge of responding to the taunt, but he held his tongue. Joe was trying to divert him down a side road. He wasn't going there. 'Joe, I want to be the manager here.'

'I'm the manager here, Mal.'

'You promised. Over and over again.'

'I still mean it. I've already spoken to the board.'

'You have?' For a moment, Malcolm's heart soared.

'I've told them when I go there's no point looking for a replacement. You're the man I want to replace me. I had to fight your corner, but I'm sure it'll all be OK in the end.'

'But when, Joe? When is that going to happen?'

'If you're the manager, Mal, then what am I?'

'You can be general manager and I'll be the team manager.'

'Well . . .' Joe was desperately searching for any way he could find to divert the conversation into a cul-de-sac.

'It worked at Sheffield Wednesday when Eric Taylor was general manager and Harry Catterick became team manager.'

'They never won anything, did they?'

'Come on, Joe. We can make it work. You and me together. More trophies.' Joe now looked unconvinced. Malcolm was on the verge of losing it. 'Joe, you promised me. Two or three times you've always said . . .'

'If I agreed, and I say *if*, I'd still make the final decision about who we buy and sell and what the team is every Saturday. That's how it's always worked.' Now it was Joe's turn to look anxious, hoping for a sign of assent from Malcolm that would confirm the continuation of their current working relationship.

'But Joe, if I'm the manager . . .'

And then, almost as if Joe had stage-managed it, Dorothy knocked on the door and put her head inside. 'Hello, Joe. I hope you don't mind, but Mr Griffiths would very much like to talk to you in his office immediately.'

'Fuck me!' exploded Malcolm.

'Tell Mr Griffiths I'll be right there.' Dorothy left in some relief. She was never sure what Malcolm Allison was going to do or say next. She was not a woman who enjoyed unpredictability in the office. Joe got to his feet. 'Mal, I know how you're feeling.'

'You do?' Malcolm sounded surprised.

'Just trust me. I'll do the right thing.'

'When?' cried Malcolm to Joe's disappearing back.

'When the time is right,' reiterated Joe. Malcolm picked up a pile of match-day programmes and hurled them at the wall. He almost ran down the steps of the main entrance to the ground, leapt into his car and drove recklessly at high speed to the Fletcher's Arms in Denton.

Ian Niven was proud of his pub. It had taken him some years to gain control of the licence from the brewers who owned the freehold, and even longer to renovate it and turn it into the pub he wanted. He had put down wall-to-wall carpeting, installed speakers for background music and bought one of those new machines that made toasted sandwiches. The 'Best Pub in Denton' award was clearly an official seal of approval, but what pleased him most was the day he'd got into a taxi in the centre of Manchester and asked the driver to take him to Denton.

'Where in Denton?' asked the driver, letting out the clutch.

'Oh, it's just a small pub. I'll tell you when we get nearer. You won't know it.'

'Try me.'

'It's called the Fletcher's Arms.'

'Oh aye. You mean the City pub?'

Niven smiled. He knew he and the Fletcher's Arms had arrived.

Malcolm Allison arrived in the Fletcher's Arms in a very different state of mind. He was angry with Joe, irritated with himself and furious with the world. Ian Niven was delighted. He always regarded Malcolm's entrance as a public statement that put his 'Best Pub in Denton' award into the shade.

'What's up, Mal?'

Malcolm was never able to disguise his real feelings in any social situation and at that moment his furrowed brow looked so thunderous that lightning might have struck the nearby A57. 'Joe's driving me fucking crazy.'

'What's he done now?'

'It's not what he's done. It's what he fucking hasn't done.'

'You talking about the manager thing again?'

'Yeah. No. He won't talk.' Malcolm tossed back the single malt Niven had poured him in one gulp and pushed his glass back across the bar. Niven reached for the bottle again and filled the glass generously.

'You know, Mal, what you really need is your own board of directors. If you had that they'd make you the manager in a minute.'

'I like Albert Alexander.'

'Everyone likes Albert Alexander. But you don't have to replace him. You just have to replace the directors.'

'Everyone loves Joe. Do you think we could find someone in Manchester who'd take his power away?'

'You can't do that till you're sure you've got a majority of the directors on your side.'

'I hate all that politics. I'm a football man.'

'I know you are, Mal. You're the best. You're the best thing that ever happened to this club, and I should know. I've been around long enough. Did I tell you about that time I went to the toilet with the directors?'

'Ian, I thought this was a respectable pub.' Malcolm grinned.

'It was when they were desperate to get Chris Muir off the board because he'd been doing something Sidney Rose didn't like. Anyway there was a court case. Now who cares about court cases? No one. But I did. I went to the court – you know, the one behind the Opera House – and I listened to every word that took place in that courtroom. Then when the directors went to the Gents I went with them. Stood next to them at the urinal. You'd be amazed what you hear in the Gents. It's when they all talked to each other. Course they didn't know who I was so they just ignored me.'

'How often did you go to the Gents then?'

'Every time they did. I must say, by the end of the day I was straining a bit.'

Malcolm laughed at the image Niven had created in his mind. 'So what did you learn?'

'I learned that they don't like Chris Muir and they'd do anything to keep him off.'

'So how does that help us?'

'Muir is desperate to get back on. If he did, he'd be on your side.'

'But they've kicked him off once. They're not going to invite him back, are they?'

'I talked to him a while ago and he explained the share situation. I've also talked to a solicitor called Michael Horwich. He's a big City fan and, more important, a big Malcolm Allison fan. He'll be able to structure the deal legally.'

'Is this getting a bit technical?'

'Blimey, Mal, if you can understand how to unlock Italian defences you can understand this all right. Albert Alexander owns about 560 shares and Eric Alexander owns about 30. Sidney Rose has got a few and John Humphreys has got a few. Simon Cussons of Imperial Leather has a fair number, and I think between him and Horwich and Chris Muir we'll have control of about 340–350 shares.'

'That's not enough to unseat the Alexanders though, is it?'

'It might be because the bulk of the rest of them are owned by the Vice Chairman, Frank Johnson. He's got 521.'

'So?'

'Chris Muir told me he might be willing to sell.'

'How many of them?'

'He needs to keep ten shares to maintain his position on the board, but he'll sell the rest.'

'So we'd have roughly 860 – enough to unseat the Alexanders and get rid of the board.'

Niven nodded and smiled.

'How much are the shares?' asked Malcolm.

'Well, I think the current market value is about two hundred quid a share.'

'So we'd need to find . . .'

'A hundred thousand quid.'

Malcolm whistled softly. 'Liverpool paid that for Tony Hateley.'

'That was a waste of money. This wouldn't be. For a hundred thousand quid we could own Manchester City. You'd be in charge. It would be your club. You wouldn't have to worry about Joe or Albert – or Walter Griffiths.'

'Christ! It would be worth doing just to get that fucking arsehole out of the place. But where do we find enough money to buy Johnson's shares?'

'I think I might know someone.'

'You're kidding.'

'Ever heard of a bloke called Joe Smith? He runs Weatherseal Windows – a double-glazing firm in Oldham. I think he might be our man.'

FIFTEEN

Joe Smith didn't know much about football, but he knew what he liked – he liked power. Weatherseal Windows wasn't the most famous company in Lancashire and double glazing wasn't the most glamorous of industries, but being in double glazing during the 1960s had made him a fortune, and with the money came some of the power he craved.

The status symbols soon followed – the big house in Prestbury, the exclusive Cheshire village that had recently become home to so many new millionaires, the Roller, the expensive divorce – but after a while it all began to pall. He had thrown himself into building up the business, but now it was established it didn't need his full attention. He didn't quite know what to do with his time and his money. What rather irritated him was that for all his considerable wealth nobody outside of his immediate circle of acquaintances knew who he was, and double glazing was regarded as a joke – at least until the cold winter nights set in.

Smith took to stopping off at the Fletcher's Arms in Denton on his journey between Prestbury and the Weatherseal Windows factory in Oldham. It was a convivial pub and he liked the landlord. He liked the landlord's wife, too. Their conversations always ended up at Manchester City. It was impossible to avoid that topic of conversation in the Fletcher's Arms. The clientele and the interior decor rather demanded it.

Ian Niven had known all about Malcolm Allison's desire to be the main man at Manchester City since 1968, and in Niven's opinion there was no more appropriate person who could ever assume the helm of his beloved football team. Malcolm was a genius. He didn't need the newspapers or even Malcolm himself to tell him that. He could see the evidence of the coach's genius with his own eyes on the field at every game, and he heard the evidence with his own ears from his customers.

THE WORST OF FRIENDS

Hiring Mike Doyle's wife, Cheryl, to work for him had been a masterstroke. Soon the other City players started making the Fletcher's Arms their local, and Niven's happiness had been completed when he realised that Malcolm Allison was making special trips to drink at his pub – when he could be persuaded to abandon the Cabaret Club in the centre of town. Malcolm's discontent at Maine Road was Niven's opportunity. He sympathised entirely with the coach's constant complaints about the elderly, out-of-touch directors and the unhelpful, unsympathetic Secretary and Joe's pusillanimous relationship with anyone in authority and players who 'cheated' and foreign coaches who were afraid to do anything but defend and hope to snatch a goal on the counter-attack.

Niven sat enthralled as Malcolm expounded his theories about changing the offside rule, about using television technology, about making the back pass to the goalkeeper illegal. This man was so far ahead of his time it was untrue, and it was a scandal that he had been relatively ignored by the world of football. He should be, at the very least, the manager of the England football team. That he was still nothing more than the coach at Manchester City was a disgrace not just to the club but also to its true supporters. If Malcolm held supreme power City wouldn't be just slugging it out with United for the position of top club in Manchester. City would be matching Santos, AC Milan and Real Madrid as one of the clubs that made the whole world sit up and take notice. A hundred thousand pounds would make the difference. Niven lost no time in contacting Joe Smith.

'City?' queried Smith as he swirled his double brandy around his glass in contemplative fashion. 'We couldn't make it United, could we?'

Niven tried to count to ten but only got as far as three. 'No we bloody couldn't!'

'All right, keep your hair on. I was only asking. It's just that United . . .'

'I really don't want to talk about Stretford Rangers, Joe!' Such was Niven's loathing of Manchester United that he couldn't bear to speak the name of the Red Devils out loud. 'This is the chance you've been waiting for. Fame and fortune, Joe.'

'I've already got the fortune.'

'All right, fame, then. But can't you see? If you can get hold of Frank Johnson's shares we've got a chance of getting rid of Joe Mercer and the old board.'

'Why do you want to get rid of Joe Mercer? I thought he was supposed to be good. Don't people like him?'

'Joe's the past; Malcolm's the future.'

'We couldn't do this by ourselves. We've got to have a coherent strategy. We'd need possible board members who all brought something different to the boardroom table.'

'You leave that to me.'

'Ian, you can't palm me off with a bunch of City fanatics who can recite games and goalscorers. I need people of real business substance.'

'Don't worry about that. I can do all the games and goalscorers you need.'

'City's no different from any other business. When I started Weatherseal Windows . . .'

But Niven was in no mood to listen to yet another recitation of the glory that was Weatherseal Windows, Oldham's Finest Double Glazing Company. 'We don't even have our own training ground, you know.'

'You don't?' Smith was incredulous. 'Where do they train?'

'All over. There's a ground in Altrincham they rent, and one in Urmston, and on Mondays they go off to Wythenshawe Park.'

'That's ridiculous. Isn't a training ground a basic requirement for a football club?'

'The City board seems happy with the current arrangements.'

'We need a vision for the future. That's how you get a business to grow.'

'You'll have your work cut out at City. That lot are stuck in the past.'

'It wouldn't be the only business I've come across that's hidebound by tradition. City sounds like one of them. I'm going to do something about it.'

Niven was genuinely excited now and his excitement transmitted itself across the table.

Smith drained his glass of brandy in a single gulp. 'So, what's next?'

'I want you to meet someone.'

There was a loud pop, and they both turned to see Malcolm Allison standing by the bar pouring champagne into three glasses and smiling broadly.

On the pitch, the cracks started to show early in the new season. Mike Summerbee failed to last the full 90 minutes of the first match at Southampton, where he was sent off for allegedly head-butting David

Walker, the Southampton defender. The City players, particularly Francis Lee, soon let Walker know exactly what they thought of his method acting. City's League form, unlike the previous two years, began promisingly, but their defence of the League Cup ended at the first attempt when they lost embarrassingly to Carlisle United.

Later that month they started along the road to recapture their European trophy, which had been won with such effort in the drenching rain of Vienna, with what should have been the gentlest of introductions – a first-round tie against the minnows of Linfield. A full-strength team could barely manage a disappointing 1–0 win at home, and it was only Francis Lee's consolation goal in a most unexpected 2–1 defeat in Belfast that allowed City to scrape through on the away-goals rule.

It was on the trip back from Budapest, where Joe and Malcolm had flown to scout Honvéd, the team they had been drawn to play in the second round, that Malcolm came up with the tactic that was to win them the tie. Relations between the men were cordial, if not much more than that, but then Joe had no idea about the takeover coalition that was taking shape behind his back. Malcolm, however, hadn't forgotten about the takeover and his ambition to usurp the crown of Maine Road, but was currently consumed by the way in which he felt they should set up the team to play in the away leg in Hungary.

'Joe, do you remember what we did when we beat Spurs away when we won the Championship?'

'You mean Summerbee dragging Mike England all over the park and leaving Bell and Young to run at Mackay.'

'Exactly. I want Francis Lee to mark their sweeper.'

'Won't that just take our centre-forward out of the game?'

'It didn't do that to Summerbee, did it? And he still scored.'

'Francis is such a key player for us.'

'I think it'll expose their defence. You saw them last night. They rely on the sweeper to get them out of trouble. If Lee marks him so he's never available they might cancel each other out, but it'll unsettle their defence. We only need a goal to take back to Maine Road and the tie's ours.'

Joe smiled. Whatever he thought about Malcolm's extracurricular activities, he had never doubted the man's tactical genius. He might come up with 24 plans of which 23 were ridiculous or impractical, but eventually he'd come up with something that could win a game. 'Sounds great, Mal. Let's try it on the training ground next week. Tony

Book can play as their sweeper. I'm sure he still remembers how to do it.'

The plan worked exactly as Malcolm had hoped. Lee scored the only goal in Hungary, and Honvéd capitulated quietly at Maine Road by an aggregate of 3–0. Yet three weeks after this latest triumph the whole club was in an uproar.

It was just after eight o'clock on a Monday morning towards the end of November when Joe Smith rang the bell of Albert Alexander's house in Gatley, in the Cheshire suburbs. The Chairman of Manchester City was eating scrambled eggs on toast in his pyjamas. He wondered if it was the cleaning lady, but his wife said she wasn't due for another hour or so. She went to the window and looked out at the middle-aged man standing on the doorstep.

'Who is it?'

'I've no idea. He looks like a businessman. He must want you.'

'It's eight o'clock in the morning. Who has a business meeting in their own house at eight o'clock in the morning?'

'Well, I'd better let him in, hadn't I?' said Mrs Alexander as the doorbell chimed again.

'Don't bring him in here. I don't want him to see me in my pyjamas.'

'What happened to that nice new pair I bought you for your birthday?'

'I like these. I've had these for years.'

'There's a hole in them. I've had to darn them twice. You go and get yourself shaved and dressed. And put your suit on.'

'Right,' said Albert, scuttling across the floor of the hall as his wife headed for the front door. As he got to the foot of the stairs he remembered something of supreme importance. 'I haven't finished my scrambled eggs. Will you keep them warm in the oven?'

The door was opened to reveal a 51-year-old businessman in a well-cut overcoat. He raised his hat to the lady. 'Good morning, madam. My name's Joe Smith. I wonder if I could have a word with Mr Alexander?'

Jim Lawton, the young and able *Daily Express* reporter who had grown close to Malcolm over the past year, was the one to break the story in his paper the next morning. On the front page, by the side of a photograph of Joe Smith and his cohorts – Chris Muir, Ian Niven, Michael Horwich and Simon Cussons – was an article that surprised not only every Manchester

City supporter but also quite a few supporters of other sides. Lawton told his avid readers that during a breakfast-time meeting at the home of City Chairman Albert Alexander, Joe Smith had revealed that his group had already received a promise from Frank Johnson to sell 510 of his 521 shares and that Smith had paid £50,000 in advance to secure it. He had also made it abundantly clear what he would do when he assumed supreme power at Maine Road.

'I will do my utmost, everything in my power, to cooperate in any way with Mr Allison to better the club. He is the greatest man in football.' There was no mention of Joe Mercer. Michael Horwich issued a similar statement of intent, focusing on the needs of the supporters, saying: 'We aim to bring greater attention to the needs of the spectators. We also want to change the idea that many directors are not in sympathy with the problems and the pressures on the men who run the team and the men who play.' The takeover group believed this was a particularly good way of bringing pressure to bear on the old men in suits.

Albert Alexander quickly summoned a board meeting and reported the facts to the rest of the board, who were just as surprised. 'I was still in my pyjamas,' complained the Chairman, who clearly remained irritated by what he felt was a two-fold breach of business etiquette on Smith's part.

'Never mind that now, Albert,' said Sidney Rose. 'I think we're all waiting to hear from the Vice Chairman.'

All eyes turned to Frank Johnson. He wasn't going to allow himself to be bullied by his fellow directors and deprived of his nest egg of £110,000. This was the figure he had mentioned to Smith, who was now baulking at the inflationary extra £10,000. 'I haven't sold anything,' Johnson said. 'I still own my shares.'

'Mr Smith told me you had made an agreement with him to sell 510 shares,' said the Chairman accusingly.

'That's not the case. He asked me would I be prepared to consider it and I said I would if the price was right. He asked what the price might be and I told him. He said he'd go away and think about it. This whole business in the press is as much a surprise to me as it is to you.'

'What about this £50,000 deposit?' The Chairman was still smarting from the perceived betrayal from his deputy.

'He said he'd do that as soon as I agreed, but as I haven't told him I have agreed he hasn't paid anything.'

'Frank, you do realise the consequences of your actions, don't you?' asked John Humphreys quietly.

'How d'you mean?'

'If you sell out to Smith, they'll have Chris Muir back.'

'He never mentioned Chris Muir to me.'

'But you've seen the picture in the *Express*, haven't you? Muir is part of that gang.'

'Smith just said Muir was a City fan. He said he'd been a season-ticket holder here for 20 years and that he'd put money into the club.' Johnson looked around belligerently. 'Well?' he demanded. 'That's what we've always been looking for, isn't it? A rich investor who has City's best interests at heart?'

'We fought a legal case to get rid of Chris Muir. Now you're going to let him back in,' remarked Sidney Rose quietly.

'They're my shares. I can do what the bloody hell I want with them,' Johnson stated firmly. He faced the unremitting hostility of the five other men in the room.

'No, you can't,' said Eric Alexander. 'You can't do it because of the covenant.' Humphreys and Rose, along with Johnson himself, turned to their youngest colleague in some bewilderment.

'What covenant?' asked Sidney Rose.

The two Alexanders smiled at each other. 'Oh, didn't I tell you about that when I brought you onto the board?' beamed the Chairman.

'Albert, what the bloody hell are you on about now?' queried Frank Johnson. The old man obviously had a trick up his sleeve.

'Tell him, Walter.'

Walter Griffiths cleared his throat and smiled thinly. If the Alexanders were evicted by these upstarts it would be the end for him, too. He was certainly not going to be driven out of the club he had run so well for so long by jumped-up little men like those pictured in the *Daily Express*. 'It's legally mandatory for any director who wishes to sell his shares to offer them for sale to the other directors before he can sell any of them to an outside party.'

'Where did that come from?' asked Johnson.

'It's been a standard part of board practice for many years.'

'Well, I never knew nowt about that.' At times of stress the solicitor reverted to the Lancashire dialect he had grown up with.

'Nevertheless, I am sure that as a lawyer you fully understand that ignorance of the law is no defence,' Griffiths replied.

THE WORST OF FRIENDS

Frank Johnson was shocked. He had expected a fight, of course, but he knew that they were his shares to dispose of as he wished. He had watched the club's recent success with more than just the general delight experienced by all City supporters, for with each trophy gained the value of his shares rose accordingly. Those shares were his nest egg, his entry to a very comfortable retirement, and he could sell them whenever he wanted. Or so he had thought. His body seemed to grow very hot very quickly, and he ran a finger round his collar. There were little beads of sweat on the back of his neck.

Albert Alexander decided to be conciliatory. He smiled at his Vice Chairman. 'Frank, we know you couldn't have thought through the implications of this sale. We knew that when we had explained everything to you you'd do the right thing.'

'Frank,' said Sidney Rose evenly, 'do you realise that if you had carried out this proposed sale you would have made Joe Mercer's job here very difficult? This man Smith wants to offer Malcolm a 20-year contract to manage the club. I mean, what do you think Joe's going to make of all this?'

The cornered solicitor rounded on the smooth doctor. 'Bloody 'ell, Sidney! Haven't you realised yet? Don't you know the bugger that's behind all this? It's all Malcolm Allison's idea.'

Joe Mercer was in bed with flu when Norah brought up the *Daily Express* and a drink of hot water with some squeezed lemon juice and a spoonful of honey.

'Who was on the phone?' he asked.

'The Chairman's secretary. They want you to come and meet the board immediately.'

'Didn't you tell them I was in bed with flu?'

'I did. Then she told me to look at the *Daily Express*.' She handed it over to him.

For a moment he stared at it blankly. 'What's all this got to do with . . . oh, bugger me!'

'Joe!' Norah's tone was mild and not particularly condemnatory. She had always thought that it was a miracle that Joe didn't swear as badly as the rest of the men in football. They rarely did it in front of her, of course, but you couldn't be around football men for 35 years and not know the way they spoke to each other. They were nearly all like that except for Stan Cullis, who was famous for not swearing at all. Maybe Joe and Stan moderated their language because they both came from Ellesmere Port on the Wirral and had come under some benign religious influence at an impressionable stage in their lives. Her reverie was broken by the sight and sound of a sneezing Joe getting out of bed.

'They're going to take over the club. They're going to have me sacked.'

'It might not be all that bad, Joe. You'll always get another job, and we've got enough money to last us for a while and . . .'

'Norah, I need a clean shirt.'

'I've just ironed your nice white one. Here's three clean hankies.'

They were all waiting for him as he drove into the car park at Maine Road. They were shouting the questions at him before he could get the car door open, and he had no answer to any of them.

'Have you spoken to Joe Smith?'

'Are you being sacked?'

'Are you going to resign, Joe?'

'Gentlemen,' said Joe with a great effort to hold onto his dignity, 'I've got the flu. I think it's quite contagious.' But not even the prospect of three days in bed with hot drinks and sweat-stained pyjamas could hold back the hordes of eager newsmen desperate for the truth. They kindly accompanied him all the way from the car park to the front door of the reception area.

'Is Malcolm behind this, Joe?'

'Has Mal spoken to you?'

'How do you feel about the club being hijacked like this?'

Joe turned to face his inquisitors. His normally relaxed smiling face was creased with the expectation of a loud sneeze. The journalists gave him space to perform to his best. The sneeze went away. 'How,' Joe asked the reporters rhetorically, 'do you start to take over a successful club?' And he sneezed loudly, resulting in a moment of dignified silence, which was broken by a journalist answering the question.

'Like this,' he said simply. 'Just the way it's happening now.'

Once Joe Mercer arrived in the boardroom Frank Johnson continued to defend himself, but he was becoming less indignant. If there really was a legal bar to selling the shares, there wasn't much he could do about it immediately. He would take counsel's opinion, of course, and somehow he'd find a way to get hold of that £110,000. He'd think about that tomorrow. Today it was important that he calmed everyone's fears.

'Look, the first thing Smith said to me was he wanted to help make City a bigger club than United.' Johnson could see that was a good start. Although they all obeyed social niceties in public with regard to United, the board of directors felt about their opposite numbers at Old Trafford precisely the way that City fans felt about the other club in town. If Joe Smith wanted to write a mission statement to convince the directors of Manchester City FC that he should be invited to join the board, jumping up and down on the prostrate body of Manchester United was an excellent way to start.

'I think we need to talk about how this consortium got the idea that Frank's shares were for sale in the first place,' said Sidney Rose. 'Joe, did Malcolm Allison ever say anything to you?'

'Nothing. As God is my witness, he said nothing about a takeover.' Yet there was something in Joe's tone of voice that left the others in no doubt that he had some relevant information.

Walter Griffiths was convinced that what Malcolm had done was a sacking offence. He pressed Joe gently but firmly. 'What do you think Malcolm's motives would have been for getting mixed up with Smith?'

'I . . . There are people Malcolm talks to who fill his head with silly ideas.'

'You mean like that chap Ian Niven?' asked the Chairman. The 78 year old was not yet in his dotage.

'Yes. He's the bloke that runs the City pub out in Denton. He's a big fan.'

'A big fan of Malcolm, you mean,' added Eric Alexander dryly. 'Horwich also claims to be a big fan of Malcolm.'

The Chairman looked at his son. 'What are they all after, do you suppose?'

'It's pretty obvious isn't it? Niven, Smith and Horwich know that Malcolm wants to be the manager here. They get him on their side so they can appeal to the fans, and then Smith throws as much money at Frank as he can afford, so that if they get Frank's shares and add them to their own they'll have control of the club. It'll be the end of all of us. Me and Dad and Grandad: we've been at City since this stadium was first built.'

'The fans wouldn't let it happen,' said the Chairman.

'Don't kid yourself, Dad. The fans are like children. Two wins and the new manager's a hero, three wins and the new board's run by a genius. God knows what they'd think if we won at Old Trafford.'

'We've won at Old Trafford,' observed Joe quietly, 'every time we've gone there in the past three seasons.' It wasn't strictly true, but it was near enough. What Joe and Malcolm had achieved together had exceeded the fans' wildest dreams. Was it all destined to end in tears?

All eyes turned to Frank Johnson again. 'I haven't promised him anything. Honestly. Just to think about it.'

'And now you've thought about it?' The Chairman scented a wounded prey.

'I won't sell.'

'You can't anyway. It's the covenant.' Walter Griffiths stared hard at Johnson. The prospect of Malcolm Allison, that loudmouthed braggart, replacing Joe as the public face of Manchester City was a prospect too terrible even to contemplate.

'It's got nothing to do with the covenant. I think he was trying to bamboozle me by not mentioning Chris Muir or Malcolm taking over from Joe,' said Johnson.

'I think we have to talk about Malcolm's role in all this.' Walter knew the board was now united in its vehement condemnation of Malcolm's behind-the-scenes chicanery. 'His position at this club is surely untenable.'

There was a murmur of assent round the boardroom table.

'Do you know,' said Albert Alexander to Joe, 'I was still in my pyjamas when that Smith fellow knocked on my door.'

'I was in *my* pyjamas an hour ago,' said Joe nostalgically, thinking back 60 minutes to an age of unparalleled innocence.

Walter Griffiths seized the moment. 'It's not my place to suggest that Malcolm Allison be sacked, but I do propose that the issue is discussed.' It was hard to distinguish between his proposal and the suggestion that he felt he could not make, but the board was in no mood for legal semantics.

'It wouldn't bother me if he went and that's a fact,' stated the Chairman baldly. Griffiths smiled inwardly. There was a good chance the much-anticipated event could happen this week, such was the outrage in the boardroom.

'Joe?' asked Sidney Rose.

Joe sneezed.

'Bless you,' came the muttered response.

Joe took out the last of Norah's clean hankies, blew his nose ceremoniously, folded up the handkerchief and put it back in his trouser pocket. 'I want to talk to him. He's impulsive. He's really not interested in boardroom politics. He's a football man, like me.'

'And he wants your job, Joe,' observed Sidney Rose.

'I don't think so. He's not a fool. He knows it's the partnership that's got us where we are. He hasn't done it all by himself. Maybe we should think about a new title for him. I'm sure another £20 a week'll quieten him down.'

'He wants to be the manager, Joe,' persisted Sidney gently. 'What's that going to do to you?'

'He can be the manager when I go. I've always said that, haven't I? Who could be better?'

'Are you planning to go now?' asked Eric Alexander.

The directors continued doggedly with their questions, and Joe felt increasingly uncomfortable. He tried to defuse the tension that was mounting with a joke. 'I tell you what. I think this flu'll be the death of me and Malcolm can have the job as soon as I've kicked the bucket.' To prove his point he sneezed very loudly again and felt once more for his sodden handkerchief.

'Does anyone know where Malcolm is?' asked the Chairman.

'He's in London. He's gone down with Francis Lee for the England friendly against East Germany.'

'Let's get the press in. I want to tell them exactly what I think about Malcolm. He's not the only one who can play games through the press. I'm going to tell them that we don't go around with our eyes shut.'

While Malcolm was watching England at Wembley, Albert Alexander was in his usual seat at the front of the directors' box at Maine Road watching City take on an Australian XI in a meaningless friendly. For the first time in the history of the club there was more interest focused on the men in the main stand than on events on the pitch. Through gritted teeth the Chairman had issued an invitation to Joe Smith to sit in the box with him as his guest, although he had been happy to be quoted in the press as saying, 'Malcolm had better watch his step in future and be very careful what he says.'

The London press soon caught up with Malcolm at Wembley – not that he ever made it difficult for the media to find him. Asked about Joe Smith, Malcolm repeated doggedly, 'Mr Smith will be good for the club.' Asked about the Chairman's warning, which had taken exactly the shape Albert Alexander had wanted, Malcolm defended himself aggressively. He had a genuine affection for the pint-sized chairman, an affection that was not reserved for anyone else who sat round the boardroom table and so intimidated Joe Mercer. He had no time for them and he didn't care who knew it. 'Ever since I have been at the club I have always supported Mr Alexander. If he wants to say derogatory things about me, that's up to him.'

The press suspected that Malcolm was on the verge of giving them the declaration of war they were spoiling for. 'Come on, Mal. Do you think the chairman of your club should say "Watch your step, Mr Allison"?'

Malcolm tried his best not to respond to the provocation. 'You can say I'm very disappointed in him,' he commented briefly, and then he settled back in his seat to watch Francis Lee give East Germany a chasing. Lee made two of the goals and scored the other in a straightforward 3–1 England victory.

Malcolm took some comfort in yet another stellar performance by the forward who had been turned into an international player by his coaching, but he was starting to feel the heat from Manchester. He had always known it was going to be uncomfortable when the limits of his ambitions became apparent, but, he reminded himself, it had been even worse sitting there passively watching the seasons tick by as Joe Mercer led Manchester City to yet another trophy with no help from anyone else. It was his time, and he'd just have to see what the week brought. One thing was for sure: the die was cast. There would be no turning back now.

SIXTEEN

In the dressing-room in the bowels of Maine Road, the players read the back pages of the newspapers with glum expressions. According to them, Frank Johnson had now changed his mind about selling his shares to Joe Smith because Smith had misled him by failing to mention that he was part of a consortium along with Chris Muir, who was anathema to the other directors. Joe Smith had apparently refused to accept the rejection and was claiming that he had a signed contract with Johnson for the sale of his shares, and he was determined to force the Vice Chairman to honour the agreement.

The players knew instinctively that whatever the outcome it wasn't going to be good news for them. The managerial partnership that had swept them to unparalleled success was fatally wounded. If the takeover happened, the Boss would be gone as well as the Chairman, whom they all liked. If it failed, there didn't seem to be any way in which the Boss and Malcolm could work together in the future.

'Shit!' said Summerbee as he and Francis Lee stared at newspaper headlines. 'It's over, isn't it?'

'What?'

'This. All this. What we've done these past few years.'

'What the fuck does Malcolm think he's doing? Shagger, have you seen this?' Lee waved a copy of the *Daily Express* at Alan Oakes, who looked morose but was doing his best to avoid thinking about the implications of the takeover.

'We've got a game against Leeds tomorrow,' said the wing-half doggedly.

'Don't you fucking well realise what's at stake here?' asked Summerbee with some passion.

'Me and Glyn lived through McDowall and Poyser and all that shit. It's what they fucking well do upstairs.'

'Exactly!' Lee stood up and virtually thrust the paper in Oakes's face. 'Do you want that shit to be happening again? After everything we've won?'

'And everything we can still win,' added Summerbee.

'Go and fucking well talk to the Boss and Malcolm. Leave me out of it,' complained Oakes. 'We're players. We've got Bremner, Giles and Hunter tomorrow.'

'Mal's had his head turned by those fucking hangers-on. He shouldn't be getting mixed up in all this,' said Summerbee.

'I'm going to see the Boss,' stated Lee decisively. 'You coming?'

He and Summerbee found Joe in his office talking to Peter Gardner about the game against Leeds. The journalist put away his notebook, but the atmosphere in the room was strained, nothing like it was usually the day before a big game. Joe still had that irrepressible grin on his wide-open face. 'Sit down, lads. If you've come for a pay rise, you're out of luck.'

It was obvious from the concerned expressions on the faces of his two most extrovert players that they had come to talk about the takeover. 'Boss, you've got to sort this thing out with Malcolm and the board.'

'Oh, it's just politics, Francis. Don't worry about it. What I want to know is why you don't play for me like you play for Alf and why Belly doesn't play for England like he does for us?'

'Boss, I'm not kidding. What's happening upstairs is bloody serious, and if you don't get control of it pretty quick it'll destroy you. And us.'

But Joe was never inclined to show the players the anxiety he was feeling inside.

'If you don't, Boss,' said Summerbee slowly, 'it's all over.'

On Friday afternoons, Stan Gibson, the houseproud groundsman, permitted the players to train on the Maine Road pitch. The first team had lost only two League games all season and looked as though they would mount a serious challenge for the Championship for the first time since they had won it in 1967–68. The following day's match at Leeds United was a fixture they would normally anticipate with some relish. Malcolm was looking forward to pitting his wits against those of Don Revie, but he sensed there was something wrong with the atmosphere amongst the players. There were no laughs. There were always laughs. It had to be something to do with the takeover news.

At the end of the session Francis Lee, Colin Bell and Mike Summerbee, the head, the heart and the soul of the team, approached him as a group.

He looked at their unusually serious faces and tried to make light of it. 'Sniffer's been looking at X-rays of your ankles so he can recognise his autograph.' Leeds United's Allan Clarke, known as 'Sniffer', was much disliked for his ankle tapping. The players ignored the attempt at humour.

Francis Lee was the first to speak. 'What the fuck's going on, Mal?'

'Eh?' Malcolm was taken aback by the players' evident hostility.

'What are you doing getting mixed up in politics?' Summerbee made it sound like he'd joined the Communist Party.

'Things have gone so well for us, Malcolm,' said Colin Bell more reasonably. 'Why are you trying to change everything?'

'Look, lads . . .' Malcolm hesitated. He hadn't expected to have to defend himself like this to the players and was unsure how to proceed. Their aggressive stance told him immediately that they were not going to desert Joe and praise Malcolm's far-sightedness in reconstituting the board of directors. 'I want to do great things with this club, with you, with all of us. This stuff in the papers, it's got nothing to do with us, what we do out on the pitch.'

'Are you trying to get rid of the Boss?' demanded Francis Lee. Lee never minced his words. It was an approach that had made him an outstanding businessman off the pitch.

'No!' protested Malcolm.

'The papers say if your takeover happens, the Boss'll leave.'

'Oh, the papers,' blustered Malcolm with relief. 'Who the fuck believes a word they say?'

'We do,' said Summerbee shortly.

In the boardroom Malcolm was under even more pressure.

'We have to sack him,' said the Chairman. 'We can't have this kind of disloyalty. He'll make a laughing stock of us in the papers.'

'Yeah, we don't need Allison for that. We can do that by ourselves,' said Frank Johnson.

The Chairman bristled. 'Those days are gone, Frank. It's my intention that Manchester City will never appear in the papers again as some kind of badly run joke.'

'Well, we'd better get this letter of dismissal written. Who's going to tell Joe?' asked Walter Griffiths.

'I'll do that,' volunteered the Chairman. 'But do we sack him before the game tomorrow or after?'

'After, surely. It's hard enough playing against Bremner, Charlton and Hunter without shooting ourselves in the foot first.'

'I think we should get on with it. Soon as Sidney gets here, we should have Malcolm in and tell him what's going on.'

Joe left the boardroom after receiving the news that Malcolm was to be sacked and went out onto the pitch looking as bleak and as sombre as anyone at the club had ever seen him. He was still suffering from the effects of the virus that had attacked him at the start of the week, but none of the players doubted that his haggard look was the result of mental rather than physical strains.

'The directors want to see you, Malcolm,' he said shortly.

'Yeah? What about?'

'You know what it's about. You're on your own now, Malcolm. I can't help you.'

'That doesn't bother me, Joe,' replied Malcolm quietly. 'I'm used to being on my own.'

They walked back across the pitch towards the tunnel as they had done hundreds of times over the past five years. Both of them remembered only too clearly their first conversation, when Joe had offered the unemployed Malcolm the job as his coach. Was this to be the last journey they would make together?

They knocked and went into the boardroom only to be told that Sidney Rose was still on his rounds at Withington Hospital and would be late. The Chairman wanted the whole board present at the meeting. Joe and Malcolm sat across from each other in silence for nearly an hour. Neither of them was capable of speaking, yet the atmosphere between the two of them managed to deteriorate still further. When Sidney Rose eventually arrived he was confronted by an angry Joe Mercer.

'Sidney, you're not fit to be a director!'

'Pardon?' Sidney Rose was astonished. He had known Joe well for five years. He had never seen him in such a state of agitation. 'And why not?' he enquired with his customary politeness.

'You've kept Malcolm waiting for an hour!'

Nobody could understand quite why Joe had leapt to Malcolm's defence in this manner – not even Joe.

When the meeting finally got under way, the atmosphere in the boardroom was less febrile than had been generally anticipated.

'Malcolm, you must tell us why you've become embroiled in matters off the field which are none of your business,' said the Chairman.

'I love this club,' answered Malcolm simply. 'But I think if we want to compete at the top level in European football we have to move with the times. And that means money. Joe Smith has got the money. I can't see what the problem is in having someone with money on the board.'

'So you think we can't run our own affairs?' Eric Alexander was not happy at being accused of guilt by association with the blinkered old men Malcolm was attacking. He was younger than the coach.

'I'm saying that we can't be small-minded. We have to think beyond Manchester.'

'Malcolm, you're employed as a coach here . . .'

'Does that mean I can't think for myself? You know what I'm saying is right. I want Manchester City to be a great club.'

Joe Mercer looked at his assistant with sad eyes. 'Malcolm, son, don't you realise? Manchester City already is a great club.'

'Do you want to be the manager here?' Walter Griffiths did not want the meeting to pussyfoot around what he regarded as the main point at issue.

'Yes. And Joe knows that.'

'And I've always said he should have the job. You gentlemen know that.'

Suddenly, and to everyone's surprise, a feeling of harmony broke out in the boardroom. Everyone had expected Malcolm Allison to leave the room as an ex-employee of Manchester City FC, but when he and Joe got up from the table no decision had been made, and there was an expectation in the air that somehow things could be patched up, and that City would go on to beat Leeds the following day.

When the directors were alone again they looked at each other with some surprise.

'How the bloody 'ell did that happen?'

'Well, if we're going to sack him we'll have to do it after the match at Elland Road,' said the Chairman.

'I'll get the letter written and you can give it to him at five o'clock.' Walter Griffiths was determined not to permit the Chairman the opportunity to vacillate any further.

'Malcolm can be quite a charmer, can't he?' observed Sidney Rose with a rueful smile.

'It doesn't change the fundamental difference at issue here. If we allow Allison to keep his job we will be taken over,' reiterated Walter Griffiths.

'I thought the covenant didn't allow Smith to . . .' began Eric Alexander.

'Never mind Smith,' interrupted his father. 'He's just a rich feller with too much time and money on his hands. I don't think he knows anything about football or this club. It's Chris Muir and Michael Horwich we're talking about here. We know what sort of men they are, and they won't rest till they have got their way. And Malcolm Allison will never stop agitating for it, and Joe Mercer will have to resign or he'll be forced out. We're directors of Manchester City Football Club. We are charged with acting in the best interests of the club. Is that what we all think is the best interests of the club?'

There was a pause for thought for almost the first time in what had been an emotionally fraught afternoon. John Humphreys spoke quietly. 'I think we should write the letter of dismissal but not give it to him till after the game. If we have another night to think about the implications of what we're doing, I think all of us'll feel happier. We've got a match to play tomorrow, and it's important the players have their minds focused on that and not what's going on here and in the papers.'

There was a silent murmur of assent, and the board meeting broke up shortly afterwards.

Joe couldn't wait to get home and talk to Norah. At all major turning points in his life he had valued her opinion. She saw football matters with a mind unclouded by the emotion of the men who were consumed by the game. She talked to him as she laid the table for dinner – tinned salmon, boiled potatoes and peas. It was one of Joe's favourites, and she knew that tonight was the time for a meal of comforting familiarity.

'What do you want, Joe?'

'I want it to go on just as it is.'

'But Malcolm doesn't. What would happen if Malcolm was sacked?'

'The players would be upset.'

'And who have you always told me is at the heart of any football club?'

'The fans.'

Norah held the pan of peas in boiling water in her hand. She had temporarily lost the response she was looking for. 'The players. You've always said the players.' She tipped the pan's contents into a colander that she held over the kitchen sink.

'Well, it's both really.'

'And what would the players think if Malcolm left?'

'I suppose it would depend on who we got in to replace him, but that doesn't matter if the board are determined to sack him.'

'Will they?'

'I think so, yes.'

'And what would stop them?'

'I can only think of one thing.'

Malcolm and Joe sat apart on the Fingland's coach taking them over the Pennines to the West Riding of Yorkshire. Both men stared out of the window at the bleak grandeur of the passing landscape shrouded in the mist of a cold, damp November afternoon. It mirrored their feelings. The terrible atmosphere between the two men inevitably affected everyone on the coach – even the players in the card school. As they passed over Saddleworth Moor, Joe got out of his seat and sat down heavily in the aisle seat next to Malcolm. He didn't look at his assistant as he tried to explain his thoughts on the previous fraught evening.

'I've been thinking it over, son, and it's got to be you and me together. We built this bloody club. We *are* this club. We can't allow sodding directors who know nothing about the game to take it away from us.'

Malcolm shot him a sideways glance and then once more turned his head to stare out of the window. He was in the vortex of a depression from which he could not extricate himself. It took an enormous amount of strength simply to utter the word, 'Right.' There was nothing else from him, no word of thanks. The breach between the two men remained as wide as ever.

Joe got up and went back to his own empty double seat, sure that his course of action had been right but unhappy at the lack of response from his coach. Were Lee and Summerbee right? Was it all over?

Leeds were always a difficult side to beat and they were now on a run that had seen them win six of their last eight matches. Bremner and Eddie Gray were back to strengthen an already dominant team and Leeds poured forward relentlessly, the usual City midfield of Doyle, Oakes and Bell seemingly powerless to resist them. Hope flared briefly when Giles most surprisingly missed a penalty and Lorimer hit a post when it seemed as if it would have been easier to score, but eight minutes after half-time Allan Clarke gave the home side the lead. Joe and Malcolm and the fans and probably the City players, too, all knew that the match was gone. They were never going to score that day.

THE WORST OF FRIENDS

The directors exchanged formal pleasantries with the Leeds directors for half an hour as Joe and Malcolm conducted an unusually unemotional post-mortem in the dressing-room. Malcolm then met his Chairman under the main stand, just before they were due back on the coach.

'Malcolm, the board have thought it over and have decided to dispense with your services.'

He didn't particularly like hearing the words, but he'd heard them before and he would no doubt hear them again in the future. Yet he still retained his fondness for the Chairman. He knew that Albert Alexander hadn't enjoyed the in-fighting that the takeover had prompted, and was sorry that he would inevitably be one of the victims however the endgame played out. 'You must do what you feel you have to.'

Albert never enjoyed these sorts of confrontations, and his health, which had been frail recently, was threatening to break down under the strain. He appreciated the fact that Malcolm appeared to be accepting his dismissal without a fight. He offered a conciliatory gesture, and since he was standing two steps above the coach he managed to place his arm paternally on the big man's shoulder. 'We've prepared a statement to be released to the press thanking you for all the hard work and many achievements at the club. Would you like to see it before it's published?'

'No thanks, Chairman. I'll be sad to leave because my heart has been with this club – you know that. It always has been, right from day one.'

Albert reached inside his jacket to search for the letter of dismissal. Walter Griffiths had ensured that the Chairman had it with him as he left the Leeds boardroom so he could seek out the coach after the game. It was at this point that a suitably sombre Joe Mercer arrived. He took one look at the two of them and knew instantly what had transpired.

'Has he been sacked?'

Albert Alexander nodded his head.

'In that case, Chairman,' said Joe slowly but carefully, 'if he goes, I go.'

The Chairman looked at his manager in shock. Didn't Joe realise that he had just sacked Allison to preserve *his* job as the manager? 'Joe, you can't mean that.'

'I do. This has been the best job of my life, but we both know how much we owe to Malcolm. We couldn't have done half of what we've achieved without him.'

Malcolm heard the words without expression. They were the same words he'd always heard from Joe Mercer, and he was only trying to save both their jobs so things would simply continue as they had always done.

The Chairman's hand left his inside pocket without producing Malcolm's letter of dismissal. 'I have to talk to the rest of the board,' he muttered, and shuffled away.

Joe looked straight into Malcolm's eyes, waiting for some acknowledgement of what he had just done, but after a second he knew it would never come. There was a short but painful pause. 'We might have Tommy Booth fit for the Arsenal game next Saturday,' said Malcolm in a low monotone. He had discovered long ago that football talk was always an excellent mask for real feelings.

'We should give him a run-out in the friendly on Wednesday then.'

Back in the Leeds hospitality room, Walter Griffiths was horrified to discover that his Chairman had failed to deliver the letter of dismissal. Malcolm Allison was still an employee of Manchester City FC.

'I couldn't do it,' the Chairman protested vehemently. 'Who wants Joe to leave?'

There was a shuffling of feet amongst the directors.

'Well, is he sacked or isn't he?' demanded the Secretary.

'I'm not sure,' confessed the Chairman. 'I told him he was sacked.'

'So he is sacked.'

'But I didn't give him the letter.'

'You're a lawyer, Frank. Is he sacked?'

'Yes, he's sacked if you tell him he's sacked. But if you've changed your mind you'd better tell him he's not sacked, quickly, otherwise he'll be managing United on Monday morning.'

'Frank, you're being a little aggressive.'

'I'm fed up. I'm fed up with the blithering and dithering on this board.'

'Then perhaps it would be best if you resigned your position as Vice Chairman.'

'Perhaps it would be best if I sold my shares to Joe Smith and cleared out altogether.'

'Perhaps it would.'

The board of directors of Manchester City, one of the two or three most successful clubs in English football, was imploding. John

Humphreys rang Sidney Rose, the director whose turn it was that week to stay at Maine Road and look after the reserve-team match, to tell him what had happened at Leeds. Sidney was sure that something would leak out over the weekend and rang Matt Busby for advice. Busby, who wielded enormous influence over the Manchester print media, assured him that he would see to it that the more sensational aspects of the events at Elland Road remained hidden from public view.

Sidney was right. The journalists knew that something had happened but weren't quite sure what. They itched to give their imaginations full rein but had to content themselves with printing the club's denials. The club denied that Malcolm Allison had been sacked. The club denied that Walter Griffiths had resigned. The club denied that Joe Mercer had resigned and that Malcolm Allison had been appointed manager in his place. The club denied that Frank Johnson had sold his shares to Joe Smith. It was like the early days of the Profumo Affair. Denials meant exactly the opposite of what they were denying. Everything was being said by implication.

The atmosphere at the club remained infected by the troubles off the pitch and that, in turn, affected matters on the pitch. City were outplayed at home by a rampant Arsenal and though the following week they went to Old Trafford and overwhelmed a poor United side, the victory was marred by a frighteningly bad injury to the popular left-back Glyn Pardoe, whose leg was horrifically broken by a reckless flying tackle from George Best. The players were so appalled by the sight of Pardoe lying on the ground in agony that most of them had to turn away. They later learned that there was a trapped artery in the leg and that Pardoe had come within six minutes of having the leg amputated. The leg was saved, but the popular 24 year old's career was effectively finished. A pall of gloom hung over the dressing-room.

Malcolm Allison was still the coach of Manchester City and Joe Mercer was still the manager, but their relationship was a constant drain on the emotions of everyone connected with them. The week after the United game, City went to Turf Moor and defeated an equally poor Burnley side by four goals to nil. At half-time, with the match already safe, Malcolm walked towards the dressing-room and fell into step with Bob Matthewson, one of the few referees that had previously played the game professionally. 'Fuck me, Bob, what about that penalty you didn't give when Francis Lee was chopped down?'

The referee, in the time-honoured tradition of referees, stared grimly ahead and prayed for the sanctuary of the officials' room to arrive quickly. Malcolm Allison was not one of those people with whom it was deemed advisable to converse about controversial decisions. Mercer, yes, but Allison, no.

Malcolm was irritated by the referee's refusal to explain why he hadn't awarded a clear-cut penalty. 'Bob, why are you such a fucking homer?'

Matthewson stopped dead in his tracks. Being called all sorts of names was part of the job description for a Saturday afternoon, but being called any kind of a cheat was anathema. Malcolm's reference to his perceived bias in favour of the home side was insupportable. 'I'm going to have to report that to the FA,' he said shortly and disappeared into the room where his shocked linesmen would no doubt be equally offended.

Malcolm dismissed the incident. He'd said worse to officials before. He'd been genuinely angry before. He convinced himself that his comment had been spoken in jest, and with City well ahead in the match who could possibly take such a comment seriously? Besides, he had other troubles, particularly on the pitch. Whether it was the horrendous tackle that broke Glyn Pardoe's leg or the breakdown in his relationship with Joe Mercer he couldn't be sure, but what he could see was his team of champions unravelling before his eyes. From the end of January they won only one more League game before the end of a season that couldn't come quickly enough for him. City finished mired in mid-table mediocrity, much as they had the previous two seasons. Those years, though, had been redeemed by three trophies in three different cup competitions.

The 1970–71 season, which had started with such high hopes, was proving to be the most disappointing one of his managerial career. Even being sacked by Plymouth came nowhere near the despair he was feeling and he slipped into a state of depression that he felt incapable of ever escaping. At the end of March he finally faced the consequences of his remarks to Bob Matthewson by attending an FA Disciplinary Committee, which charged him with bringing the game into disrepute. This time Joe Mercer didn't bother to show his traditional support by attending the hearing in the hope of mitigating the sentence. His absence was duly noted, and Malcolm suffered the most draconian of punishments.

The FA did not accept his argument that his remarks to the referee had been intended as light-hearted. Impugning the integrity of the referee was one of the most serious charges that could brought against any player or manager, and this, added to Malcolm's lengthy record of previous convictions, determined the FA to make an example of him. He was banned from actively carrying out his duties at the club for 12 months and was fined £2,000 – half his annual wages before tax. Ten months of the sentence was suspended until December 1973, three years after the original offence had taken place.

In theory it made life simpler for Joe Mercer, who looked forward to two months in which the brooding presence of his unhappy assistant would not be felt around the club. In practice their relationship managed to deteriorate still further, even with Malcolm forbidden to come to Maine Road or the training ground. Over Easter the team played poorly and lost two games in two days. Malcolm knew that Joe would be panicking at his failure to arrest the decline that had started in January. Joe hadn't been helped by bad injuries to Heslop, Summerbee and Oakes as well as Pardoe, which had kept them out for some weeks, but it was obvious to the manager that the team could not go to Newcastle on Easter Monday and lose again. It was two days before the European Cup-Winners' Cup semi-final first leg at Chelsea and the morale of the team would sink beneath the floor if they had to approach it knowing they had just lost three times in four days. He would play his strongest team and hope they could replicate the famous triumph of 1968 and secure a vital win.

Malcolm had exactly the reverse idea. The Cup-Winners' Cup could be retained and the whole season could be redeemed. They had already humiliated Chelsea in London in the FA Cup, and that memory would be at the back of the Chelsea players' minds. All Joe had to do was to flood the team with reserves at Newcastle and ensure that his key men were fit to play on the Wednesday at Stamford Bridge. Defeat at Newcastle meant nothing in the wider scheme of things. If they finished thirteenth in the League instead of tenth who would care as long as they retained that precious European trophy? The day after City's defeat by Huddersfield at Leeds Road, Malcolm rang Joe to make sure he was going to pick a team that rested most of the first-team regulars.

'Well, I'm not going to play Francis Lee or Freddie Hill,' Joe started.

'Good.'

'Because they're both injured.'

'Shit!'

'Calm down. Sidney said they'd both be fit for Wednesday. Probably.'

'Let that be a warning to you, Joe. You're going to leave the others out, aren't you?'

Joe was starting to get very irritated with Malcolm. Why didn't he just go and lie on a beach somewhere and let him get on with managing the team? This back-seat driving was annoying him intensely. 'What others?'

'Bell, Doyle, Book, Young.'

'I'll have to leave Bookie and Young back in Manchester. They're both injured, too.'

'Joe! For Christ's sake! Just play the reserve team, will you?'

'I can't do that. The club'll get fined.'

'The club won't care if we beat Chelsea and win the Cup again.'

'Malcolm, you're suspended. We shouldn't even be having this conversation.'

'You'll fuck the whole thing up if you play Bell and Doyle.'

'I want to win. It's important.'

'It's important for you, you mean. You don't want to lose three games in a row because then people will think you're a crap manager and I'm the one who won everything for you . . .'

Joe put the phone down, shaking. Norah came into the hall because she had recognised the change of tone in her husband's voice. He hadn't shouted back at Malcolm, but she was so attuned to him that she knew something had happened to make him lose his equanimity. 'What is it, Joe?'

'It's nothing, love. Really.'

'Is it Malcolm?'

'How did you know?'

'You can't go on like this, Joe. It's going to make you ill again.'

'I'm fine. Stop fussing.'

'Joe, I can hear you at night. Your breathing is so laboured.'

'I'm just snoring.'

'And when I asked you to sweep the kitchen floor you had to sit down after a minute.'

'What can I do, Norah? I'm a football manager. It's all I've ever wanted to be since I stopped playing.'

'Does Malcolm want your job?'

'No. We're in it together. We always have been. Malcolm's not stupid. He knows he needs me. He wants more responsibility, but he doesn't want my job. Anyway, the board has told him he can't have it. Not till I'm good and ready to go.'

'But if he wants more responsibility how will he get that if he's not going to be the manager?'

'As long as the Chairman and the Secretary and Sidney Rose are still there, Malcolm'll have to wait. I've already saved his job half a dozen times.'

'But Joe, this new board . . .'

'There is no new board. Not yet. I've got till the end of the season without Malcolm interfering. Let's see what happens in the League and in Europe. Then they'll know I'm still the manager there.'

Norah shook her head doubtfully and went back to the kitchen. Joe was such a clever man, such a shrewd man, she couldn't understand why he was refusing to recognise what was under his nose. She knew that Malcolm wouldn't rest until he was the manager of Manchester City, but if what Joe was doing was better for his health then she could accept it. The trouble was that she felt his health would suffer whether he was pushed out of his job or if he jumped first. Maybe, she thought as she took off her rubber gloves, something wonderful would happen and City would finish the season in style.

At Newcastle on Easter Monday, City fought out a goalless draw but, just as Malcolm had feared, both Bell and Doyle were badly injured and ruled out of the game against Chelsea 48 hours later. Malcolm was incensed. Joe knew that Malcolm would be calling and tried hard to avoid talking to him on the telephone, but eventually the coach slipped under the protective wire and, predictably, lambasted him unmercifully. 'You're full of fucking ego . . .'

'That's rich, coming from you,' said Joe, not without justification.

'I told you, I fucking told you what would happen if you picked Bell and Doyle.'

'We have an obligation to the fans. We can't just palm them off with kids and reserves . . .'

'You've fucked up the whole season. Just because you think you can do it on your own. Well, you fucking can't. Everyone knows you fucking can't. You wouldn't have won a fucking thing without me. You're not a fucking manager any more. The players think you're a fucking joke . . .'

Joe put the phone down while Malcolm was still in mid-rant. He tried to clear the hurtful comments from his mind but he couldn't. Was he finished? Was he too old? Did the players really think he was a bit of a joke? Would he have won nothing without Malcolm? His mind was reeling.

He smiled at the assembled pressmen the next day as he announced the patched-up team that would play Chelsea. 'God bless this ship and all who sail in her!' he joked. The press loved it, for they loved Joe. Genial Joe, with his heart as big as a lion's; Courageous Joe, who played on at the top level till he was 40 and only retired because his leg was broken; Genius Joe, who came back from obscurity and illness to transform the fortunes of an old, broken-down club and turned Manchester City into everyone's second-favourite team.

They were kind to Joe when his ramshackle team lost in the first leg at Chelsea to a Derek Smethurst goal. City had fought hard and gallantly, but lost. As they did at Maine Road in the second leg, where they regained the services of the not yet fully fit Summerbee but lost those of Corrigan and Booth. A disastrous season came to a downbeat end. Joe was typically gracious afterwards. 'We can't argue about it – they played very well. We played better after half-time, but we couldn't break through. Full marks to Chelsea: they deserved it.'

Malcolm was never a man for such magnanimity, but Joe and Matt Busby would write in the match-day programme about welcoming the opposition and 'may the best team win', and they would mean it. Different generations, different philosophies. Matt had announced his intention to stand down at the end of the season. He had tried it the previous year, but his successor Wilf McGuinness had failed so spectacularly that Matt had been forced to return and shepherd his ageing team to First-Division safety. The last match of the season was to be a now meaningless derby, and Joe was delighted to be asked by Eamonn Andrews to be a guest on Matt's *This is Your Life*. The big red book was to be presented to the United manager before the kick-off. Joe felt it entirely appropriate. Matt had been an adornment to the game and his passing from it was a landmark. Of course, Matt was five years older than Joe and he wasn't ready to go like Matt clearly was, but he understood that they were both of a generation that appreciated sporting grace under pressure. Malcolm saw exactly the reverse – that such sporting generosity merely confirmed that men like Busby and Mercer belonged to the past. The future was about winning first and all that 'may the best team win' shit was just so much bollocks. Malcolm was pleased that Frank O'Farrell, his old mate from Upton Park, had been named as the new United manager. He liked the idea that his disciples were moving into positions of importance in the game.

A week after they went out of the European Cup-Winners' Cup, City entertained Liverpool in the League. The previous season almost fifty thousand people had crammed into the ground to watch this fixture, for Liverpool was only thirty miles down the East Lancs Road and the battle between two of the country's top teams had been eagerly anticipated. Now fewer than 18,000 could summon up the enthusiasm to watch City play their Merseyside rivals. It seemed as though City were doomed to return to the obscurity from which Joe and Malcolm had rescued them five years before.

In the boardroom there was a similar feeling of anticlimax. When Joe had saved Malcolm's job after the confrontation at Elland Road, he had won the battle but lost the war. Now much the same was happening in the boardroom. Various directors made trips to the Inns of Court in London to solicit counsel's opinion, all of which concurred that if the agreement between Joe Smith and Frank Johnson had been made in good faith between two parties then the covenant was not strong enough to invalidate the sale. Within a month of the takeover story appearing on the front page of the *Daily Express* it became clear that the legal covenant that the Chairman believed would be a bar to the sale of Johnson's shares would offer no real protection to a man as determined as Smith and the men who supported him.

Sidney Rose and John Humphreys met to discuss their strategy. They had both been invited onto the board in 1966 and had known little but the good times.

'We could produce a man of our own.'

'What good would that do?'

'Then whatever Smith voted for would be nullified by our man. The vote will always reflect the fact that we retain the majority.'

'We'd need more than one.'

'Why's that?'

'Albert's not a well man. He wants Eric to become Chairman and as soon as that happens he'll probably resign.'

'Well, it's logical, I suppose, and it preserves the continuity of tradition.'

John Humphreys was thinking further ahead. 'And that group won't be happy just getting Smith onto the board. The pressure will continue to intensify. Niven'll want to be on, Muir, Horwich: all of them. We can't have a board of 25.'

'They won't all be coming on at the same time. We'll tell them no more than one a year, and then every time they nominate one of their lot, we'll put up our own candidate.'

'"The animals went in two by two, hurrah,"' sang John tunelessly.

Sidney smiled. 'Something like that. Once they see they can't ride roughshod over us they might just get fed up and take over some other club.'

'Hmm.' John Humphreys wasn't entirely persuaded by that argument but still thought the tactic of acquiring their own men to be the best way to proceed. 'We should talk to Walter,' he continued. 'He mentioned some people with money who might be interested.'

'Oh, I know one of them.'

'Who is it?'

'Robert Harris. He's on the board at Great Universal Stores.'

John Humphreys brightened appreciably. 'That *is* good news. I've met Robert. Apparently Isaac Wolfson rates him very highly.'

'I think God must rate Isaac Wolfson very highly.'

'Why's that?'

'He's the only man apart from Jesus Christ to have colleges named after him at Oxford and Cambridge.'

John didn't much care for jokes about Oxbridge colleges and responded with a dour Mancunian observation. 'Jesus Christ wouldn't be much use to us round here,' he muttered.

'He's got no money you mean?'

'No, I mean Malcolm would manage to fall out with him anyway.'

Sidney laughed. 'Maybe, but we could certainly use him to bring peace and harmony to Joe and Malcolm.'

'Well, funnily enough, one of the blokes Walter talked to me about wants to act as a peacemaker.'

'Between Joe and Malcolm?'

'No. I mean between the various factions on the board when Smith and Niven get on.'

'I think Jesus Christ might be a better choice for that job.'

The Alexanders liked the plan that John Humphreys and Sidney Rose presented to them and asked Walter Griffiths to bring in Robert Harris and anybody else he thought would make a valuable addition to the board. They would interview them, explain the strategy and see what materialised. As long as the potential directors were men of substance and integrity, it wasn't necessary that they were City supporters or even football fans, for that matter. Or so they thought.

Great Universal Stores was certainly a name of substance, so the candidature of Robert Harris was quickly approved. The name of Nigel

THE WORST OF FRIENDS

Howard was suggested. Howard had been the captain of Lancashire County Cricket Club and had led them to a share of the County Championship in 1950. He had also captained England on a tour of India and played for Cheshire at golf and hockey. It would have been impossible to conceive of a more suitable and less contentious name in Lancashire sport, in addition to which he had been a success in the textile business and was chairman of the Cricket Committee at Old Trafford.

'Well, we can't have him,' said John Humphreys decisively.

'Why on earth not?' wondered Eric Alexander.

'He's a committee man at Old Trafford.'

'Old Trafford Cricket Ground!' said Eric through clenched teeth.

'You know what the bloody fans are like round here. They'll think he's a United spy.'

In vain did the other directors protest. Nigel Howard would not become a director of Manchester City.

By the time of the next board meeting, Walter Griffiths had taken great care to ensure that his new candidate had nothing in his background that could possibly be tainted by any association whatsoever with the despised enemy from Stretford. 'He's a local man, self-made, built a string of successful shops that sell television sets.'

'Any football experience?' asked Eric Alexander.

'Yes, he's been chairman of Altrincham.'

'Just non-League then?' The Chairman was sceptical. He didn't want some amateur cluttering up the boardroom.

'But he's been a big City supporter down the years.'

'All right, Walter, wheel him in.'

At the far end of the boardroom was a room that was referred to as 'the inner sanctum'. Walter Griffiths stood up and opened the door, beckoning to the man who was nervously sitting there. An unprepossessing man wearing built-up shoes and sporting a comb-over that Bobby Charlton would have disdained came into the boardroom.

'Gentlemen,' beamed the Secretary, 'may I introduce to you Mr Peter Swales.'

The nervous would-be director sat down at the boardroom table and looked around at what he was determined would become his very own court. He was fed up of selling television sets and opening shops. This was what he wanted: real power, and power at the heart of Manchester, interviews in the papers and on television. When he got control of this club who knew how far he could rise in the world? He would be somebody. He would be . . . He choked off the fantasy before it took complete control of his mind and went on to answer with ease such questions as the directors tossed in his direction. He had been thoroughly briefed beforehand by Walter Griffiths. It was obvious that the majority of the board members simply wanted someone to join their ranks who would arouse no controversy and support the current board in its attempts to withstand the pressure that would be exerted by the takeover group.

'Please understand, Mr Swales,' Eric Alexander said very seriously, 'if this board does make you an offer to join our ranks we would expect from you the most absolute loyalty.'

'Of course. You'll get it from me, gentlemen. Don't you worry about that.'

'It seems inevitable that Mr Smith will become a member of the board in the close season, as will Simon Cussons of Imperial Leather.'

'Anyone from your side?'

'We've offered a position to Robert Harris of Great Universal Stores.'

'An excellent choice,' said Swales, who had never heard of the man.

'We would expect you to vote consistently with us on any matter in which Cussons and Smith vote against us.'

'I understand.'

'And on no account are you to reveal this strategy to anyone – particularly the press.'

'You can trust me, gentlemen.'

The interview with Swales concluded shortly afterwards. He stood up and shook hands with all the directors, picked up his coat from the inner sanctum and left. As the board of directors came to a formal decision to offer a directorship to Peter J. Swales, the man under discussion was driving happily towards Prestbury into the teeth of an unseasonable gale and the driving rain of a foul night that could have been mistaken for mid-winter.

He drove through the gates of a large house, stepped out of the car and walked briskly to the front door as the rain blew into his face and down the back of his shirt collar. He pushed the buzzer. Somewhere deep in the bowels of the house he could hear a bell sound. It was a long wait, and twice more, as he stamped his feet on the doorstep to maintain the circulation of blood, the cold blast of a gusting wind blew another squall of rain into his face. Eventually the door was opened by the house's owner, a smiling Joe Smith. They shook hands and Smith escorted Swales into the lounge, where the visitor began to warm his backside in front of the open fire that roared in the grate.

'Bloody daft weather, this,' said Swales, noting with approval the other man's impatience and anxiety. 'It's supposed to be summer out there.'

'Well?' asked Smith impatiently. 'What did they say?'

1970-71: MANAGER JOE MERCER

1	AUG	15	(A)	SOUTHAMPTON	D	1–1	BELL	24,599
2		19	(A)	CRYSTAL P	W	1–0	OAKES	33,118
3		22	(H)	BURNLEY	D	0–0		36,599
4		26	(H)	BLACKPOOL	W	2–0	BELL, LEE	37,598
5		29	(A)	EVERTON	W	1–0	BELL	50,724
6	SEP	5	(H)	WEST BROM A	W	4–1	BELL 2, SUMMERBEE, LEE	30,549
7		12	(A)	NOTTINGHAM F	W	1–0	DOYLE	28,896
8		19	(H)	STOKE C	W	4–1	BOOK, LEE, YOUNG, OPP OWN-GOAL	35,473
9		26	(A)	TOTTENHAM H	L	0–2		42,490
10	OCT	3	(H)	NEWCASTLE U	D	1–1	DOYLE	33,159
11		10	(A)	CHELSEA	D	1–1	BELL	51,903
12		17	(H)	SOUTHAMPTON	D	1–1	LEE	31,998
13		24	(A)	WOLVES	L	0–3		32,700
14		31	(H)	IPSWICH T	W	2–0	BELL, LEE	27,317
15	NOV	7	(A)	COVENTRY C	L	1–2	BELL	25,287
16		14	(H)	DERBY C	D	1–1	BELL	31,817
17		21	(H)	WEST HAM U	W	2–0	LEE 2	28,485
18		28	(A)	LEEDS U	L	0–1		43,511
19	DEC	5	(H)	ARSENAL	L	0–2		33,027
20		12	(A)	MANCHESTER U	W	4–1	LEE 3, DOYLE	52,636
21		19	(A)	BURNLEY	W	4–0	BELL 2, SUMMERBEE, LEE	19,917
22		26	(H)	HUDDERSFIELD T	D	1–1	BELL	40,091
23	JAN	9	(H)	CRYSTAL P	W	1–0	BOOK	27,442
24		12	(A)	LIVERPOOL	D	0–0		45,985
25		16	(A)	BLACKPOOL	D	3–3	SUMMERBEE 2, BELL	29,356
26		30	(H)	LEEDS U	L	0–2		43,517
27	FEB	6	(A)	ARSENAL	L	0–1		36,122
28		20	(A)	WEST HAM U	D	0–0		30,168
29		26	(A)	IPSWICH T	L	0–2		20,685
30	MAR	6	(H)	WOLVES	D	0–0		24,663
31		13	(A)	DERBY C	D	0–0		31,987
32		20	(H)	COVENTRY C	D	1–1	LEE	22,120
33		27	(A)	WEST BROM A	D	0–0		20,100
34	APR	3	(H)	EVERTON	W	3–0	DOYLE, BOOTH, HILL	26,885
35		9	(H)	NOTTINGHAM F	L	1–3	DOYLE	33,772
36		10	(A)	HUDDERSFIELD T	L	0–1		21,992
37		12	(A)	NEWCASTLE U	D	0–0		29,040
38		17	(H)	CHELSEA	D	1–1	LEE	26,120
39		24	(A)	STOKE C	L	0–2		14,836
40		26	(H)	LIVERPOOL	D	2–2	CARTER, OPP OWN-GOAL	17,975
41	MAY	1	(H)	TOTTENHAM H	L	0–1		19,674
42		5	(H)	MANCHESTER U	L	3–4	MELLOR, LEE, HILL	43,636

FINAL LEAGUE POSITION: 11TH IN DIVISION ONE

FA CUP

3	JAN	2	(H)	WIGAN A	W	1–0
4		23	(A)	CHELSEA	W	3–0
5	FEB	17	(H)	ARSENAL	L	1–2

LEAGUE CUP

2	SEP	9	(A)	CARLISLE U	L	1–2

SEVENTEEN

The new season, like the flowers that bloom in the spring, brought with it the promise of merry sunshine. The new, covered North Stand was finally open to the public after two painful years of construction. It had been erected on the ruins of the old open terracing of the Scoreboard End, known as such because it had boasted an old wooden hut which had the half-time scores posted on its front some time around quarter past four on matchday afternoons. Stan Gibson had laid out a new pitch to replace the one that had dissolved too easily into a heap of mud, and he had made it two yards wider. Good players played better on the best pitches. Malcolm had finally managed to secure the signature of Wyn Davies, whom he had admired since he had first arrived at the club. With Summerbee on the right and young Ian Mellor on the left to supply the crosses, he was convinced that Lee and Davies together would be a strike force to be feared.

Joe put up little resistance to the signing of Davies. He could see Malcolm's reasoning very clearly and could find little fault in it, though he was pleased that the board had made sure that it was he who did the negotiating with Newcastle. After all, he was still the manager of the club. It was a different matter, though, when Malcolm brought up the subject of Rodney Marsh. The conversation was spiky, irritable and unsatisfactory to both parties. They'd had their differences before, of course, notably over Tony Coleman, but then the sum of money involved had been only £12,000. Rodney Marsh was going to cost a fortune, and Joe didn't like either the amount of money that Queens Park Rangers wanted for the player or the player himself.

Wyn Davies was an honest, hard-working professional who had served his time at Bolton and Newcastle, not among the fleshpots of London, where Rodney Marsh was reputed to dwell with appropriate flamboyance. Davies had worked successfully with Francis Lee when they were together at Burnden Park, and there was some enthusiasm for his signing amongst the players. The prospect of Davies's arrival during pre-season training together with the emergence of Ian Mellor as Malcolm's preferred favourite for the left-wing position made Neil Young uneasy as to his future with the club he had supported as a boy and joined as a teenager.

After a patchy second half to the 1969–70 season, when he had been dropped for the League Cup final, Young had regained his form and place: he had scored the first goal and gained the penalty that won the Cup-Winners' Cup in Vienna. However, the previous season he had suffered badly from injury, like most of the rest of the team, and had played in only 24 games. The telling statistic, though, was that he had scored only once in those twenty-four games: his worst season ever. He knew that being a popular hero with the fans was no defence against Malcolm's displeasure. He had never been much of a tackler; in fact, for a tall man he had very little physical presence on the field, and unlike Summerbee, Lee and Coleman, he was never prepared to go looking for pre-emptive trouble.

After one of the violent spells of sprinting that he hated but knew were vital for his own game, which relied greatly on the ability to lose his marker over five yards on the edge of the box and fire home accurately, he slouched on the ground with the others as Malcolm outlined his plans for the season. Young was slightly surprised to see Malcolm pointing at him, especially as the dressing-room talk that morning had centred exclusively on the imminent arrival of Wyn Davies.

'You,' said Malcolm, pointing directly at the man whose left-foot shot had won the FA Cup, 'are going to have your best season yet.'

Young sat bolt upright in surprise. This was more like it!

'How many goals did you get when we won the League?' Young looked blank. He had no idea.

'Nineteen,' came a voice from the back of the group. Everyone turned to stare at the young man who had volunteered the information. He was a university postgraduate student who had joined the squad for pre-season training with the intention of writing a behind-the-scenes book about the club. Joe Mercer had given him permission to train with the players but had omitted to tell the coach. The young man had proudly shown Malcolm the manager's letter granting him unrestricted access to all parts of the club. It elicited a response that could hardly be described as warm until the coach asked which university he was attending. 'Cambridge,' said the student. Malcolm softened briefly as thoughts of his time there nearly a decade before flooded back.

'I used to coach there.'

'I know,' said the student. 'They still talk about you there,' he added, lying through his teeth. All the players that Malcolm had coached had long since left. Malcolm's first thought had been that Joe Mercer had planted the student as a spy in order to report back on Malcolm's movements. As a consequence he regarded him with intense suspicion. But he smiled briefly as the postgraduate piped up with the information.

'Thank you, Poet,' said Malcolm. Nicknames were de rigueur. 'Youngy, if you scored 19 that year, I want more than 20 from you this year.'

There was a buzz of renewed vigour and excitement around the place. Although Bell wasn't yet fully fit, everyone else was. It was the first time for nearly a year that the first team had had a full complement from which Joe and Malcolm could choose. After the catastrophic end to the previous season it seemed as if everyone was determined to start all over again, and this time they would not only make a serious challenge for the League Championship but would also sustain that challenge from August to May: something they had been unable to do in the past three seasons.

Malcolm had always prided himself on having the fittest set of players in England, but he was quick to seize on any innovation that would give him the slightest advantage. A conversation with Dr John Books at the University of Salford soon convinced him that science was the way forward. The players, grumbling and unconvinced, were then sent off to the University, where they were asked to step onto a treadmill. Running at various speeds, their heart rates were monitored and their bodies poked, prodded and measured until Malcolm had a printout of what each player was capable of doing. He didn't bother to tell Joe Mercer what he was doing. As far as he was concerned it was none of Joe Mercer's business.

Joe rarely made an appearance on the training field now, and when he did he looked incongruous in his sports jacket, tie and proper shoes. He had always appreciated that training was Malcolm's domain, but now it was like a foreign kingdom to him. Although he would always get a smile from Oakes and Doyle, and Lee, Bell and Summerbee, he knew that he didn't have the same relationship with the younger players. Tony Towers, Derek Jeffries, Ian Mellor and Frank Carrodus were players that Malcolm had brought through. Joe felt unsure of his welcome amongst them and preferred to stay around Maine Road. He was becoming increasingly fearful and unhappy.

'But, Joe,' said Norah as she served up his bacon and eggs at the kitchen table, 'when you've felt this way before it was because you had a bad team and were losing.'

'I know.'

'Now you're winning, and they want you out. I don't understand.'

Joe munched quietly for a moment. 'Neither do I, love.'

'Is it Malcolm or the board?'

'I get the feeling that the board is fed up of the constant fights. If all it takes is for Malcolm to be made manager to stop it, then that's what they'll do.'

'But Albert's always been such a supporter of yours . . .'

'Albert's 78 and not well. I don't think he's got the strength to keep on fighting.'

On 9 October, the Board met to issue a statement of managerial restructuring. Sidney Rose took one look at it and said dismissively, 'This makes no sense.'

'We think it will work,' said Eric Alexander defensively.

'Malcolm is to be responsible for all team matters?'

'That's right.'

'But Joe Mercer is to remain as the manager?'

'Perfect, isn't it?'

'There are two managers then.'

'No. Joe's the manager. Read it again.'

'I don't need to read it again. All Joe will want to know is who makes the final decision on transfers and who picks the team on Saturdays?'

'Well, Malcolm's going to be responsible for all team matters so I suppose it'll be Malcolm.'

'So in what sense is Joe the manager?'

'He's the manager of the club.'

Joe knew it was important that he be seen to accept the new state of affairs at the club as graciously as possible. He met the press as Genial Joe and told anyone who cared to listen that it was only fitting that Malcolm should have this new title after all the fine work he had done.

'What's Malcolm going to call you now?' asked a voice.

'I suppose he'll call me "Joe" instead of "Boss", but I'll still be here to advise him from time to time.'

It was a masterly performance by Genial Joe, and behind the constant smile it was impossible to detect the heart-searching that had preceded it. Malcolm was also true to himself, unable to grasp that he should echo the magnanimity that Joe Mercer had just displayed. Instead he spoke briefly about how long he had waited to be made the manager of the team and how much he was looking forward to walking out at Wembley ahead of the Manchester City Cup-final side. He simply had no idea that by refusing to react in the same spirit of generosity he was starting to lose the fans that had been the bedrock of his support for six years. When asked after his first match in charge, a scrappy 1–0 home win over Everton, what sort of manager he would make, he replied without a second thought: 'Probably the best ever.'

Some of the more perceptive fans were becoming uneasy. This statement wasn't like the humorous 'We'll probably be the first team to play on Mars' or 'We'll terrify the cowards of Europe' claims that Malcolm had made the day after the Championship triumph at Newcastle. Those comic declarations had been made in praise of the team. Malcolm wasn't talking about the team now; he was talking about himself. Shankly, Revie, Busby, Clough and Stein would never have made that mistake, and Joe Mercer certainly didn't. If Malcolm resented the fact that despite his acquisition of total power Joe Mercer still remained the preferred public face of Manchester City, he had only himself to blame.

Within a few weeks, more changes were announced. Albert Alexander retired from the board due to ill health, and Eric became Chairman, the youngest in the First Division. Joe Smith became Vice Chairman in succession to Sidney Rose, and the board began to draft a marginally more realistic ten-year contract for Malcolm Allison at twelve thousand pounds per annum. A new title for Joe Mercer would clearly have to be found, but the discussion left the decision in abeyance. Shortly afterwards, following the success of having two managers, the club decided to have two captains. Colin Bell was announced as the team captain with Tony Book being promoted to club captain.

If matters were confused and contradictory off the field, at least on the field the League campaign was going well. Superficially, as far as the players were concerned, not a lot had changed. Malcolm was with them in training, and they saw Joe at the ground and on match days. It had been that way for a while, so they tried hard to pretend that the announcement of a managerial change was purely cosmetic. On the field results went their way, and from late August until the beginning of December City lost only one game and were genuine title challengers once more.

They went away empty-handed from the Baseball Ground, where Brian Clough and Peter Taylor were doing to Derby County exactly what Joe Mercer and Malcolm Allison had once done to Manchester City. The players heard on the grapevine that the relationships between Clough and Taylor and Clough and the board were as volatile as anything at Maine Road, but Derby were now their main rivals for the title, along with Leeds and Liverpool. City quickly recovered from the defeat and again embarked on a long unbeaten run that took them clear at the top of the League. They had only to hold their nerve and a second Championship was guaranteed.

The success that City were having was starting to eat away at Joe Mercer. Thrilled as he was for the players and everyone at the club, he wouldn't have been human if he hadn't wondered if this string of successes was not somehow connected to his own increasing marginalisation. Malcolm scarcely talked to him at all now, and he missed the cosy familiarity of their chats about football. What he heard came from third parties: Ken Barnes, Johnny Hart or Harry Godwin, or one of the directors who could still be bothered to come and talk to him – usually Sidney Rose. Albert Alexander had gone, and it was clear to Joe that it wouldn't be long before the new board assumed full power. If Malcolm had a ten-year or twenty-year contract to be the manager of Manchester City where did that leave him?

In December, before the match with Ipswich Malcolm was presented with a gallon of whisky and a cheque for £100 as a reward for being named Bell's Manager of the Month for November. It had been the first month for which he was eligible as a manager in his own right. Joe sat in the front row of the directors' box and looked on, applauding the triumph of his successor. He had a small sensation of how Malcolm must have felt watching him when he had walked out at the head of the team at all those cup finals.

After the game, which City won easily 4–0, the party of players, officials and press left for Manchester Airport from where they flew to Malta for four days of training in the sun and a friendly match against part-timers Floriana at the Gzira Stadium in Valletta. The night before the match, the City party was finishing its dinner when voices were raised in the dining room. Everyone turned to see, to their horror, Joe Mercer with his back against the wall both literally and figuratively as

Malcolm Allison loomed over him, barely able to restrain the urge to inflict physical pain. All other voices died away and an eerie, transfixed silence was broken by the sound of Mercer and Allison going at each other hammer and tongs.

'You're old. You're past it. You're living on past glories. You're living on *my* glories!'

'The players don't respect you any more, Malcolm. You've lost it. And until you understand what a manager is, you'll never be one.'

'You're fucking nothing, *nothing* without me!' yelled the incensed Malcolm.

'I picked you up off the scrapheap.' Joe defended himself with vigour.

'Everything we've won is down to me.'

'I suppose the players had nowt to do with it.'

'I bought the fucking players.'

'Nobody would've given you a bloody job in this game if it wasn't for me.'

'You're finished. Why don't you leave?'

'If I go, how long do you think you'll survive without me?'

'Watch me. Just you fucking watch me. I'll win this Championship on my own, and everyone'll know it was me that done it. Me! Not you, me!'

It was the first time that anybody had seen what they had long suspected was significant tension between the two men spill over into genuine rancour, bordering on venomous hatred. The two men were quickly separated. There were other diners in the room, but they were locals or tourists and they quickly resumed their conversations in a vain attempt to pretend that the row had never happened. Peter Gardner of the *Manchester Evening News* was one of the observers, but the current standard working practice among sports journalists was that they wrote about the sport and didn't tell tales out of school. In any case, he had genuine affection for both men and didn't see how his readers' lives would be in any way improved by the knowledge that the two men who had carried their club to such glory now couldn't stand to be in the same room as each other.

Both men were shaken by the row but Malcolm shrugged it off as one more step towards the inevitable parting, and by now he was quite sure that Joe would be the one to leave first. Joe, however, was not going down without a fight – but he'd do his fighting inside the club.

THE WORST OF FRIENDS

His chance came at the beginning of March. City were stretching their lead at the top of the First Division, but the 2–1 home win over West Brom attracted a crowd of only 25,000 into a ground that could still hold 55,000, even though the new all-seated North Stand held nearly 10,000 fewer than the old Scoreboard End terrace it had replaced.

Malcolm looked at the attendance figures at Old Trafford and ran his fingers through his hair in frustration. His side was far better than the team across town that was in terminal decline, yet the general perception, backed by the crowd figures, was that City had footballing class but they didn't have showbiz style. He'd rather have Lee, Bell and Summerbee on his team than Law, Best and Charlton any day, but in George Best United held an ace – an erratic, unreliable ace, but an ace nonetheless. Bestie brought United a unique glamour. Malcolm was desperate for some of that. He had to acquire someone for Manchester City who could match or, better still, eclipse what United had. Only one player would do that for him – Rodney Marsh of Queens Park Rangers.

Joe had already warned Malcolm against the purchase. 'Mal, you don't want those fancy back-heelers here.'

'I do. I want Marsh.' Malcolm's stubbornness towards Joe was now matched by his taciturnity.

'It's unfair to the rest of the team. They'll have to do his running for him.'

Malcolm just shrugged. He knew there would be a price to pay for acquiring the stylish Marsh. The two managers were now entrenched in their positions.

'If the board ask me what he's worth I'll tell them,' said Joe.

'I'm the manager. I decide who we sign and who we don't.'

The old, easy, freewheeling conversations about players were long gone. When the board came to Joe just before transfer-deadline day in March, he strongly advised against the purchase of Rodney Marsh.

Gordon Jago, who was desperately trying to keep hold of Marsh for QPR as he manoeuvred to get the west London club back up to the First Division, was appalled by Malcolm's naked ambition. The City manager had clearly approached Marsh, and Marsh was understandably anxious to go to a top First-Division club where he could win a League Championship medal in a matter of a couple of months as well as pocket a proportion of the transfer fee. In vain did Joe Mercer counsel once more against the Marsh transfer. He had thought it a poor deal at £140,000 earlier in the season. Now he could only stand by and watch as Malcolm harassed 'his' board into the decision, telling them that he had agreed a deal with Jim Gregory, the QPR chairman, at £180,000. The board told the new manager a fact of managerial life. If he wanted Marsh that badly he'd have to sell someone, probably two players bearing in mind what Marsh was likely to cost them on a weekly basis.

David Connor and Neil Young were sold to Preston North End for small fees in order to free up the money that the club would have to find to pay their new star. Young and Connor had been products of the City youth team, but Connor now had a suspect injury record and Young, far from scoring a good proportion of the twenty goals Malcolm had demanded, had in fact scored no goals in five appearances.

Malcolm was so anxious to acquire Marsh that he couldn't wait to usher his two old stagers out the back door, even though he resented the manner in which the board had wrung the concession out of him. The truth was that he was already fed up with this new board, which had recently presented him with a contract that his solicitor had told him was so full of problems it was virtually meaningless. But the board could see Malcolm's reasoning and decided that when City won the Championship they would be back in the European Cup, and the foreign revenue would soon start to pay off the debt that Marsh's purchase would incur. City were four points ahead of Leeds at the top of the First Division when the board failed to prevent the wily Jim Gregory from squeezing another twenty thousand pounds out of them to make the final transfer fee two hundred thousand pounds.

Malcolm went to Ringway Airport to greet his new signing in front of the cameras. His stomach lurched as he saw the familiar face of the QPR star coming towards him. Noting the way that Marsh's smart brown leather coat clung to his thighs, he could tell immediately that Marsh was overweight. When he started training he wasn't the first player to be physically sick, but he was the first player to be sick quite so frequently. Malcolm decided that he wouldn't play him on Saturday in the match at Everton. He would wait until the home game the following week. It would give him time to get some of the excess weight off Marsh, and it would help to fan the flames of publicity that had surrounded him and the club since the signing had been announced.

The players were not surprised to see the most expensive footballer in the country being sick all over Wythenshawe Park. They knew what a shock to the system the intensity of Malcolm's training routines could be for a newcomer. Still, there was no sympathy. They had all run that particular gauntlet, and it was the best and fastest way of getting someone fit. They all knew of Marsh's skill but they worried that he didn't belong in a Manchester City side that had been used to playing in a fast, direct style. In addition there was the inevitable ill-feeling emanating from whichever player would be dropped to make way for the new signing.

Tony Towers shook Marsh's hand at training without much of a smile. He knew he was destined for the chop despite having been one of the most consistent of players since the turn of the year. He shook it much more warmly when he substituted an exhausted Marsh in the second half of the home match against Chelsea. It came as no surprise to any of the players that the pace of the game had completely passed Marsh by. When Malcolm had arrived at the ground at 11.30 a.m. he discovered that a white-faced Rodney Marsh had been there since 10 a.m. It was the Ken Mulhearn debut all over again. He hadn't realised his new signing would be quite so badly affected by the pressure. But then who knew what anybody else was really like underneath? The whole world thought Malcolm had a huge ego, but that Robert de Ropp book *The Master Game* had taught him that ego can be an obstacle to success. Over the years since reading that he had tried to keep his in check, though the rest of the world believed the reverse.

On the other hand, a crowd of 53,322 had turned up to watch Rodney Marsh have no impact on the game, and City had scrambled a 1–0 win to maintain their lead at the top of the table. Probably the only negative thoughts in the ground were those retained by Joe Mercer, who had sat at the front of the directors' box and noted that the team no longer had any penetration down the left-hand side. More significantly, whenever Marsh got the ball he held it up too long so that the City attackers and midfield players who were used to charging upfield and exploiting the gaps in the opposition defence were forced to hold their positions to avoid being caught offside, thus giving the opposition defence time to recover.

Marsh retained his place in a dull, scoreless draw at Newcastle, where even Malcolm could see that his new signing was badly out of sorts. Points continued to slip away, and shortly after Easter they had fallen to third in the table, a point behind Derby County. There were five games to go. Joe was taking very little pleasure from watching the train heading for the buffers at top speed. He tried to intercede with Malcolm but the conversation was spiky, edgy, each of them concerned to defend his own position.

'It's not working, Malcolm.'

'Too early to tell.'

'You can see as well as I can. Marsh wants to stick the ball between people's legs. That's not the way we play.'

'He's not fit enough.'

'Even more reason to drop him.'

'He'll get fitter.'

'We can leave him out till the end of the season. Get him fit in pre-season and let him settle in properly.'

'I can get 60 minutes out of him and then sub him.'

'Malcolm, if you want my advice . . .'

'I don't want your fucking advice. I never want to listen to your fucking advice again!' He stormed off. It was how most conversations between the two men had been finishing since the glory that was Vienna.

Joe looked at his disappearing back and his heart sank. There was only one way this relationship was going to finish and that was in his total humiliation. It had already started. Although he was still technically the manager of the club, it was clear that he was no longer valued. Oh, he was liked all right, maybe loved, by everyone from Lee and Bell to the groundstaff lads and the tea ladies. But he wasn't valued. He was just 'Good old Joe' now.

The new board had been very considerate – or so they must have thought – but the fact was that they had replaced that often repeated concept of 'a job for life' with a three-year contract at a salary which was equivalent to a pay cut of 33⅓ per cent. He knew all about the government's battles to control inflation with the prices and incomes policy, but he didn't think the Trades Union Congress would be particularly impressed if any of their unions had been offered a new pay deal on those terms. What hurt him even more was that Malcolm had apparently told the board that whatever title was to be offered to him it could no longer contain the word 'manager' in it. Malcolm Allison was the manager of Manchester City. Joe Mercer was . . . nobody really knew. Sidney Rose tried to calm his nerves.

'I don't think there's a place for me at this club any longer, Sidney.'

'Nonsense, Joe. You're the best public relations officer this club has ever had.' It was true, of course. Joe's famous laid-back attitude and smiling face had long been the reason why City's press profile had been so positive. That and the team's results, of course, and Malcolm . . .

THE WORST OF FRIENDS

Joe had learned a long time ago that football was the best and worst of games. It was astonishing that it could provide so much enjoyment yet also cause so much misery. Yes, Joe was a happy, smiling fellow, never too proud and remote to appreciate that the public paid his wages. He owed it to them to be a happy, smiling fellow, shaking hands, doffing his trilby to ladies, acknowledging the shouts of 'Hello Joe!' whenever he and Norah went out shopping in town. Football had given him everything: a long and distinguished playing career, and now, finally, a successful seven years as a manager. He had done everything in the game and it had rewarded him.

Seven years? There was something biblical about that. There was his time at Sheffield United and Aston Villa – seven years of managerial failure with very little in the way of success. Now there was seven years at City with almost unbroken success – even the disaster that this season was turning out to be could hardly be classified as a failure if you were a City supporter. The team was delivering goals and points and excitement. Did it matter that his pride had been dented? He tried hard to get past all these petty humiliations, but it was difficult.

'What's your new title, Joe?' asked Peter Gardner innocently when the managerial takeover was announced. Joe had known young Gardner since his first day on the job and he'd always liked the man. Gardner knew the difference between a football reporter and a scandal-sheet hack. He'd seen things over the years that would have shocked many supporters, but he hadn't printed them and he was always welcome on the team bus. Joe knew well the pivotal importance of the club reporter from the local paper and in his opinion Gardner was one of the better ones. That was why he felt able to explode at the question.

'Title?' he repeated. 'Do you know what that lot want to call me?'

Gardner was surprised at Joe's unexpected vehemence.

'They want to call me their Public Relations Officer.'

'What? You're going to be the PRO?'

'All my life I've been either Joe Mercer the footballer or Joe Mercer the manager. I never thought I'd end up as Joe Mercer the PRO.'

'They can't mean that, Joe.'

'You ask Sidney Rose. He just told me.'

'He must mean you're great at PR. It's not a job description.'

'Well, I'm not the bloody manager, am I? So what am I?' and he wandered away, distraught.

Gardner's mind recalled the incident in Valletta a few weeks earlier.

He had suspected that was the end of the relationship and this was the confirmation. He felt unutterably bereft. If Joe Mercer left Manchester City, particularly in circumstances like these, it would be one of the saddest days in the history of the club. He was not a City supporter himself. Having been raised in Lancaster, Blackpool had been his local side, but their defeat by Manchester United in the 1948 Cup final had produced in him a virulent dislike of the side from Old Trafford and he had enjoyed City's frequent recent triumphs over United as much as any City fan.

Joe continued to go to the ground and chat to people as he had always done, but it was now becoming something of an effort. For years it had been his job to cheer up everyone else when things were going badly; now he seemed almost incapable of doing even that, so badly was he hurting inside. He enjoyed watching his side win, of course, and after the Easter Passion play, when they had lost two vital games, the team returned to winning ways. Marsh scored two simple goals in a comfortable 3–1 win over West Ham, and then Malcolm did exactly what Joe (and many others) had been telling him to do for a couple of weeks – he dropped Rodney Marsh.

Malcolm felt that it took more raw courage to drop Marsh for the derby match at Old Trafford than it had to persuade the directors to write the cheque for £200,000 in the first place. He told the player he was dropped to the substitutes' bench and couldn't help but notice the brief look of relief that flashed across his face. Marsh did a good job of pretending that nothing fazed him, but it didn't require much in the way of psychological insight to work out that he was feeling the mounting pressure of being held personally responsible if his new club were to lose the Championship.

Malcolm then called over Tony Towers, who had expected that his restoration to the team the previous week in place of the injured Doyle would be a temporary affair since nothing short of an amputation would cause the regular right-half to miss a derby match. 'Growler, you're playing tonight.' The brief look of delight that passed over the young lad's face was soon replaced by the grim expression he'd worn since the day Rodney Marsh had come into the club and stolen his place.

'You should never have dropped me,' Towers said and trotted back to tell his mate Derek Jeffries the glad tidings.

A rebuke was on the tip of Malcolm's tongue, but he restrained himself. In days past he would probably have let rip, but he had felt slightly disorientated since assuming total control of team affairs from Joe. He noticed he didn't laugh as much as he used to, he didn't join in the fun in the dressing-room the way he had always done. In short, he was depressed. It was odd for him to feel quite so down when his side was still within striking distance of the Championship. It wasn't that he doubted his own judgement. He had never done that. It was just that the world was showing a disconcerting tendency to disagree with his judgements and so arrange matters that it looked as though he had been wrong.

At Old Trafford, everything went right. A scrappy, goalless first half was followed by an exciting second in which United took the lead, but Francis Lee scored twice and to cap it all Malcolm brought on his famous substitute with a quarter of an hour left. Colin Bell, who yet again became the man of the match in an Old Trafford derby, created a chance for Marsh, which the new signing took with cool aplomb, and the match finished as that ground-breaking game four years before had finished: in a 3–1 victory. Manchester belonged to the Blues, and now there were only three games left. One of them was at home against Derby, so it was almost inevitable that if they won them all they would finish at the top of the table.

But they didn't. As in 1968, the triumph at Old Trafford was followed by an uncharacteristically hesitant performance. City took the lead at relegation-threatened Coventry through Tony Towers, but Malcolm pulled Summerbee back into midfield, stranding Lee and Davies without proper support. The result was that the side began to defend too deeply against a Coventry side that scented City's lack of confidence. The home side equalised ten minutes from time, and another vital point had slipped away. Everyone was deeply disappointed. This wasn't the way end-of-season title races were supposed to finish.

After the game Joe fell into conversation with Derrick Robbins, the Coventry chairman. 'I think you'll be safe now, Chairman.'

'We needed that point. Cantwell nearly took us down.'

'Sorry to hear it didn't work out with Noel. He and Malcolm were good friends.'

'I know. You remember, Noel tried to bring him here.'

Joe had temporarily forgotten Malcolm's flirtation with Coventry in the 1968–69 season. He smiled, his standard reaction to the realisation that bits of his memory seemed to be floating away from him on a worryingly regular basis. It was the stress, of course. 'Your lads really stuck at it today. Cloughie couldn't have got more out of them.'

'You heard he and Taylor wanted to come here.'

'Football's a small world. We all know each other's business.'

'Can you believe that they would come here when it's you or them for the title?'

'Leeds and Liverpool might think they have a shout.'

'Would you leave City three games from the end of the season?'

'Brian likes a fat wallet.'

'You can say that again. He's money daft, that one. I must say, when I saw what he was like I didn't care for him. I even felt a little sorry for Sam Longson. Never thought I'd say that.'

'You'll be all right here. Bob Dennison's doing a decent job for you.'

'Bob's fine, but we've agreed that he's just a caretaker till the end of the season.' There was a pause as Robbins weighed up his approach. Joe had an inkling that the conversation was turning in his direction. 'I don't suppose you'd be interested in the job?' It was a hopeful punt from Robbins, but everyone in football knew that Malcolm had supplanted Joe at Maine Road and he realised that life there must be awkward for Joe at the very least.

'What job would that be?'

'Well, manager, of course.' Robbins was encouraged that Joe hadn't dismissed the suggestion out of hand.

'I'm too old, aren't I? What would you want with an old man like me?'

'Too old? Bloody hell, Joe, you're only 57.' Robbins had done his homework. He knew Joe's age would be an issue one way or another.

'That's like 97 in football.'

'I was thinking about Gordon Milne as coach.'

'Now that's a good idea. He was manager at Wigan Athletic when they nearly turned us over in the third round a couple of years back.'

'England like him, too. He's involved in their youth set-up.'

'Bit short of League experience, though, as a manager.'

'But you're not.'

'Eh?'

'I was thinking. You as the manager here, Gordon as your assistant. Like when you and Malcolm first started.'

'Who makes the decisions?' asked Joe quickly.

'Which decisions?'

'Who picks the team?'

'You do.'

THE WORST OF FRIENDS

'Who buys and sells the players?'

'You do. You're the manager. In name *and* in deed.' Joe wasn't going to commit himself that day, but Robbins knew he had his man.

Joe's heart lightened. A fresh start, a new chairman, a bright young man to take the training and who would respect his knowledge of the game, a set of fans without too many expectations of immediate honours, no more Malcolm, no more Joe Smith and the takeover and the constant talk of new directors on the board. Derrick Robbins ran a tight ship at Coventry. As long as their relationship was OK, he'd be fine. No more going home to Norah as if he were carrying the weight of the world on his shoulders. No more waking up in the morning feeling as if the weight of the world was on his chest.

The match against Ipswich on the following Tuesday evening would settle matters. If they won at Portman Road and beat Derby at home Malcolm and Joe both thought they would have enough to see off Leeds and Liverpool, but if they lost they were finished. Marsh was back. This was why Malcolm had bought him: the big player for the big occasion. This was why Marsh had signed: for the chance to score the goals that would win a Championship title. Alan Oakes was relegated to the position of substitute as Malcolm threw his troops into battle with instructions to attack. What else could they do? He'd chosen a forward line of Summerbee, Bell, Davies, Lee and Marsh. It was all or nothing.

It was nothing. The home side was equally fired up for the occasion, just like Newcastle had been four years before, but this time it was City that had to come from behind. Trevor Whymark beat Ronnie Healey with a spectacular overhead kick in the first half, but Summerbee equalised ten minutes after half-time from a corner taken by Tony Book. This is where it starts, thought Malcolm. This is where all that training pays off, this is where the class of those players will show. It was like a ten thousand metres race with four runners still bunched together as the bell rang.

Bell rang all right, but there was no one home. Colin Bell shot past Laurie Sivell but was frustrated to see his goal-bound shot palmed onto the bar by Harper, the Ipswich full-back. All eyes turned expectantly to the referee, Mr Homewood, who waved 'play on'. Harper then went up to the other end, where he proved just as destructive as he headed home what transpired was the winning goal. Appeals for a penalty after a blatant foul on Bell were dismissed by Mr Homewood, who had already decided not to take his summer holiday in Manchester that year. Even the normally mild-mannered Tony Book was incensed at the palpable injustice and spoke as many words in his sometimes impenetrable West Country accent as were necessary to get himself reported to the Football Association.

Summerbee and Davies clashed heads as they both went for the same cross. Malcolm watched his team becoming increasingly desperate. He could hardly complain. They felt as he did, as the travelling supporters did. Davies left the field to have stitches inserted in the badly gashed wound above his eye. The disgruntled Oakes came on for the last throw of the dice. But however the dice rolled, it was not the number they needed. Ipswich held firm. They'd enjoyed some luck, but the irresistible force that had swept City to triumph in 1968 was nowhere to be seen. It was over.

In the dressing-room Malcolm had nothing to say. He was so depressed that the words simply would not form in his mind. The season that had begun amidst such high hopes in August was ending in tears and emptiness. The players had nothing to show for their efforts. Eyes turned in the direction of Rodney Marsh. The players might say nothing but the fans certainly would. Yet they all knew that City's failure wasn't entirely Marsh's fault. Some of it, probably most of it, belonged to the man who had so publicly declared him to be the icing on the cake. They had the icing all right, but the cake had crumbled on the plate.

Asked for his opinion on whether the signing of Rodney Marsh had cost City the Championship, Joe contented himself with the observation, 'Two hundred thousand pounds is a lot of money to spend to throw away a championship.' It was a measure of how alienated Joe now felt that he could be persuaded to say something as acerbic as that. The Joe of 12 months previously, the Joe of 'God bless this ship and all who sail in her', would just have smiled and said football was a team game. Teams win together and lose together, and there was always next year. Not now.

On Saturday morning, Joe drove into the ground for the last game of the season against title rivals Derby County to see Malcolm's car parked in his traditional space. He parked elsewhere and ran into one of the ground attendants as he walked towards the social club, where everybody had lunch on match days. 'Hello, Billy.'

'Hello, Joe. Are we going to thump them today?' It was his traditional greeting.

'Course we are,' said Joe and smiled. 'Listen, is that Malcolm's car in my spot?'

Billy looked a little embarrassed. 'I don't know,' he mumbled and couldn't look the manager in the face.

Joe knew instantly that this was no accident. 'Did someone say something to you?'

'Bob told me they were giving you another space.'

'Where?'

'Back of the Platt Lane Stand.'

Joe looked grim. What stronger sign could there be that the Revolution was about to send him to the guillotine?

The match took place in bright spring sunshine on a glorious warm afternoon at the end of April. Determined to bury the memory of the distressing Tuesday night at Portman Road, Malcolm Allison's rampant Manchester City surgically and predictably took apart Derby County and butchered them to make a Roman holiday. The chief tormentor was, of course, Rodney Marsh, who delighted the 55,000-capacity crowd with his full repertoire of flicks and tricks. It was a glorious, meaningless irrelevance. City were top of Division One, but they had completed their programme and the other three teams still had games to play. All they could do was stand and watch helplessly as they were overhauled. In the end it was Derby County, the team so completely outplayed by Marsh and the laughing cavaliers, who won the coveted title. City finished a point behind in fourth place on goal average, their highest position in the League for seventeen years apart from 1968, but it could have been fourteenth for all the joy it brought to Maine Road.

Football grounds out of season can be gloomy places despite basking in summer sunshine. They seem to lack a purpose to their very existence. Even in the depths of winter, when the pitch is unfit for play, there is a notice somewhere on the ground proclaiming the details of the next match. The new season's fixtures were not to be announced until June, and when Joe drove into Maine Road because he just loved being around a football club whatever time of the year it was, he couldn't help but be affected by the strange melancholy that hung in the atmosphere. He parked directly outside the ground on the forecourt and walked up the front steps past the girl at reception. He could have sworn he saw a look of relief on her face as the phone on her desk rang just as he approached her. She seemed very busy and barely had time to flash him the briefest of welcoming smiles. He climbed the stairs and turned down the corridor towards his office. A man in overalls was moving his furniture out of it. Joe felt as though he had stumbled upon a robbery in his own home. 'What are you doing?'

'Been told to get rid of all this furniture.'

'Who by? Why?' Joe was overwhelmed by the humiliating and public nature of his displacement.

'Dunno. Just know someone else's moving in here.'

Joe turned round and left the building. He jumped back into his car and drove the short distance to St Werbergh's Road in record time. Without even pausing to discover if Norah was home, he picked up the telephone and dialled.

'Hello, I'd like to speak to Derrick Robbins . . . Chairman, good morning, this is Joe Mercer . . .'

THE WORST OF FRIENDS

1971–72: MANAGER JOE MERCER UNTIL 9 OCTOBER.
THEREAFTER TEAM MANAGER MALCOLM ALLISON, GENERAL MANAGER JOE MERCER

1	AUG	14	(H)	LEEDS	L	0–1			38,566
2		18	(H)	CRYSTAL P	W	4–0	LEE 2, DAVIES, BOOTH		27,103
3		21	(A)	CHELSEA	D	2–2	LEE 2		38,425
4		24	(A)	WOLVES	L	1–2	LEE		26,663
5		28	(H)	TOTTENHAM H	W	4–0	BELL, SUMMERBEE, DAVIES, LEE		36,483
6	SEP	1	(H)	LIVERPOOL	W	1–0	MELLOR		45,144
7		4	(A)	LEICESTER C	D	0–0			25,238
8		11	(H)	NEWCASTLE U	W	2–1	BELL, LEE		32,710
9		18	(A)	NOTTINGHAM F	D	2–2	DAVIES, LEE		21,488
10		25	(H)	SOUTHAMPTON	W	3–0	BELL, DAVIES, LEE		27,897
11	OCT	2	(A)	WEST BROM A	W	2–0	LEE, CONNOR		25,834
12		9	(H)	EVERTON	W	1–0	LEE		33,538
13		16	(A)	LEEDS U	L	0–3			36,004
14		23	(H)	SHEFFIELD U	W	2–1	DOYLE, LEE		41,688
15		30	(A)	HUDDERSFIELD T	D	1–1	CARTER		20,153
16	NOV	6	(H)	MANCHESTER U	D	3–3	SUMMERBEE, BELL, LEE		63,326
17		13	(A)	ARSENAL	W	2–1	MELLOR, BELL		47,443
18		20	(A)	WEST HAM U	W	2–0	DAVIES, LEE		33,694
19		27	(H)	COVENTRY C	W	4–0	BELL 2, LEE 2		31,003
20	DEC	4	(A)	DERBY C	L	1–3	LEE		35,354
21		11	(H)	IPSWICH T	W	4–0	BELL, DAVIES, LEE, MELLOR		26,900
22		18	(H)	LEICESTER C	D	1–1	LEE		29,524
23		27	(A)	STOKE C	W	3–1	BOOK, LEE, TOWERS		43,007
24	JAN	1	(H)	NOTTINGHAM F	D	2–2	DAVIES, LEE		38,777
25		8	(A)	TOTTENHAM H	D	1–1	DAVIES		36,470
26		22	(A)	CRYSTAL P	W	2–1	LEE, OPP OWN-GOAL		31,480
27		29	(H)	WOLVES	W	5–2	LEE 3, BOOTH, TOWERS		37,639
28	FEB	12	(A)	SHEFFIELD U	D	3–3	LEE 2, BELL		38,184
29		19	(H)	HUDDERSFIELD T	W	1–0	BOOTH		36,421
30		26	(A)	LIVERPOOL	L	0–3			50,074
31	MAR	1	(H)	WEST BROM A	W	2–1	BELL 2		25,677
32		4	(H)	ARSENAL	W	2–0	LEE 2		44,213
33		11	(A)	EVERTON	W	2–1	HILL, OPP OWN-GOAL		44,646
34		18	(H)	CHELSEA	W	1–0	BOOTH		53,322
35		25	(A)	NEWCASTLE U	D	0–0			37,460
36	APR	1	(H)	STOKE C	L	1–2	LEE		49,392
37		3	(A)	SOUTHAMPTON	L	0–2			27,374
38		8	(H)	WEST HAM U	W	3–1	MARSH 2, BELL		38,491
39		12	(A)	MANCHESTER U	W	3–1	LEE 2, MARSH		56,000
40		15	(A)	COVENTRY C	D	1–1	TOWERS		34,225
41		18	(A)	IPSWICH T	L	1–2	SUMMERBEE		24,365
42		22	(H)	DERBY C	W	2–0	LEE, MARSH		55,026

FINAL LEAGUE POSITION: 4TH IN DIVISION ONE

FA CUP

3	JAN	15	(H)	MIDDLESBROUGH	D	1–1
R		18	(A)	MIDDLESBROUGH	L	0–1

LEAGUE CUP

2	SEP	8	(H)	WOLVES	W	4–3
3	OCT	5	(A)	BOLTON W	L	0–3

EIGHTEEN

'**W**ho wants to go on television and tell everyone?' asked Eric Alexander at the board meeting. He felt a little let down, as did Sidney Rose, at the suddenness of Joe's departure. Both of them believed that they had fought hard for Joe to retain some measure of status at the club. Joe hadn't discussed his potential move to Coventry with either of them, and had only told Sidney when he stopped at a phone box at the Knutsford service station as he was driving down the M6 to Highfield Road to discuss the terms of his new contract.

Peter Swales volunteered to go on television. 'We as a board had a simple decision to make: Joe Mercer or Malcolm Allison? And we chose Malcolm Allison.' This was the first sight most City supporters had had of the new power in the boardroom. Having been used to the easy charm of Joe Mercer and the thrilling bombast of Malcolm Allison, it was not easy for them to accept that this was to be the new face of Manchester City.

Swales knew he couldn't be accused of being a Malcolm man in the way that Ian Niven was unquestionably a Malcolm man. In fact, despite acting decisively during the takeover that resulted in Malcolm finally achieving the power he had craved, Peter Swales didn't care much for the new manager at all. In particular, he didn't like Malcolm's insatiable desire for personal publicity. It rather got in the way of his own insatiable desire for personal publicity. Still, there was work to be done and Swales was determined to carry through the reformation of Manchester City to its logical conclusion.

As Hitler had made a habit of invading countries on a Sunday morning, when defences were least prepared, so the new board sacked Walter Griffiths on a Sunday morning around the turn of the year. Walter had not been enjoying life at Maine Road for a while, but this wasn't the way he would have chosen to go. Albert Alexander was long gone, and his son Eric seemed likely to depart soon, too, leaving only Sidney Rose as a director with whom he could get on.

Joe's departure had hit Walter hard. Joe was Old School, like him. Walter's favourite manager had been Les McDowall, who had been at the helm for 13 years, his time pretty much coinciding with the Conservative government of Churchill, Eden and Macmillan. McDowall left office as the Profumo Affair broke and public manners and social deference disappeared. Walter Griffiths was not surprised to learn that Malcolm Allison had been sleeping with Christine Keeler. In fact, he wouldn't have been surprised to learn that Malcolm had somehow been involved in passing those state secrets to the Russian naval attaché.

The takeover group had always wanted Walter Griffiths out. Chris Muir, the aggressive Scotsman, had harboured a fierce resentment at the way in which he had been ejected from the board in the past, and he had vowed to take his revenge on the man whom he regarded as the primary mover in his removal from office. Peter Swales, too, wanted to see the end of Walter Griffiths as soon as possible. If he was to take supreme power, as he had always intended, Walter Griffiths was going to be an obstacle.

Walter wasn't well – something to do with his neck or his spine; they weren't greatly interested. He wasn't any longer the upright uptight figure who had ruled the corridors of Maine Road for so many years, and like sharks scenting blood they waited until their enemy was at his weakest before attacking. There would be no public demonstration on behalf of Walter Griffiths. The fans scarcely recognised the name, let alone knew what he did. It sounded as if he did the typing. He could be easily replaced.

He was. Bernard Halford was scarcely 30 years old, but he had been singlehandedly running the administration at Oldham Athletic since Ken Bates had bought the club in 1965. He was much admired in the game as a first-rate administrator, and the new City board was delighted to acquire his services. They paraded him in front of Malcolm. 'See what we've done for you,' they crowed. Malcolm Allison had cried, 'Who will rid me of this turbulent priest?' and Walter Griffiths lay lifeless on the floor of the Maine Road boardroom. Six months later, when he had recovered his health, Walter Griffiths was resurrected to take over the vacancy at Oldham Athletic. Bernard Halford was to remain at Manchester City for nearly 40 years.

The new Secretary was not disconcerted by the behaviour patterns of the manager that had so upset the previous Secretary. An extra seat would be held on the train or the plane travelling to away matches in case the manager turned up with a bunny girl, as he was wont to do. Halford negotiated deals with the hotels and bars when the extravagant drinks bills arrived without warning on his desk. If half a dozen tickets that had been promised for guests that Malcolm had neglected to inform anyone else about had to be found at a quarter to three on a Saturday afternoon, Bernard Halford found them.

It was a new era. Malcolm had the power he wanted on the pitch, no immediate hassles from the boardroom and the position of number-one team in Manchester. United were declining at such a rapid rate that they sacked his old West Ham teammate Frank O'Farrell in December 1972 after a humiliating 5–0 thrashing at Crystal Palace under the unblinking eyes of the *Match of the Day* television cameras. But Malcolm was Malcolm, and Malcolm was, just now, deeply – perhaps clinically – depressed. It had all meant so much to him once. Now it meant almost nothing.

This depression had afflicted him occasionally throughout his life. It descended unopposed during the 1972–73 season and squeezed all the joy of his new position out of him. Home attendances were back to hovering around the thirty thousand mark as they had been four or five years ago, before the great run of trophies. His team of all the talents lost five of the first six matches of the season. They went to Bury and lost in the third round of the League Cup. Malcolm was so depressed that he hadn't turned up for training or at Maine Road for three days before the game. Then City went to Coventry and lost, and he had to watch the adoration of Joe Mercer by the crowd all over again.

Joe had left Manchester City smelling of roses, and he had done it in the most charming way possible. On television he had, with consummate ease, made Peter Swales look like a fool. 'I've had a lot of blows in my time but you must never have animosity,' he told his interviewer, 'because you're the one it hurts rather than anyone else. Things happen. That's history now.' Joe went out as he had come in, with the respect and the love of everyone he touched. His only criticism of Malcolm was more like a wistful regret: 'Malcolm seems to have stopped listening.' It was true enough and said without any malice. He made the usual noises of wishing the club and the supporters well in the future, and treasured the memories of their successful times. Joe Mercer had the instinctive diplomatic gifts to have been elected president of any country in the world.

Malcolm had been coaching in Cape Town when he had heard the news that Joe had gone to manage Coventry. He was relieved that Joe was out of his hair but, as ever, he seemed incapable of understanding that the situation required words of tribute to a great manager and a wonderful partnership. Instead he seemed to rub Joe's face in the dirt.

'Before I left Manchester to come to South Africa I told Mercer all there was to be told.' Mercer? He can't remember the man's first name? 'He knew exactly where he stood. Mercer knows how I feel.' Mercer again? Does the man have no political antennae at all? Then the killer phrase: 'In effect he was relegated to opening the mail.' Oh Mal, for such a clever man in so many ways you can be a really dumb sonofabitch. This was the Malcolm who abandoned his crashed Jaguar in Bolton, the Malcolm who thought it would be a good idea to go to bed with the wife of one of the Plymouth directors while he was managing there, the Malcolm of the unpaid bar and hotel bills and the repossessed cars.

Perhaps if City had started the season with five wins in their first six games instead of five defeats, some of the more short-sighted fans with the memory span of a gnat might have been able to forget such unnecessarily cruel words. But Joe Mercer held such an honoured position in the hearts and minds of the City supporters that even that was unlikely, and Malcolm's churlishness contrasted badly with Joe's generosity of spirit. When Coventry beat City at Highfield Road in the middle of October, the home side had been enthusiastically applauded by the travelling supporters. Anything that was good for Joe Mercer was good for the whole world. Malcolm seethed impotently. Peter Swales wondered how long it would be before Allison left and a new manager, perhaps one more easily influenced by him, could be installed. He wanted the Chairman's job, and with that went the responsibility of appointing the manager. Malcolm Allison wouldn't have been his choice.

By the time the return match against Coventry was played the following March, Swales was significantly closer to achieving his wishes. Eric Alexander had agreed to stand down as Chairman and Joe Smith, whose money effectively controlled the club, was a lazy bugger with no interest in the hard slog of a Chairman's working week. It had been simple to persuade Smith and the rest of the board to appoint him as Chairman in waiting. Swales would have to wait for another six months or so, but the job was within his grasp. Today, Manchester City; tomorrow, the world, he thought with satisfaction. Well, if not the world then at least one of the influential FA committees.

Swales was even closer to seeing the end of Malcolm Allison than he knew. He wasn't enjoying being the manager in sole charge of Manchester City half as much as he had imagined he would. He constantly felt exhausted, not so much physically as emotionally. His marriage to the long-suffering Beth had finally collapsed, and his affairs with Barbara and the Brazilian girl Claudia had petered out. He was seeing more of Serena, who had moved to London, but he wasn't proud of using women like Kleenex. He knew he had been a rotten husband and father, but he wasn't like other men. There was no element of domesticity in him. He enjoyed the challenge new women provided him with, but once achieved the relationship rarely lasted long. It caused him the occasional pang of discomfort when one of them decided she couldn't take his lifestyle any longer, but by and large there was always one of them around somewhere to provide solace when it was needed.

No, it wasn't the lack of women or family that was causing his soul-searching. These bloody directors were proving a severe disappointment. They had promised him the earth but had failed to deliver. They had their feet under the table now and had carefully distanced themselves from him when results started to go against him. Three days before Joe came back to Maine Road with his Coventry side, against his wishes the board sold Spider Mellor to Norwich City for £65,000 just to balance the books. He was outraged. It was one thing to deny him transfer funds for a player he fancied, but to sell a player he liked without consulting him made him feel much worse than when Albert Alexander had told him they wouldn't have the money to buy Colin Bell for eight months. The board, *his* fucking board, had betrayed him. None of those bastards would have even been on the board if it hadn't been for him and Ian Niven. He felt impotent and humiliated.

Niven was still Malcolm's biggest fan, but he hadn't made it onto the board as yet. Besides, what good was his support when the smarmy television-set salesman was going to be the Chairman? Malcolm knew instinctively that there would be a problem there. It wasn't the way it had been with old Albert. All right, they had had their differences around the time of the Leeds match when he had been sacked for five minutes, but he had always liked Albert and it seemed to him that he was the perfect model of a football club chairman. He stayed in the background and let the manager manage. That wasn't going to be the way of Peter Swales, he could tell.

Even the contract wasn't the real cause of his deep-seated unhappiness. He had just run out of things to say to the players. He had never thought his vast reserve of enthusiasm could ever be exhausted, but it was. He looked at them in the dressing-room and saw their upturned, expectant faces staring at him. Even the bright ones, the ones who could express themselves on the field and in the dressing-room like Francis Lee and Mike Summerbee, expected him to come up with something original before every match. He couldn't, not any longer. He knew them so well. He'd said everything he had to say a hundred times before. They had all listened to it before, so what was the point of saying it all again merely for the satisfaction of saying something? Maybe he should let Johnny Hart do it. What he needed was a young Malcolm Allison. Fuck me, he thought. I'm turning into Joe Mercer.

Now he sat in his accustomed seat over the tunnel and watched his crowd acclaim the real Joe Mercer. Their cheers stuck in his gullet. There was another roar, that old familiar roar, as the City players came out of the tunnel and kicked a couple of balls towards the goal at the Platt Lane end. The Kippax started first as they stared down the tunnel and were the first to glimpse their beloved pale-blue shirts. Then the North Stand got to their feet, picking up their cue from the reaction in the Kippax, until the whole ground was up and applauding their heroes, but in his currently depressed state of mind it felt devoid of sincerity to Malcolm. All he could see were the empty seats, the gaps in the terraces on either side of the Kippax. He knew the ground was full if those places were taken. They weren't. Not today. City fans drove him crazy with their late appearances. At ten to three, the ground seemed almost empty – certainly fewer than twenty thousand in it – but by the time the referee blew his whistle to start the game, there had in the past been regular crowds of more than forty thousand. Today, perhaps inevitably considering the bad results of late, there were scarcely thirty thousand people in a ground that could hold nearly twice that number.

Malcolm kept his gaze fixed on the pitch, watching as Colin Bell shook hands with the Coventry skipper and tossed the coin. He knew what was going to happen, and he thought that if he resolutely refused to turn round he could somehow ignore it. As the coin fell to earth he sensed that 30,000 football fans were looking only at the centre of the main stand. If they were looking for a reaction from him, they weren't going to get it.

As the slight, familiar figure of Joe Mercer emerged at the back of the directors' box and made its way towards the front, a low growl of approval spread around the stadium. The growl grew louder in intensity to become a full-throated cheer, accompanied by the sound of 30,000 pairs of hands still clapping their appreciation for one man. The ovation on the pitch hadn't satisfied them entirely. Tears welled up in Joe's eyes once more. It surprised him, for he had neither thought of himself as a particularly sentimental man nor of football as a sentimental game. It was hard and it was tough and he had willingly devoted his whole life to it, even though it kicked you in the teeth so often and so undeservedly, but here at Maine Road he was confronted by the stark realisation that this crowd loved him. He had long suspected that the fans' adulation was only skin-deep; it would be there so long as he was the manager of a successful club and it would disappear the day that the team declined or he left to go elsewhere. But it hadn't gone, and here was the final, incontestable proof. These people loved him. Shyly, he acknowledged the continuing tumultuous reception with a brief wave and sat down thankfully in the third row, but still the applause continued.

'You'd better stand up again, love,' said Norah smiling, 'else they'll never be able to kick off.'

Joe stood up and gestured to the crowd to quieten down. On the pitch, the players looked up to the main stand. They knew what was going on, and they glowed inside, too. They might be professional footballers, but they were human beings first and they understood why the crowd felt so passionately about this man because they felt the same way themselves. In the front row, Malcolm Allison stared grimly ahead.

Eventually, the referee blew his whistle and Coventry kicked off. The crowd's roar became focused on the game. Joe's heart was light. Of course he wanted the two points that victory would bring; more than that he desperately needed the two points given Coventry's dire position in the League, but nothing that might happen during the rest of the afternoon could ever dim the memory of this sublime moment of total vindication.

Malcolm also wanted the two points. He didn't need them the way that Joe's Coventry needed them, but his desire for victory that day was as great as anything he had experienced that entire season. He was destined for disappointment. As they had done so often this season, his City players failed to perform. Tommy Booth scored but Coventry did so twice, and when Francis Lee missed a penalty he knew it was going to be Joe's day, not his. And so it was. Genial Joe had done the double over him, and the defeats hurt more because Malcolm had been unable to do what he had previously done so well – inspire his players on the big occasion. How often in recent times, he couldn't help thinking, had it been somebody else's glory instead of his – Brian Clough's last May, Bob Stokoe's last month, Joe's today.

Why? Why had fortune, which had smiled on him for so long, suddenly deserted him? No, not deserted him – abandoned him. When that fool of a doctor told him his playing days were over, when Plymouth told him to fuck off and never come back, when Fenerbahçe humiliated him in Istanbul, he had never doubted for a moment his ultimate victory, his walk with Destiny. Television stardom, screwing Christine Keeler, the flirtation with Agnelli and Juventus: they were all Meant To Be. He would go on from managing Manchester City to victory in the European Cup to winning the World Cup with his England team – not the miserable wingless wonders of Alf Ramsey scrambling desperate results in the security of Wembley, but going to the Maracana Stadium in Rio and the Bernabeu in Madrid and winning there with his own brand of cavalier attacking football played by bright, young, enthusiastic disciples.

He had believed in all this even on that miserable day in Leeds when the directors had tried to sack him but found they couldn't. He had believed it when Rodney Marsh turned up fat and unfit and they handed the Championship to Clough's Derby. He believed it when the hate mail arrived after Joe fled to Coventry. He was destined for greatness. It wasn't much of an excuse for behaving like a rotten husband and father, he knew, but he had always felt himself in the grip of a greater power. It wasn't much consolation to Beth and the kids and the other women he'd known and left, but it was the most powerful emotion in his life and he had had no option but to obey its dictates. But what about now? Now, after this season which had promised so much and delivered so little, after the public humiliation inflicted by Joe Mercer's Coventry of all unlikely teams, after the collapse of his marriage and the inevitability of the jeers and the obscenities, the spitting and the hate mail, the calls for his head in the papers, on the streets, in the pubs, in the boardroom. How much did he need of all this? How much could he take of all this?

The following week, when he travelled with his team to Upton Park, where they lost yet again, he stayed on in London to see Ray Bloye, the chairman of Crystal Palace, who offered him the manager's job at

Selhurst Park. He turned it down, though he liked Bloye personally. He came back to Manchester, but he was still unable to halt the series of defeats that were making him physically ill. The following Saturday, Arsenal came to Maine Road and won; on the Tuesday night Chelsea came and won. Four defeats in a row, five in the last six matches. City were humiliatingly mired in the bottom half of the League after missing the Championship by a point last year. Malcolm was desperate. Malcolm had had enough. He felt as though he hadn't laughed or smiled in a year. He went back to the flat and rang Ray Bloye.

On Friday, 30 March, a still disconsolate Malcolm Allison sat opposite Bernard Halford in the office that had once belonged to the hated Walter Griffiths. 'I'm off now,' he said shortly. He had made his decision, but it had afforded him little pleasure. Bernard was busy with the inevitable Friday demand for tickets for the following day's match.

'Right,' said Halford. 'I'll see you tomorrow.'

'No. I'm off. Now.'

The Secretary looked up, alarmed.

'I'm going to manage Crystal Palace.' Malcolm stood up, shook hands with the bemused Secretary and left Maine Road without so much as a backward glance. It was easy to walk away because his feelings for the place had evaporated. The love affair had been over for some time. He just hadn't realised it. He didn't know it for sure until Joe had come back and shown him.

He was going as he had arrived – quietly, without fuss. The fuss would start as soon as the papers got hold of the news he had just given to the players and the staff. No doubt in Coventry they would be cracking open the champagne. No, not Joe. No champagne for Joe. A nice pot of tea and a couple of Norah's special fairy cakes. That would be the Mercer household's idea of celebration.

It was a blustery day in early spring as he got back into the yellow E-Type. The smell of the new leather interior was starting to fade – like his dreams. Like his life. He drove out of Maine Road and onto Princess Parkway, which led, according to the signpost, to the M6 and the South, leaving Manchester behind him. Manchester that day was as Manchester always seemed to be: a miserable, cold, grey town, deprived of the cotton industry that had made it great, unsure of where it was going. Manchester United, the club that for 20 years had given the town its glory while it lamented its lost empire and searched vainly for a new role, were heading inexorably for the Second Division. Malcolm could have made Manchester City the greatest club in the land, in the world, in history. Lesser men, men with personal ambition but none of his vision, had prevented him from securing it.

Inside the stadium offices, Peter Swales saw Ian Niven coming towards him along the corridor outside the boardroom. 'Your mate's off,' Swales said briefly, neatly distancing himself from the turmoil the club was to be plunged into by Malcolm's departure. Had to be good for him, he thought. They'd all be looking for leadership now, and who was better fitted to provide it?

The following day, Johnny Hart's Manchester City beat Don Revie's Leeds United 1–0. *Vive le Roi!*

1972–73: MANAGER MALCOLM ALLISON UNTIL 30 MARCH. THEREAFTER JOHNNY HART

1	AUG	12	(A)	LIVERPOOL	L	0–2		55,383
2		16	(H)	EVERTON	L	0–1		38,676
3		19	(H)	NORWICH C	W	3–0	LEE 2, BELL	31,171
4		23	(A)	DERBY C	L	0–1		31,173
5		26	(A)	CHELSEA	L	1–2	MELLOR	30,845
6		29	(A)	CRYSTAL P	L	0–1		24,731
7	SEP	2	(H)	LEICESTER C	W	1–0	MARSH	27,233
8		9	(A)	BIRMINGHAM C	L	1–4	TOWERS	32,983
9		16	(H)	TOTTENHAM H	W	2–1	MARSH 2	31,755
10		23	(A)	STOKE C	(A)	1–5	LEE	26,448
11		30	(H)	WEST BROM A	W	2–1	BOOTH, LEE	27,332
12	OCT	7	(H)	WOLVES	D	1–1	MARSH	31,201
13		14	(A)	COVENTRY C	L	2–3	SUMMERBEE, MARSH	24,560
14		21	(H)	WEST HAM U	W	4–3	MARSH 2, SUMMERBEE, TOWERS	30,890
15		28	(A)	ARSENAL	D	0–0		45,536
16	NOV	4	(H)	DERBY C	W	4–0	BELL, MARSH, CARRODUS, OPP OWN-GOAL	35,829
17		11	(A)	EVERTON	W	3–2	LEE 2, OPP OWN-GOAL	32,924
18		18	(H)	MANCHESTER U	W	3–0	BELL 2, OPP OWN-GOAL	52,050
19		25	(A)	LEEDS U	L	0–3		39,879
20	DEC	2	(H)	IPSWICH T	D	1–1	LEE	27,839
21		9	(A)	SHEFFIELD U	D	1–1	BELL	19,208
22		16	(H)	SOUTHAMPTON	W	2–1	MARSH 2	24,825
23		23	(A)	NEWCASTLE U	L	1–2	MELLOR	28,249
24		26	(H)	STOKE C	D	1–1	MELLOR	36,334
25		30	(A)	NORWICH C	D	1–1	TOWERS	24,203
26	JAN	20	(A)	LEICESTER C	D	1–1	BELL	18,761
27		27	(H)	BIRMINGHAM C	W	1–0	DONACHIE	31,882
28	FEB	10	(A)	TOTTENHAM H	W	3–2	LEE 2, MARSH	30,944
29		17	(H)	LIVERPOOL	D	1–1	BOOTH	41,709
30	MAR	3	(A)	WOLVES	L	1–5	MARSH	25,047
31		6	(A)	SOUTHAMPTON	D	1–1	LEE	16,188
32		10	(H)	COVENTRY C	L	1–2	BOOTH	30,448
33		17	(A)	WEST HAM U	L	1–2	DOYLE	30,156
34		24	(H)	ARSENAL	L	1–2	BOOTH	32,031
35		27	(H)	CHELSEA	L	0–1		23,973
36		31	(H)	LEEDS U	W	1–0	TOWERS	35,772
37	APR	7	(A)	IPSWICH T	D	1–1	OAKES	19,109
38		14	(H)	SHEFFIELD U	W	3–1	BELL, MARSH, LEE	26,811
39		18	(H)	NEWCASTLE U	W	2–0	BOOTH, MARSH	25,156
40		21	(A)	MANCHESTER U	D	0–0		61,500
41		25	(A)	WEST BROM A	W	2–1	LEE, TOWERS	21,193
42		28	(H)	CRYSTAL P	L	2–3	LEE 2	34,784

FINAL LEAGUE POSITION: 11TH IN DIVISION ONE

FA CUP

3	JAN	13	(H)	STOKE C	W	3–2	
4	FEB	3	(A)	LIVERPOOL	D	0–0	
R		7	(H)	LIVERPOOL	W	2–0	
5		24	(H)	SUNDERLAND	D	2–2	
R		27	(A)	SUNDERLAND	L	1–3	

LEAGUE CUP

2	SEP	6	(H)	ROCHDALE	W	4–0	
3	OCT	3	(A)	BURY	L	0–2	

EPILOGUE

There is a sadness that affects the declining years of most people, particularly those who have achieved most in life. For Joe Mercer there was one more glorious triumph, a swansong that everyone in football applauded. Between the end of Alf Ramsey's time in charge of England on 1 May 1974 and Don Revie's appointment as his full-time successor in the autumn of that year, Joe Mercer was asked to look after the England team for seven matches. Thereafter Joe was a regular, smiling figure at football grounds all around the country for over ten years, before he began to slip behind the curtain of dementia. He died on his birthday in 1990 at the age of 76, remembered fondly by the supporters of every club with whom he had had dealings.

For Malcolm, the contrast could not have been greater. He guided Crystal Palace to two consecutive relegations and then left the country. When he returned he doubled back on himself, going in rapid succession from Plymouth to Manchester City to Crystal Palace again, each stay more disastrous than the last. His brain never stopped buzzing; plans and tactics and innovations poured from him in a torrent to the bemusement of his players and the frustration of the fans. There was a brief moment of public triumph in Palace's FA Cup run to the semi-final when they were languishing in the Third Division, and in Portugal, where he did the Cup and League double with Sporting Lisbon. He fell out with the directors in Lisbon as he had fallen out with the directors at every club he managed. His appearances in the police courts for unpaid bills and wild, unpredictable social behaviour mounted up, and wives and girlfriends and potential employers became understandably wary of him.

There was no Joe Mercer to restrain his excesses once he had left Manchester, and he became increasingly an object of pity. His career continued remorselessly downwards after his second stint at Crystal Palace. He went from Middlesbrough to Bristol Rovers to Fisher Athletic. His private life offered no comfort. He rebounded from Serena to Sally and from Sally to Lynn until he entered an old age that was ravaged by illness. The champagne that he had consumed in industrial quantities during his working life took its revenge as he declined into alcoholism and destitution. Now he, too, succumbed to the ravages of dementia.

But, however sad the ending, the fact is that Malcolm Allison made an impact on the lives of others. He was, in his time, the finest football coach that England had ever produced. With Joe Mercer he created a football team that has lingered these past 40 years in the memory of those who saw it. For many of them, it was the Garden of Eden before the Fall, the elegiac recollection of high summer in Edwardian England. Together Joe Mercer and Malcolm Allison forged a friendship and a working relationship that was the most rewarding of their professional lives. They couldn't sustain it through the problems created not by failure but by success. Individually neither of them achieved anything as great as their joint accomplishments. The best of friends became the worst of friends. It was the tragedy of success.